A CULTURAL HISTORY OF THE HOME

VOLUME 5

A Cultural History of the Home
General Editor: Amanda Flather

Volume 1
A Cultural History of the Home in Antiquity
Edited by Andrew Wallace-Hadrill and Joanne Berry

Volume 2
A Cultural History of the Home in the Medieval Age
Edited by Katherine L. French

Volume 3
A Cultural History of the Home in the Renaissance
Edited by Amanda Flather

Volume 4
A Cultural History of the Home in the Age of Enlightenment
Edited by Clive Edwards

Volume 5
A Cultural History of the Home in the Age of Empire
Edited by Jane Hamlett

Volume 6
A Cultural History of the Home in the Modern Age
Edited by Despina Stratigakos

A CULTURAL HISTORY OF THE HOME
IN THE AGE OF EMPIRE

Edited by Jane Hamlett

BLOOMSBURY ACADEMIC
LONDON • NEW YORK • OXFORD • NEW DELHI • SYDNEY

BLOOMSBURY ACADEMIC
Bloomsbury Publishing Plc
50 Bedford Square, London, WC1B 3DP, UK
1385 Broadway, New York, NY 10018, USA
29 Earlsfort Terrace, Dublin 2, Ireland

BLOOMSBURY, BLOOMSBURY ACADEMIC and the Diana logo are trademarks of
Bloomsbury Publishing Plc

First published in Great Britain 2021
This edition published in Great Britain, 2024

Copyright © Bloomsbury Publishing, 2021

Jane Hamlett has asserted her right under the Copyright, Designs and Patents Act,
1988, to be identified as Editor of this work.

Cover image © Heritage Images /Getty Images

All rights reserved. No part of this publication may be reproduced or transmitted in any form or by any means, electronic or mechanical, including photocopying, recording, or any information storage or retrieval system, without prior permission in writing from the publishers.

Bloomsbury Publishing Plc does not have any control over, or responsibility for, any third-party websites referred to or in this book. All internet addresses given in this book were correct at the time of going to press. The author and publisher regret any inconvenience caused if addresses have changed or sites have ceased to exist, but can accept no responsibility for any such changes.

A catalogue record for this book is available from the British Library.

A catalog record for this book is available from the Library of Congress.

ISBN: HB: 978-1-4725-8429-8
       Set: 978-1-4725-8441-0
       PB: 978-1-3504-1226-2
       Set: 978-1-3504-1235-4

Series: The Cultural Histories Series

Typeset by RefineCatch Limited, Bungay, Suffolk
Printed and bound in Great Britain

To find out more about our authors and books visit www.bloomsbury.com
and sign up for our newsletters.

CONTENTS

List of Illustrations   vii

Series Preface   x

Introduction: The Home in the West in the Age of Empire   1
Jane Hamlett

1   The Meaning of Home: The Ideal and its Limits in England and the Colonies   19
Margaret Ponsonby

2   Family and Household: Domestic Service in Colonial India   43
Fae Dussart

3   The House: Inside and Outside Villas and Terraces in England   67
Lesley Hoskins and Rebecca Preston

4   Furniture and Furnishings: Transnational Production and Consumption Networks in East Africa   89
Britta Schilling

5   Home and Work: Housework and Paid Work in British Homes   111
Victoria Kelley

6   Gender and Home: Domestic Spaces and Families in North America   133
Rebecca J. Fraser

7   Hospitality and Home: Dining Spaces and Practices in England
    and North America   157
    Jane Hamlett and Marie Drews

8   Religion and the Home: Lived Religion in Working-Class
    Households   179
    Lucinda Matthews-Jones

NOTES   203
BIBLIOGRAPHY   209
NOTES ON CONTRIBUTORS   235
INDEX   239

ILLUSTRATIONS

CHAPTER 1

1.1	The fear of homelessness, engraving, 1870.	22
1.2	The parlour or drawing room, engraving	23
1.3	The family Christmas, engraving, 1868.	24
1.4	The working-class home with material comforts threatened by alcohol, etching, G. Cruikshank, 1847	26
1.5	Contrasting styles for drawing rooms, H.J. Jennings, *Our Homes and How to Beautify Them*, 1902	29
1.6	'Our Magistrate's Wife', George Franklin Atkinson, *Curry and Rice*, *c.* 1860	40

CHAPTER 2

2.1	Planter's bungalow, Allahabad, India, 1877. Photograph, 1877	47
2.2	A British family celebrating Christmas in India, *c.* 1900. 'Indian Christmas', by E.K. Johnson	49
2.3	A British officer in India receives a pedicure from an Indian servant, photograph, undated	50
2.4	A European lady and her family attended by an Ayah, or Nurse, drawing by Charles D'Oyly	54

CHAPTER 3

3.1	Detached villa at Calverley Estate, Tunbridge Wells, John Britton, 1832	70
3.2	Rock Park, Cheshire	72

3.3 A typical four-roomed 'Through-House', Manchester, *c.* 1900 — 79
3.4 Postcard view of Cranford Park, Ilford, Essex, *c.* 1918 — 81
3.5 Recent view of Corbyn Street, Islington, London, *c.* 1870 — 84

CHAPTER 4

4.1 Sir Harry Johnston's dining room in Entebbe, Uganda, *c.* 1902 — 96
4.2 Dining room of William McGregor and Isabel Ross in Nairobi, *c.* 1909–16 — 99
4.3 Zanzibar chest in the home of David LeBreton, England, Photograph, 2014 — 101
4.4 Sitting room in the home of Kurt von Schleinitz, German East Africa, *c.* 1907–14 — 107
4.5 Daudi Chwa II with Regents, Uganda, *c.* 1908 — 108

CHAPTER 5

5.1 Domestic irons, 1914 — 117
5.2 Borax Extract of Soap show-card advertisement, *c.* 1900 — 118
5.3 Woodheyes Park, near Manchester — 124
5.4 Anna Blunden, *For Only One Short Hour*, 1854 — 129

CHAPTER 6

6.1 Nineteenth-century home of the middle classes — 141
6.2 Sarah Hicks Williams, *c.* 1850s — 143
6.3 The Old Plantation Home — 145
6.4 Slave quarters on the Hopsewee Plantation — 147
6.5 Hammatt Billings, 'Chloe and Mrs Shelby' — 148
6.6 Southern Planter Home — 151
6.7 'Four Oaks' Old Plantation Home — 151

CHAPTER 7

7.1 The ideal drawing and dining room — 162
7.2 Cakes from *Mrs Beeton's Cookery Book and Household Guide* — 165
7.3 Ideal five o'clock tea, illustration, 1891 — 166
7.4 At dinner, St. Marylebone Workhouse, *c.* 1901 — 174
7.5 Interior of the dining hall at Holloway Sanatorium, 1881 — 176

CHAPTER 8

8.1	John Bunyan's *Pilgrim's Progress*	188
8.2	Front cover of *Foxe's Book of Martyrs*	190
8.3	'Awesome' images from *Foxe's Book of Martyrs*	191
8.4	'A Child's Prayer', *Hymns and Pictures*	193
8.5	Postcard showing a church parade in Preston	196
8.6	Fragment of temperance crockery	198

SERIES PREFACE

A Cultural History of the Home is an authoritative, interdisciplinary, six-volume series investigating the changing meaning of home, both as an idea and as a place to live, from ancient times until the present. Each volume follows the same basic structure and begins with an overview of the cultural, social, political and economic factors that shaped ideas and requirements of home in the period under consideration. Experts examine important aspects of the cultural history of home under eight main headings: the meaning of home; house and home; family and home; gender and home; work and home; furniture and furnishings; religion and home; hospitality and home. A single volume can be read to obtain a thorough knowledge of the period or one of the eight themes can be followed through history by reading the relevant chapter in each of the six volumes, providing an understanding of developments over the longer term.

Individual volumes in the series will cover six historical periods:

Volume 1: *A Cultural History of the Home in Antiquity* (500 BC–800 AD)
Volume 2: *A Cultural History of the Home in the Medieval Age* (800–1450)
Volume 3: *A Cultural History of the Home in the Renaissance* (1450–1650)
Volume 4: *A Cultural History of the Home in the Age of Enlightenment* (1650–1800)
Volume 5: *A Cultural History of the Home in the Age of Empire* (1800–1920)
Volume 6: *A Cultural History of the Home in the Modern Age* (1920–2000+)

Amanda Flather

Introduction: The Home in the West in the Age of Empire

JANE HAMLETT

During the nineteenth century, the home, as a cultural construct and a set of lived practices, became more powerful in the western world than ever before. The modernization of farming and the industrialization of Western Europe (which took place at different paces in different times and places) changed the working lives of many men and women and led to a reorganization of their domestic lives. Where commercial and industrial activities were most developed, more people than ever before made their homes in towns and cities. Scientific advances and the increasing mass production of goods also changed homes materially, bringing in domestic technologies and a plethora of new things. Often linked to these socio-economic and material changes were shifts in the way social relationships were understood, which influenced home life. People from all walks of life began to invest more materially and temporally in domestic space, and they developed new ideas about it: buying more goods but also placing greater emphasis on an ideal of the male breadwinner, which stressed the need for women to maintain the domestic material fabric and emotional environment. While most western homes were based on the patriarchal family, over the century the authority of fathers was challenged, perhaps most notably in assertion of the legal rights for married women. Children, too, were seen differently. Childhood was viewed as a separate period of life to be celebrated, but also something that was increasingly regulated by the state. With the growth of middle-class groups, an increasing number of families across the West employed domestic servants. How domestic workers were seen in relation to the household also changed, with the gradual removal of slavery and the decline of indentured labour. New domestic practices, particularly in relation to space and time, were developed to try to make sense of new kinds of home. Yet these were combined with older domestic rituals, on occasions such as birth, marriage and death, which created a sense of continuity and longevity in home life.

Understanding change across such a vast geographical area is challenging, especially as the boundaries of the West proved so elastic and expansive in this era. Europe's global trading connections were long established, and empire in its economic form was present in the eighteenth century, but it was only in the second half of the nineteenth that it was established politically. By 1914, the states of Western and Central Europe are thought to have controlled roughly 84 percent of lands around the globe (Hamerow 1983: 389). Not only did the acquisition of empires lead to the establishment of Western European homes in new terrains, but it also buttressed the way in which Europeans saw themselves, as the guardians of superior cultures, patriarchal relationships and living practices. Significant numbers of Europeans settled in colonial holdings, mainly Australia, New Zealand, Canada and some parts of Africa. Huge streams of migrants also flowed from Northern Europe to the USA, especially in times of economic difficulty. Indeed, more migrants headed for the States; in the last decade before the First World War, 56 percent of migrants whose destinations were known went to America, with only six percent going to Canada, four percent to Australia and one percent to New Zealand (Hamerow 1983: 84). The multiplicity of homes and living practices created by Europeans of different nationalities, social groups and religions across a vast and expanding geographical terrain defies easy categorization. This book deals with this by focusing primarily on the Anglophone world, with studies of Britain, the United States of America and the British Empire including colonial India and British East Africa. This introduction puts these studies within a broad overview, exploring the nature of home and the major changes that influenced it across Western Europe,[1] the USA and their empires as a whole, providing context for the geographically focused chapters presented in the rest of this book.

The title of this book, and of this series, denotes the fact that the home is now seen as a cultural phenomenon. Historians view the home as a powerful cultural construct that shaped how people thought about themselves and their daily living practices. Talking about a culture of home also draws attention to its historical specificity. Ideas of what home means, and even the use of the word itself, vary according to period and place. How this worked across the nineteenth-century West will be discussed later on. In general, this book adopts a broad definition of what home comprised, considering it as an idealized cultural construction and as a lived experience in a physical place surrounded by family members and material things. This introduction will focus on five different aspects of home: as an ideal that was represented and celebrated in print and visual culture; as a place or location; as the nexus of family relationships; as a material entity; and finally as a set of lived practices that we might call domesticities. The rest of this essay considers to what extent we can see a shared sense of home emerging across Western Europe and the USA, by examining these different constituents of home. Across these regions, homes were shaped by industrialization and urbanization, by empires created by political and military means, and resettlement driven by war and economic disaster; but I will also stress the power of the home and family to create a sense of security and stability amid change, and the role of the patriarchal family, domestic relationships and rituals in creating continuous cultures of home that were handed down between generations.

To deal with the vast territories that were claimed as part of European empires in this era, this essay and this book look at the domestic lives of those who moved to these places. While the focus of this discussion is the home lives of the colonizers and settlers, it is important to remember that these new homes were not built in a vacuum – their establishment often rested on doing considerable damage to and even destroying the ways of life of people who already lived there (Banivanua Mar and Edmonds 2010: 1–10). The living arrangements of indigenous peoples are not fully explored here, partly for reasons of space but also because there was a specific idea of home and its practices that reached across the European West and its outposts that was promoted by white imperialists. Indigenous peoples in contrast often had very different and varied ideas of family relationships, gendered hierarchies and ways of living (Nash and Strobel 2006: xvii). It is important to acknowledge this and in this introduction I will discuss the ways in which their interactions with settlers produced new domestic forms and practices.

THE IDEA OF HOME

How far was there a common idea of home across the West? Amongst Western Europeans and settlers in the United States and the colonies there was a basic understanding of the household as somewhere where blood families or working groups of people lived. However, there were differences in the way that home, as a cultural idea, was understood, which can be seen in different language formations. The word 'home' has been used in English since at least the late medieval period (Kowaleski and Goldberg 2008). By the eighteenth century, it entered the dictionaries in the form that it is used today, and meant the place one was emotionally attached to, as well as where one lived (Harvey 2009). In France, however, there was no direct translation for the English word for 'home', and, in the early nineteenth century, the French middle classes began to use this

English word, along with other English domestic phrases such as 'baby' and 'comfort' (Perrot 1990: 10, 343). Often, understandings of home were linked to a sense of place – both national and local. Again the Germans had no equivalent of the English word 'home', instead they had *'heimat'*, the homeland – an idea, closely bound to the recently forged German state, that gained political significance from the late nineteenth century (Umbach and Hüppauf 2005: 10). Different sections of society also used language differently. Until the twentieth century, the landscape was a crucial part of the social world of the French peasantry, and home was not just a physical space but a particular *'terroir'*, 'the same word for house also designated the associated farmland' (Perrot 1990: 347–48). In the late eighteenth and early nineteenth centuries, the British working classes used the word home differently to other social groups – in applications for poor relief it was used to denote a place of origin, rather than a particular house or space (Snell 2012). This difference in the use of language reflected the transitory nature of the domestic arrangements of the poor, a quest for permanence and stability fulfilled by identification with a place rather than the temporary and uncertain shelter offered by rented rooms. Perhaps the most complex use of the word emerges in the writings of colonialists and settlers who often had a dual idea of home – of the country of origin, the motherland, as well as the newly settled colonial space (Perry 2010). These individuals might use the word home in a number of different ways, expressing the complexity of cultures of home across time and space in the nineteenth century.

Home, then, was understood differently across Western Europe and North America. But the version of home that historians have placed most emphasis on is the shared 'cult of domesticity' propagated in print culture in this era, predominantly by the European and American middle classes. A striking aspect of the development of societies across national boundaries was the growth of the middle classes or bourgeoisie. The celebration of virtuous domestic life, in which husband and wife adhered to gendered roles and brought up children in a Christian home, became the touchstone for middle-class families across vast geographical areas. How far this happened and when was linked to socio-economic change. In Sweden, for example, this middle-class celebration of home occurred in the final decades of the century when society was in transition due to industrialization (Löfgren 2003). The ideal bourgeois home was celebrated in the literary and visual culture across the West. It seems to have been most prominent in the English-speaking world (Oldenziel and Hård 2013: 61), and Chapters 1 and 6 of this book demonstrate its reach and power across Britain and its colonies and the USA. Even French culture, always somewhat apart from British cosines, saw a celebration of family relationships with popular publications such as *Monsieur, Madame et Bebe* (1866) playing up French fatherhood (Robertson 1982: 16). Britain, France and Spain all produced an increasing amount of advice for middle-class homemakers over the century, promoting highly decorated spaces for both public display and family intimacy (Cohen 2006; Tiersten 2001: 115; Cruz 2011: 52). Yet once we begin to look closely at how this idea worked across a broad geographical reach, we can see significant differences in how home was constructed in relation to gender, religion, social class and empire.

Visions of the home across the West shared an essentialist view of gender roles, and a basic idea of the world as divided into public and private spheres. This was famously articulated in British culture in Coventry Patmore's poem, 'The Angel in the House', which celebrates a meekly submissive wife, who tends husband and home (1860). This idea appeared in slightly different forms – in France the domestic angel was known as the 'Femme de Foyer', in the USA her followers formed 'the cult of true womanhood', while in Spain the middle classes celebrated the 'Angel del Hogar' (Welter 1966; Nash 1999: 8). However, the imagined woman in the home was always connected to a public world outside, which was configured according to national politics and identities. In France, female participation in the public world was imagined in the context of the Republican state, in which the shopping activities of moral citizens formed an outlet for acceptable participation in the creation of a wider social good (Asquer 2012: 576). In the US middle-class home, the concept of moral motherhood was particularly powerful, and sometimes portrayed as superior to the morality of men (Grier 1997: 6–7). Chapter 6 of this book traces the delineation of domestic womanhood in the United States, revealing that while there was a basic shared ideal, this was appropriated in different ways by the northeastern middle classes and the Confederate slave-owning households of the South. And while British colonists tried to avoid over-intervention in Indian home life, and Indians sought to use it as a means of preserving a sense of independence, in the heavily charged atmosphere of empire 'the institution of the family, together with the home that inhabited it, came to assume enormous political significance' (Ansari 2004). Across the US and Europe, the representation of gendered power relations in the home shifted in the final decades of the nineteenth century, with advice literature increasingly stressing female authority (Cohen 2006: 106–10; Tiersten 2001: 155–56). In Britain, this was part of a larger social transformation that saw more women enter secondary and higher education, and take on a larger number of roles in the workplace.

Religion was at the heart of new idealizations of the home, but religious differences across the West created competing versions of this ideal. There was a growing sense of religious toleration in Western Europe in the nineteenth century. After 1815, there was a gradual move for legal equality for Catholics in Protestant countries, Protestants in Catholic countries and for Jews in both (Hamerow 1983: 418). Diverse religious practices were given room to flourish, and could transform the home and its environment. The relationship between the state and religion could powerfully affect family life. In Italy, for example, the influence of the Catholic Church led to a continuation of the indissolubility of marriage when other European countries were beginning to allow divorce (Willson 2004: 6–7). Such divisions were also powerful within the Anglophone world. In Protestant and Catholic North America, there was a basic idea that the Christian home worked towards the salvation of the family (McDannell 1986: 19). Yet Catholics and Protestants had different ideas about how the home could function as ritual or sacred space – elite Catholics had domestic oratories while lower down the social scale altars were erected in the homes of the sick (McDannell 1986: 42, 66–70). While we know how crucial religion was to the idea of home, we know less about how it entered everyday domestic life. Chapter 8 shows us how this happened in English working-class homes. In Britain, there were important differences between Anglican and non-conformist domestic practices – with the latter placing more emphasis on worship in the home itself, especially before non-conformist groups were able to set up official church organizations. Again Chapter 8 reveals just how important these differences were for working-class families, giving domestic religion a degree of agency and fluidity that helped maintain its vitality.

The ideal of the home was a key means of promoting status and identity for newly emergent middle classes across the West. Yet there were different ideas about how to achieve a home of distinction – in Spain, and in France, truly distinguished apartments were only found on the first floor of large blocks (Cruz 2011: 62). In England, however, according to the architect Robert Kerr, social distinction was vested in the possession of a detached house with an appropriate number of rooms (Kerr 1871: 66). How this was realized in English villa homes is explored in Chapter 3. Across cultures, middle-class standards of domesticity were used to criticize the poor, and there were also some attempts to use them to help them, through the provision of model housing or special accommodation, even if these were often insensitive to real feelings and needs (Hamlett 2015). While it was important across cultures to use domesticity to draw boundaries between different class groups, there were subtle differences in how these lines were drawn. In British culture, the lower middle classes – an increasingly large group in the late nineteenth century, including shopkeepers and clerks – were often critiqued for their failure to conform to contemporary ideas of domestic respectability, and were portrayed as naïve or uncultured (Crossick and Haupt 1995: 98). Yet in France, Germany and Belgium, a different political climate created trade union movements that promoted a positive image of the petite bourgeoisie – holding up the small shopkeeping family as an idealized form of domesticity (Segalen 1996: 400). According to historians of the North American home, visions of social distinction created by living practices were particularly inclusive in the US, with advice manuals and novels expounding a vision of the 'refined' North American abode that could be realized in every farmhouse (Bushman 1992: 247, 276–79; Grier 1988: viii).

Across the nineteenth-century West, domestic ideals were a potent tool for the powerful. In the British Empire, the idea of home was often mobilized in the construction of imperial dominance (Burton 2003: 8). The homes of colonists were increasingly seen as a site for the reproduction of imperial power relations (Blunt 1999). Chapter 2 of this book, focused on British households in the Indian Empire, explores this through interactions between colonial families and indigenous servants, arguing that imperial domesticity was fundamental to the colonists' narrative of dominance, but also to their more ambiguous attempts to forge a new identity for themselves. Critiques of indigenous living practices also drew on domestic ideals, with depictions of the zenana[2] used to bolster a sense of western moral authority (Burton 2003: 8). Both memsahibs and Indian women and their domestic roles were the subject of intense cultural discussion and extensive representation as they were powerful symbols in the construction of cultural imperialism (Sen 2002). Across the European empires, there were some commonalities in the use of domestic ideology to justify colonial activities: ideas of gender and the patriarchal authority of the home were often key – the colonizers were often cast as parent figures, the colonized as children (Clancy-Smith and Gouda 1998: 8). Yet there were some subtle differences. The French and Dutch governments had different approaches to how they administered their colonies and how much they attempted to transform their subjects, influenced by different political traditions and ideas about the value of indigenous cultures (Clancy-Smith and Gouda 1998: 9–14).

HOME AND PLACE

The place in which a home is situated has a fundamental effect on its nature. The location of living places was intrinsically related to the occupations of household members. As we have seen, the local landscape, language, customs and practices affected the conceptualization of home. This aspect of the home changed for many people in the nineteenth century. Millions of Europeans moved into cities for the first time or emigrated to the colonies and the US. The pace of urban growth varied, usually in response to different forms of industrialization. As large-scale industrialization took place first in England, it was English cities that were the first to expand. By the middle of the nineteenth century, more English people lived in cities and towns than in the countryside, yet this did not happen in Scotland for another forty years (Hamerow 1983: 107). Elsewhere, industrialization gathered speed later on. In Germany, it picked up pace in the decades after unification, with the population of Berlin doubling between 1871 and 1905 (Salmi 2008: 90). In France, although Paris saw much growth, the rural population remained more stable throughout the century, partly because the French system of landholding allowed more division of lands between younger sons (Hamerow 1983: 104). In parts of Southern

Europe, the situation was further complicated by the fact that it was customary for rural workers to reside in 'agri-towns' (Kertzer and Barbagli 2002: xii). Again in the US, large cities grew very rapidly, although many people continued to live on small farms (Atkins 2007: 84). While this was an era of urban expansion, the majority of people still lived in rural homes, whose nature and location were not transformed by industrialization (Shammas 2002: xiii).

In some places, new kinds of homes emerged as towns and cities grew. In European cities, housing did not keep pace with population growth (Hamerow 1983: 112). Urban workers often lived in cramped and insanitary conditions, packed together in crumbling and decrepit housing stock. When cities were modernized, little attention was paid to where working people lived (Perrot 1990: 395). For the lower classes in Britain, one of the major differences in urban and rural living was a move into shared accommodation of some kind. Poor Londoners often lived in 'furnished rooms' or common lodging houses. These were usually paid for on a weekly or nightly basis, making it difficult to establish the sense of residential security and longevity associated with the middle-class ideal of home. Despite the privations of these places and their lack of privacy, there is some evidence that shared material strategies and sociability allowed their residents to forge a sense of shared moral identity and even find comfort (Hamlett 2015: 131). Although industrialization is often associated with a separation of home and workplace (and the emergence of the nuclear family), this is not what happened in a lot of places. Alongside the growth of factories, small-scale enterprises continued to be run close to home across Europe. The combination of home and workshop was well established in nineteenth-century industry, as, for example, in the metal trades of the English Midlands or the tinsmiths of Lyon (Crossick and Haupt 1995: 91).

The relationship between work and place also had an important impact on middle-class homes, but this was not straightforward. In some urban centres, the middle-class response to industrialization was to remove themselves from the horrors of urban expansion. If we look at England, where urban expansion was at its greatest in the nineteenth century, there was a growth in the suburbs of many towns and cities. However, this took place at different rates in different places (Hamlett 2010: 30). And even in London, which saw a huge amount of suburban growth, it was not a simple case of the middle classes moving outwards: often workers and middle classes moved outwards together as service industries grew up around new forms of middle-class housing (White 2007: 82). As we will see in Chapter 3, suburban villas were usually situated away from industrial dirt and noise, but often deliberately remained connected to the public worlds of trade and commerce that created them. Many lower middling families continued to live alongside the places they worked: small shopkeepers, who continued to be significant in late-nineteenth-century Britain, are a case in point. In Germany, where industrialization took place later on, and in France where the shift from rural to urban was less sharp, this situation was even more pronounced (Hamerow 1983: 113; Perrot 1990: 117). For many people, the practice of having a small business, closely connected to family life if not actually on the premises of the home, remained a normal experience. Even in the homes of leading colonial administrators, running the Empire also often took place in domestic space (Perry 2010: 74).

A smaller but significant group of people saw a profound change in where they lived through the experience of migration. Although large numbers of people had moved to new continents in previous centuries, the nineteenth century saw the first voluntary mass migrations of people overseas. Economic destitution, political persecution and despair were motivating factors, but people were also propelled by the hope of a better life. Migration was also made more attractive by the growing ease of transport and communication: steamships, newspapers and the telegraph meant that migrants reached their destinations more easily and could stay in touch when they got there. Increasing literacy levels and a speedier postal service also meant that family ties were not completely cut by such moves (Kertzer and Barbagli 2002: xiii). In colonial families, weekly letter writing became an important and established practice (Buettner 2004: 130). Even those on the margins of society might muster pen and paper to communicate with home (Casella, Cornwall and Frost 2001). At first, most migrants came from industrial Western Europe, especially the UK and Germany, but this altered later in the century with more people coming from the south and east, and in particular from Italy and Austria-Hungary as those countries industrialized (Hamerow 1983: 85–86). Despite new opportunities opened up by the acquisition of colonial territories under new European empires, most Europeans chose to make new homes in the US. Approximately 35 million of the 50 million Europeans who emigrated between 1820 and 1920 came to the US (Gerber 2011: 2).

For those who established new homes on different continents, there was an important difference between temporary and permanent settlement. People moving to the US and settlers in Australia, Canada, New Zealand and some parts of Africa usually intended to remain there (Buettner 2004: 22). These intentions were not always realized. Failure of employment, illness or simply the desire to return home might result in re-immigration. Between 1908 and 1923, approximately three million European immigrants to the US re-immigrated (Gerber 2011: 69). All the same, those who stayed in the colonies for only a few years tended to have a different attitude to domestic life there. The middle-class families who engaged (often over a number of generations) with the British Raj created specific forms of class, racial and national identity that were produced by their transient status, a 'cultural hybridity' created by movement back and forth between home and Empire (Buettner 2004: 2–4). For those who intended to stay, conventional domestic practices took on a powerful new meaning as they were used to create a sense of security and duration. As is shown in the discussion of the domestic practices of female settlers across the British Empire in Chapter 1, long-term homemaking activities such as gardening could be a means of establishing permanency and expressing their intent to remain.

WHO WAS HOME?

Homes were also made by and understood according to who lived in them. In the western bourgeois ideal, there was a strong identification between immediate blood families – mothers, fathers and children – and the idea of home as a lived domestic space. In practical terms, domestic life was shaped by who lived in the household. However, historically, there were major differences in household formation across Europe and between different class and occupational groups, creating different domestic dynamics. Crucially, the establishment of homes did not always take place at the same point in the life-cycle, and was often closely related to the means by which a family earned their livelihood. In Western Europe, homes tended to be formed on marriage, whereas this was less often the case in middle Europe and seldom in Mediterranean countries (Laslett 1983: 526–27). In the latter places, households were often composed of more than one nuclear family group, with young brides moving in with in-laws, and siblings and their families co-habiting. These arrangements made a substantial difference to how home was experienced: in England couples tended to set up by themselves, whereas a Mediterranean bride would be more likely to move in with her mother-in-law (Laslett 1983: 351; Robertson 1982: 166). But as recent studies have pointed out, geographical and national divisions were not straightforward, and there was considerable variety in the way that households were formed between regions, and working conditions. In Italy, for example, sharecroppers tended to live in complex households that generated a large number of workers, whereas waged labourers doing similar jobs usually worked as individuals and found separate housing (Kertzer 2002: 45). There were also marked differences for families working in different kinds of industry. In Lancashire cotton towns, where women were employed in factories, grandparents might share the home to provide additional childcare, whereas in the heavy industries such as coal mining it was far more common for the father to be the main wage labourer and for the family to live in a 'nuclear' form (Segalen 1996: 388).

The number of people living in a home made a huge difference to life within it, especially when we consider that many lived in relatively small spaces. This was influenced by changing demographic patterns. The death rate declined, but so did fertility. Again, these changes were experienced very differently across the social spectrum. Overall, nineteenth-century Europe saw a population expansion because of the growing availability of foodstuffs (Hamerow 1983: 65). However, mortality rates amongst the poor remained high for most of the century and impoverished families everywhere faced difficult conditions that challenged their ability to stay together. In 1833, for example, between 20 and 30 percent of all children born in France were placed in institutional care by their parents (Hamerow 1983: 79). Poorer women might have had many children, but infant mortality remained high. Amongst the better-housed and well-nourished middle classes, both children and parents had a greater chance of survival. In these homes, it is likely that there would be large numbers of children, creating what Leonore Davidoff has called the 'long family', a nuclear family consisting of a large sibling group (2012: 78–107). During the second half of the century, the middle classes across Europe saw a drop in infant mortality, probably because they were deliberately limiting family size through sexual abstinence (Hamerow 1983: 72, 76). This happened first in France, although it also spread quickly in the US (Kertzer and Barbagli 2002: xxiii; McDannell 1986: 8). Family life lived in a small home, with large numbers of siblings, sharing and squabbling over space, was very different to that in a home where space could be carefully parcelled out between individuals. Of course, many people did not live in conventional family households, nuclear or otherwise. For much of the century, adults, too, were more likely to die in midlife, creating large numbers of families headed by a widow or widower (Anderson 1990: 29–30). There were also many men and women who did not marry, and Chapter 1 explores how these people constructed their living spaces in the face of a culture that privileged the ideal of home as a family space.

Across Western Europe there were growing numbers of domestic servants in the homes of the middle classes (Salmi 2008: 77), but there was also significant variation in the kinds of workers who resided in homes. Western European households were more likely to employ live-in workers from outside the family (Laslett 1983: 526–27). Many households contained different kinds of workers attached to family businesses. Over the period, there was an uneven decline in live-in apprentices, but there remained a strong tendency to employ workers at certain points in the life-cycle (Crossick and Haupt 1995: 103–5). In England, the number of domestic servants steadily grew with the middle classes, peaking in the 1870s, with single-servant households being most common (McBride 1976: 40; McBride 1978). Here, from the early part of the century, there was a move away from the conception of the servant as part of the household family, to an understanding of the servant as a salaried employee (McBride 1976: 33). Everywhere, the presence of homeworkers was a means of conveying social status, yet the significance of this was very different according to political and national contexts. This emerges strongly in Chapters 2 and 6 of this book, which show the roles played by Indian servants and American slaves in the construction of wider systems of power and authority. The ideal of a separation of home and work had to be configured differently in the slave-owning households in the southern US. There also seem to have been national differences in servant-keeping practices across Europe. Travellers were often struck by the apparent fact that German women did more housework and had fewer domestic servants (Muthesius [1904] 2007: 9; Robertson 1982).

As people moved across national boundaries, to build empires and to settle in new lands, this created different kinds of households. The household and family were transformed partly by the process of movement and settling itself, but in some circumstances settlers might intermarry with indigenous populations, creating new family forms and patterns. Over the course of the nineteenth century, intermarriage between settlers and indigenous groups became less acceptable to colonial governments across Europe (Clancy-Smith and Gouda 1998: 8). Yet there were many places where intermarriage did occur, creating hybrid families (Wanhalla 2012). Migrating and moving across vast distances often involved sharing or setting up household with others in a way that would not have taken place in the home country. Men who moved out to India often rented together and shared domestic expenses (Jones 2007: 16). The elite families who governed the Empire might find themselves spread out over several continents. Adele Perry has referred to the example of a family group who encompassed the Caribbean, North America and the UK, with childhoods split between metropolitan and colonial space, as the 'trans-local family' (2010: 71). Elite Anglo-Indian living practices were transformed by spending time in India, but also moving back and forth between colony and mother country. It was particularly important to these families to maintain their status by having their children educated and/or brought up in England (Buettner 2004: 14). For these families, separation between parent and child became the norm, and fragile intimacies were maintained through regular letters and an exchange of objects (Buettner 2004: 130–37).

HOME AS A MATERIAL SPACE

During the nineteenth century, a vast number of new homes were built, and older buildings refashioned. The homes of the well-off had much in common, and the gap between rich and poor remained the most significant differentiating factor across the West. Yet there were also national and regional variations in the design and construction of homes. Climate made a difference: in England, for example, open fireplaces were seen as a sufficient heating source, whereas in Northern Europe and the northern US, stoves were essential (Oldenziel and Hård 2013: 59–60). A notable difference between housing stock in England and the rest of Europe and some American cities was the absence of apartment blocks in city centres and the predominance of the terraced house (Muthesius 1982: 3). English villas and terraces, and the living practices they fostered, are explored further in Chapter 3. There were a wide variety of housing forms across the vast territories of the US. In more rural areas, new balloon frame technologies were used to create wooden exteriors partly fashioned by the availability of timber but also by a new aesthetic vision of the refined American family farm (Bushman 1992: 247–49). For settlers across North America and the Empire, the necessity of adapting to local conditions and the availability of materials could produce new housing forms: the 'sod houses' created by settlers in Nebraska are a good example of this (Vollenbröker 2014: 296).

To what extent can we see a transnational bourgeois home emerging in this period? Certainly there were technological developments that spread across Europe and America. Changes in scientific ideas in relation to the home had a transnational circulation. There were also movements for hygiene reform across Europe (Oldenziel and Hård 2013: 65). In British and Spanish domestic advice there was a drive against dust, and furniture and furnishings that might harbour it, including traditional four-poster beds, were banned (Neiswander 2008: 66; Cruz 2011: 66). Increasingly, it was possible to buy similar or the same goods across the West. Decorative domestic items had already been flowing through trade networks for several centuries (Gerritsen and Riello 2016). But what was new was the change in methods of production, often leading to larger numbers of goods being produced at a lower cost, as well as the development of networks required for their distribution (Benson 1994; Grier 1988: 9). Global trade networks also grew and strengthened. Exports of manufactured things from Britain to its settler colonies increased in the second half of the nineteenth century and migrant demand for goods from 'home' strengthened, even though foreign and domestic things were increasingly available (Magee and Thompson 2010: 117). This was particularly the case in New Zealand and South Africa (Magee and Thompson 2010: 120). Yet as we see in Chapter 3 of this book, domestic goods in British East Africa came from a complex range of places and producers. Increasingly, the colonial domestic interior was composed of a 'bricolage' of objects, representing a cosmopolitan style of decorating that was shared between European and even local indigenous elites.

Across different nations and regions in middle-class homes there was a new, shared emphasis on the importance and decoration of living rooms (although they had different names and subtly different functions). English drawing rooms, American parlours and Italian *salottos* were seen as the public face of home, and were increasingly elaborately decorated (Logan 2001; Grier 1988; Caesar 2004). From the mid-century onwards, these rooms were densely and heavily decorated, furniture was draped and large numbers of ornaments introduced. These interiors were strongly associated with the sins of the Victorian age that prompted the modernist critique (Reed 1996). Later on, there was a shared trend for oriental objects in an attempt to create greater individuality within the interior (Oldenziel and Hård 2013: 63–64; Perrot 1990: 346). Yet there was also a new emphasis on the family significance of these spaces. If there was enough room for an additional sitting room alongside the grand salon in French bourgeois homes, it was usually devoted to the *petit salon*, which provided an informal space for family intimacy (Tiersten 2001: 168). The Spanish meanwhile celebrated the *gabinette* (family room) alongside the *sala principal* (public room) (Cruz 2011: 73).

The choice of things for the home could also express clear cultural, political and national differences. This is evident in styles of furnishing, and their association with particular national identities. In the Henry James novel *The Europeans* (1879), the title characters' reactions to the decoration of the American homes they visit conveys a powerful sense of cultural difference. This period is thought to have seen the emergence of a distinctively North American style, positioned against the moral excesses of the European aristocracy, epitomized by the rocker in the parlour, which expressed comfort, refinement and 'homeyness' (Bushman 1992: 272). However, French historic styles remained popular across Europe in the nineteenth century, and France continued to be seen as a leader in matters of taste (Cruz 2011: 63). Yet for the French themselves, an exact duplication of historic style was politically problematic due to its association with the *ancien régime*. Instead, a modern version emerged, streamlined and lightweight, but replicating its essential features (Tiersten 2001: 159–61). European-wide stylistic trends were often given a national twist. In early-twentieth-century Sweden, for example, Carl Larsson's designs combined arts and crafts with eighteenth-century style to create a distinctive National Romantic interior (Facos 1996). Within nations, too, different groups might have their own particular takes on national style. Leora Auslander (2015) has looked closely at a photograph album produced by a bourgeois German Jewish family around 1910: in this house the dining room was furnished heavily in an almost caricatured version of traditional Bohemian style. This pressured minority groups to use furniture to assert a sense of belonging in a nation in which they were increasingly sidelined. National styles might take on different meanings in colonial homes, or colonists might create their own versions, drawing inspiration and domestic objects from many sources, as shown in Chapter 3. There were also significant differences in the physical and material nature of homes in the British Empire, created by different climates and material circumstances, but also by the ideas and newly emerging identities of the colonists.

DOMESTIC PRACTICES

The nineteenth century, then, saw the arrival of new objects and ideas about what should be done with them. To a certain extent, these goods were circulated transnationally creating shared domestic practices. Yet new things were also co-opted into older and continuous rituals that varied according to nation and region, and the kind of household that people lived in. New forms of spatial organization and etiquette emerged, but there was also continuity in rituals related to the life-cycle and particularly in practices handed down from mother to daughter. Often highlighted as new to the period, is the growing rationalization of bourgeois homes, with strict timetables and a new ordering of household space that assigned separate spaces to family members and servants and placed increasing emphasis on the precise function of rooms. Chapter 3 shows just how fundamental the idea of privacy was to the design of new forms of English housing. Yet, as with decorative choice, we can see national and local differences in the way that people chose to organize space in the home. The French aristocracy were reputedly less obsessive than the English about dividing up space (Girouard 2000: 309–11). In Anglo-Indian homes, rooms were named by their location rather than a specific use, suggesting a more flexible use of space (Jones 2007: 114). Lower down the scale, advice literature encouraged the British middle classes to aspire to domestic divisions, but inventory evidence suggests they rarely had the opportunity to do so (Hamlett 2010: 43). Naming rooms after their supposed function might also be lip service to convention; the lived reality of most middle-class British homes was very far from the upper-class ideal. There is evidence, too, that the new timetables for home management were difficult to implement, particularly when they involved servants (Hamlett 2010: 56).

The Victorian home has often been seen as rigidly regulated, and the location of a new range of social forms and etiquette practices that ensured the maintenance of new standards of gentility. These are associated with the newly emergent middle classes and bourgeoisie, who have been portrayed as ultra-anxious to relay and maintain their new-found social status. In Britain, there was a new emphasis on rules around paying social calls, the use of calling cards, and return visits (Davidoff 1973: 41–49). Visitors would be expected to be conversant with the norms of social etiquette and to confidently handle the phalanx of cutlery that lay on the dining room table. These rituals were played out in different ways in the colonies and in frontier territory. More settled societies in India and South Africa developed even more elaborate calling practices, perhaps because of the frequent arrival of incomers trying to establish themselves in these nascent societies (Lawrence 2012: 80; Jones 2007: 16). Yet on the US prairies settlers who ate out of doors challenged conventional dining rules (Vollenbröker 2014: 305). Even in Britain, supposedly the stronghold of buttoned-up domestic etiquette, people had different takes. In the early twentieth century, for example, in farming households in the West Country, everyone (masters and servants) ate together as a family. It was only when visitors came to call that more conventional dining practices were adhered to (Hamlett 2010: 58). Women were also adept in adapting domestic conventions to suit broader purposes. Headmistresses, for example, often adopted the conventional practice of holding a weekly 'At Home' to legitimize public gatherings that furthered their professional role (Hamlett 2015: 92).

We also need to think about how new practices sat alongside older domestic rituals. As in the early-modern period, the different stages of the life-cycle and the development of the family remained fundamental to activities within the home. One important commonality across geographical areas and social groups was the fact that birth and death usually took place in the home. In cases of illness, deaths were usually something that the whole family could prepare for, gathering around the death bed. It was also common for bodies to be displayed in the home before funerals (Strange 2005: 66). In Thomas Mann's *The Magic Mountain* (1927), the central character's contemplation of his grandfather's body, laid out in state in the dining room, is a defining moment in his early life. These rituals would have been different in working-class homes, where lack of space necessitated proximity to the deceased (Strange 2005: 69). For childbirth, too, the better-off tended to mark out special spaces for lying in within the home, which would have not have been an option for those with more limited resources (Adams 1996: 115). More national variation is evident in domestic practices that related to marriage. For the well-off everywhere, and for some working people in Western Europe and America, marriage tended to coincide with the establishment of a new home. In homes where a bride was simply an addition to a larger household, her arrival was marked in different ways – sometimes only by taking in her wardrobe and trousseau, but in some areas of France a new room or kitchen might be added to the main house (Segalen 2002: 13–14). There were also cultural differences in childcare practices that had implications for the organization of domestic space. In the early part of the period, the French were more likely to send children out to wet nurses (Robertson 1982: 14–15, 410), yet while the English did not do this, the middle classes were particularly keen on spatial separation between parents and children, with the nursery being distinctively British (Löfgren 2003: 145; Robertson 1982: 424). For the labouring classes, reliance on institutions for the care of infants was also a much greater phenomenon on the Continent (Tapaninen 2004).

Finally, we also need to consider the means by which domestic practices and ideas were transmitted between generations. In particular, homes were often created by women who established and maintained feminine cultures, handing them down to their daughters. Hand-worked objects are often underestimated, but they were at least as – if not more – important to their feminine creators as the mass-produced items that arrived in this era. In France, the creation of the trousseau marked an important point in a woman's life-cycle and was a powerful expression of her relationship with her mother (Fine 1984). English drawing rooms were often filled with hand-worked objects. Wedding lists from the period reveal that the exchange of hand-worked things might be a means of establishing and maintaining a circle of friends and kin (Hamlett 2010: 78–82). Sewing did, of course, reinforce conservative ideals of femininity, but could also offer agency. Sewing was an increasingly important part of the education of English working-class girls, and could provide a surprisingly wide range of opportunities for social expression (Richmond 2016). Sewing in plantation households reinforced the suppression of slaves, yet slave women could acquire and use these skills to provide for their families, acquiring a little power in the face of complete social oppression (Kennedy 2010: 127). As women moved out to temporary or permanent homes in the colonies, needlework was used in new ways to try to maintain or establish bonds. In the American West, migrating women often carried scrap bags containing remnants of material from generations of women, to be transformed into quilts that kept the memory of their families alive when they reached their new homes (Vollenbröker 2014: 296).

CONCLUSION

The home, then, was increasingly celebrated in the nineteenth century by the growing middle classes in both Europe and the USA. Yet once we move away from this social group, understandings of what home meant become more diverse. An appreciation of the meaning of home across this very broad social swathe needs to take account of differences of language, social group and locality. There was significant variation in the location of homes, the composition of households, what homes contained and what people did in them. While the nineteenth century is often characterized by the idea of an industrial revolution and the rapid growth of cities, we need to remember that many people in Western Europe and North America continued to live in rural homes. The occupation of families made a crucial difference to who resided in the household, with workers engaged in certain trades or farming methods continuing to live together in large households, as pooling resources remained economically effective. Different social groups also tended to have different sized families, which would have made a great deal of difference to the lived experience of home. And while more people had access to a greater number of household goods than ever before, there remained distinct national ideas of style. Decorative choice was a key means of expressing cultural difference. Many households developed new domestic practices and forms of etiquette, which were most evident in bourgeois homes across Western Europe. Yet across the board the home continued to be organized around key moments in the life-cycle, with birth, death and marriage being the focuses of ritual material exchange and practices that took their forms according to local customs and traditions.

While it is essential to be aware of this variety, this volume demonstrates the power of home as a shared idea across the Anglophone Western world; something that reached its peak in the age in which that world itself was aggressively expanding its boundaries. Nonetheless, the following chapters emphasize the limits of this idea and the different ways that it was constructed by different societies and cultures, as well as its practical limits when we consider the everyday lives of Britons and Americans. While studies of home have usually focused mainly on the middle classes, the homes of working people (which made up the vast majority of dwellings) are given more emphasis here. For the millions of people who did not live in conventional family households, whose working lives continued to impinge on the domestic, or who could not afford to keep a mother at home and furnish a parlour and dining room, the ideal home remained just that, an ideal. The chapters in this book each explore a different aspect of home in detail, demonstrating how a greater understanding of the cultural history of home can bring us closer to people's past lives and identities.

CHAPTER ONE

The Meaning of Home: The Ideal and its Limits in England and the Colonies

MARGARET PONSONBY

Name Jo . . . No father, no mother, no friends. Never been to school. What's home?
—Charles Dickens, 1853

With these words the beadle summed up the life of Jo the crossing sweeper in *Bleak House*, and thereby revealed a terrible deficiency in his life; as an unloved orphan sleeping in a squalid derelict house, he had never had a home and did not even understand the concept. Dickens produced a poignant portrayal of destitution in the character of Jo that perhaps now seems somewhat sentimental but for his readers in the mid-nineteenth century, was entirely appropriate to convey the horror of Jo's situation – to have never experienced a home. During the Victorian period, the concept of the home achieved a potent image that formed the core of family life; a place of safety, moral rectitude, domesticity, warmth, comfort, and love. While the ideal was difficult if not impossible to achieve, especially for the poor and those on the margins of society like Jo, still the image was strongly expressed through the novels of the age as well as through advice literature, paintings, popular songs, and poetry. This concept took physical form in the furnishings of the home that were ascribed symbolic roles rather than simply fulfilling practical needs. The years 1800–1920 encompass the main period of growth of this meaning of home, through the major manifestation of the concept and its decline when in the late nineteenth and early twentieth century, the beginnings of the modern idea of home were discernible in household organization and furnishings.

The reasons for the development of the Victorian concept of the home are complex but must surely be linked to the upheaval of the industrial age. Previously, society had been led by the aristocracy but by the early nineteenth century the middle classes had emerged to take the lead; economically, politically and socially (Davidoff and Hall 1997: 21). The middle classes could be critical of the extravagance of the aristocracy with their lavish lifestyle that revolved around show, and instead they valued sober domesticity. However, rapid industrialization and urbanization brought social turbulence, and although the middle classes were aspirational they were often financially and culturally insecure. Davidoff and Hall suggest that the 'middle class was being forged at a time of exceptional turmoil and threatening economic and political disorder' (1997: 30). This resulted in an urgent need to strengthen the established order within families and the role of the individual particularly with regard to gender roles. A religious revival that emphasized the importance of the nuclear family and its moral well-being increased the focus on the domestic abode as a physical space to be created, controlled and scrutinized; within the household and by society at large. This style of homemaking placed the wife and mother at its centre, the 'Angel in the House' who would care for the practical needs of the family but also its spiritual well-being.

Alongside these developments was the huge expansion in the production of goods, and simultaneously of retailing, which made a variety of furnishings available that in the past would only have been consumed by the very wealthy (Briggs 1990). The increase in production was mirrored by an increase in consumption and the middle classes were the chief protagonists. Deborah Cohen suggests that they ceased to associate the acquisition of goods with self-indulgence and instead defined consumption of the right kind 'as a moral act' (2006: 30). By the mid-century, the middle classes used consumption for the home to consolidate their identity. They created a space that was meant to express the solidity of their economic position, their respectability and social status, and the cohesion of the family unit. Their homes needed to fulfil a dual purpose, to be a private domestic space that provided safety and a moral setting for the family but also to provide a semi-public role for invited guests with an opportunity to display taste and position (Grier 1988: 2). The tensions that this dual purpose created were somewhat resolved by the symbolic associations of home furnishings that were provided by increased commercial production but also through amateur 'home-made' creations.

The growth of the middle classes and their influence on homemaking was prevalent throughout Britain and affected people living in rural and urban localities, traditional cultural centres and the newly industrialized towns.

However, although the ideal was widespread, how it was translated varied and was dependent on where people lived, their position in society, even with variations within the middle class that made people more or less able or desirous to put the ideal into effect. The powerful and widespread image that was encompassed by the Victorian ideal of the home was not the same as lived experience. This chapter will begin by outlining the concept of the ideal home portrayed in cultural representations and how this was to be translated into physical and symbolic form through the furnishing of the house. It will then go on to explore how the reality of home was created in less than ideal circumstances that both disrupted the ideal image but at the same time demonstrated the power of the concept of home. The meaning of home was both emotional and physical, and achieving its creation was desired by many whatever the circumstances; by single people as well as families, by people in institutions as well as individual homes, and in far flung corners of empire as well as in England.

THE IDEAL HOME

The nineteenth century produced a wealth of representations of home that influenced the practice of homemaking. The concept of home was expressed most vividly in the Victorian period in the cultural media of the age, novels, paintings, songs and poetry. The prevalence of the imagery, its detail and sentimental nature all testify to the importance given to the meaning of home by the Victorians. Coventry Patmore's poem of the 1850s 'The Angel in the House' celebrated the perfect wife and coined the ubiquitous phrase to describe her. The song 'Home Sweet Home' with sheet music was published in 1852 and could be sung by the family around the piano in their own parlour. Victorian narrative paintings and the cheaper and widely popular prints produced from them delighted in telling stories that often illustrated the meaning of home, such as the idealized cottage scenes by Frederick Daniel Hardy or the dangers of losing the home as in the Past and Present series by Augustus Egg (Thomas 2000: 39, 67–81) (Figure 1.1). Sad scenes depicting destitution and loss were made more poignant by the interior being depicted without the accoutrements of home. Many middle-class Victorian interiors would have featured one or more paintings or prints of this kind; their small size made them ideal for the domestic setting and their moral, sentimental and uplifting narratives could be consumed by the whole family (Aynsley and Grant 2006).

The centre of the home was visualized as the parlour, or in more wealthy homes, the drawing room (Figure 1.2). These variations of sitting room, as Lesley Hoskins (2014) has demonstrated, were not interchangeable and had subtle hierarchical differences, the latter featuring more specialized furnishings

FIGURE 1.1: The fear of homelessness. Engraving from 1870 of a poor homeless family on the streets of London in the nineteenth century. © Duncan Walker / Getty Images.

FIGURE 1.2: The heart of the home: the parlour or drawing room. Engraving of a Victorian drawing room at Brahan Castle. © Duncan1890 / Getty Images.

than a parlour, which probably needed to have several functions. It was in the sitting room that the family gathered and spent leisure time together and the arrangement of the room encouraged shared activities. If they were not gathered around a piano, then the fashion for a central table also served this purpose. Often with the only oil lamp in the room, it provided a space for reading, drawing, sewing and other activities that might be performed individually but were an opportunity for being together, perhaps while one member of the family read aloud. Although nineteenth-century family life might seem rigid by today's standards, it was less formal than earlier periods even at the level of the wealthy in society in their country houses, and this was expressed and encouraged by the furnishing of homes (Girouard 1978: 231). Ideology was given material form: Victorian furniture was often rounded in shape with luxurious curves and a great deal of upholstery. When buttoned spring upholstery became widely available from the 1840s, a range of chairs, couches and sofas were produced which were comfortable and allowed a relaxed posture but also looked comfortable. Around the mid-nineteenth century, interiors, in particular living rooms, employed furnishings that used copious amounts of fabric, often with a soft finish, such as plush velvets, and with fancy trimmings. Textiles were used to soften the architectural shell of rooms, draped over tables and chairs, layers of curtains at windows, lambrequins placed over doors and mantelpieces. All of these elements made the interior look warm and cosy and emphasized the difference between work and home. The ideal parlour provided physical comfort but was also a visual expression of comfort and ease.

Christmas was the time of year in particular when the ideal of the home came into its own in the nineteenth century. Christine Lalumia suggests that the revival of Christmas by the Victorians was, like the creation of home, a reaction to the social changes that England was undergoing and as a 'cultural anchor' for the middle class (2001: 23–24). The Victorians 'repackaged' many of the traditions associated with Christmas such as burning the yule log and singing carols but in doing so they formulated the potent image of Christmas as a family celebration at home as well as a religious festival. The royal family were seen as the perfect example to the rest of the population and the picture, reproduced in the *Illustrated London News*, of them gathered around their decorated tree at Windsor in 1848 provided the image to emulate (Lalumia 2001: 26) (Figure 1.3).

The visual and literary image of the ideal and cosy parlour or drawing room in Victorian homes was not the same thing as how families lived in their homes. As Thad Logan reminds us, 'all representations of the parlor – whether graphic or linguistic – are partisan, strategic and embedded in history' (2001: 2). The image portrayed of the home around the mid-century was conformist in nature;

FIGURE 1.3: The family Christmas. Engraving from 1868 after the painting by Thomas Webster. © Duncan Walker / Getty Images.

one style of homemaking that all should aspire to. The ideal home was a family home with father, mother and children who all understood their role within the structure of the household. The material culture of the home was employed as a physical expression of the relationships of the inmates of the house and their place in society. This produced a moral obligation on the part of the parents to create an interior that fulfilled this task, with the degree of fulfilment varying according to social status. Rooms were given specific roles and were to be used by particular members of the household and the furnishings should express this, whether it was gendered usage of morning room or library, age-related usage as in the nursery or schoolroom, or status usage as in the correct divisions between family and servants. The zoning of the interior encompassed the segregation of the sleeping arrangements of the sexes and was taken to extremes in some of the large country houses built in the nineteenth century (Kerr 1864; Franklin 1981).

In addition, interiors needed to be clean and well-maintained, particularly once the means of transmitting infectious diseases was understood. By the later nineteenth century, interior furnishings and decoration evolved to reflect these concerns with washable wallpapers, a reduction of crevices that harboured dust, and the removal of heavy curtains around beds and at windows (Neiswander 2008: 58–59). It was at this time that wooden beds gave way to metal ones, since they were easier to clean, and newly built middle-class housing began to routinely include a bathroom, although washing often continued to take place in bedrooms using a washstand and bowl (Hoskins 2014: 344; Smith 2007). The cultural practices of cleaning the home expressed in physical terms the hard work that was dispensed to protect the inmates from dirt and disease, both the physical bacterial threat and the moral contamination (Kelley 2009b). To fail to create the ideal home cast a shadow over the inmates – over their financial strength and credit worthiness but also their morality and religious worth.

It was also the case that the ideals of homemaking could be used as a yardstick by charitable organizations for dealing with the working class and for people on the fringes of society, whether they deserved help or not. Numerous Victorian philanthropists financed model housing as a method of providing help for the poor but it was always accompanied by a great many rules and regulations (Burnett 1978). These were to ensure that the recipients lived sober, religious and moral lives, and helped them to become hardworking, good citizens. For working-class and poor people who fell outside the definition of worthy or who broke the law, part of their punishment was to be deprived of the trappings of home as, for example, in the newly built workhouses. The working class were often portrayed in paintings and prints in this way; happy, moral and enjoying a home, or dejected, depraved and lacking all of the effects of domestic life (Figure 1.4).

FIGURE 1.4: The working-class home with material comforts threatened by alcohol. Etching by G. Cruikshank, 1847, after himself. © Wellcome Library, London.

ADVICE FOR HOMEMAKERS

The rise of a middle class that was at the forefront of the changes in society in the early nineteenth century also produced a large number of families that had risen quite quickly without a strong background of education and refinement. Their perception of their own shortcomings made them a ready audience for advice literature, especially as printed materials were on the increase and available at lower prices (Beetham 1996). A great many books were published during the century to cater for this perceived need to create a home 'correctly'. A consideration of the style of presenting this advice and how it changed over the nineteenth century is useful for thinking about the relationship between the idea of the ideal home and how that ideal should be translated into the material culture of the domestic interior. There were differences of opinion on certain issues by advice writers, and ideas of what the home should consist changed over time. But there was a basic consensus in these writings as to what the ideal home was, focused on the middle-class model of breadwinner husband with a wife whose central occupation was home and family.

During the first half of the nineteenth century, a link was made between the choice and consumption of objects for the home and the formation of character. How to make the right decision about home furnishings was expressed in emphatic language in advice literature (Grier 1988: 7). The art critic John Ruskin, whose books were sold in large numbers, set the bar high for cultivating the correct taste in home furnishings as well as architecture and art. 'Taste', he declared, 'is not only a part and an index of morality, it is the ONLY morality . . . Tell me what you like, and I'll tell you who you are' (quoted in Young 2003: 173). Such a comment might well make any unsure young wife desperate for advice on what she should like.

Much of the advice literature in the period up to the 1860s was prescriptive in nature, sometimes taking the form of a conversation between an older and more experienced woman and a younger, recently married one. Examples of this style include Mrs Williams Parkes's *Domestic Duties* (1828) and Alexis Soyer's *The Modern Housewife or Ménagére* (1849). The advice was often difficult to translate into concrete choices of furnishings, since it stressed the importance of the home atmosphere that should be created as well as how it should be furnished, the need for richness in the public rooms without being showy and opulent, and since this was a middle-class audience, the need for the best quality that could be afforded but without going into debt. A warning was often included on the danger of trying to aim too high, for example in *Cassell's Household Guide*: 'living in a fine house with very straitened means frequently entails great discomfort, and it is in most cases excessively imprudent' (1870: 2). Rather more useful as a guide to furnishing were the books produced by John Claudius Loudon, which offered several different levels of consumption with the corresponding furnishings, copiously illustrated, for every room of the house at each level (e.g. 1833). Although it is not possible to be sure how influential advice literature was on homemaking activities, the increased quantity of this published material during the century and the prevalence of remarkably similar advice suggest that it reflects broadly accepted attitudes to what constituted a home and how it should be organized and furnished. British advice manuals were also widely consumed in the colonies, demonstrating the prevalence of at least a desire to follow similar ideals in homemaking, as will be examined below (Lawrence 2012: 99).

The 'separate spheres' of the public world of work and the private world of the home, albeit imperfect and not absolute, also 'underpinned the discourse of design advice' for the home and its organisation into gendered spaces (Keeble 2013: 32). Rooms were designated male and female according to how they were to be used and were furnished accordingly. The principal male domain was the dining room and the principal female room was the drawing room. All the advice literature that flourished in the early to mid-nineteenth century described how these rooms were to be furnished and how the gendered nature of the interiors was to be expressed. The 'masculinity' of the dining room should be expressed through the polished and carved mahogany furniture and plain woollen curtains, while the 'feminine' drawing room should use lighter colours with upholstered furniture and chintz, velvet or silk textiles (Kinchin 1996). Increasingly in the nineteenth century, the design of objects was designated for male or female use, which increased the need for consumption as well as expressing the gendered nature of individual rooms and how they were to be used (Young 2003: 177; Forty 1987, ch. 4).

From the 1870s the advice took a somewhat different form, reflecting perhaps the maturing of the middle-class position in society and the development of the notion that expressing taste was an opportunity for individuality. Rather than the heavy moralistic tone of earlier publications, the later part of the century presented homemaking advice in consumerist terms (Ferry 2003). Some books were written in collaboration with furniture manufacturers and reflected the style of their productions, while illustrated catalogues for department stores might carry furnishing advice, as in the late-nineteenth-century examples produced by Liberty's (Ashmore 2008). Rather than following one fashion, consumers could now choose what style reflected their 'lifestyle'. H.J. Jennings, for example, writing in 1902, offered readers a range of different styles for their drawing rooms (Jennings 1902: 173–200) (Figure 1.5). These developments are clearly discernible in the advent of the *Daily Mail* Ideal Homes exhibition in 1908, which displayed furnished houses and all the latest products to purchase for the home (Sugg-Ryan 1997).

There is some debate over what advice literature tells us about who controlled homemaking decisions. Cohen (2006) is particularly adamant that men were at the forefront of determining the purchase of furnishings and were even the main audience for advice literature; by contrast, Logan (2001) associates women with the homemaking process. Advice literature often stressed the emotional responsibility of household management as well as the practical requirements, so for example in 1823 readers were told that 'to make a home the agreeable retreat of a husband, fatigued by intercourse with a bustling world; to be his enlightened companion, and the chosen friend of his ear; these are woman's duties, and her highest honor' (Eaton 1823: x). In texts like this one, it was mostly women who created the tenor, the visual style of the interior apart from in the male preserves such as the study or library. The division of responsibilities was highlighted by Disraeli in his novel *Coningsby* when he declared that 'woman alone can organize a drawing room; man succeeds sometimes in a library' (quoted in Tristram 1989: 59). Even in advice literature in the 1870s, women were still being admonished that to them fell the duty to invest in the home by increasing its refinement and beauty (Orrinsmith 1877).

Print culture featured many patterns and instructions for women to use for making textile items that would add a 'homely' touch to interiors such as

FIGURE 1.5: Contrasting styles for drawing rooms. 'White Panelled Drawing Room with Old English Furniture' and 'Adams Drawing Room'. From H.J. Jennings (1902), *Our Homes and How to Beautify Them*, 2nd edition, London: Harrison, 179 and 188.

embroidered cushions, pictures, footstools and fire screens. Berlin wool work was promoted as a simple method of embroidery that in addition was available in kit form with the design already printed on canvas (Edwards 2006: 12). Some women practised a variety of crafts out of necessity and publications such as *The Workwoman's Guide* (Anon. 1838) provided instructions for them to follow. However, many magazines aimed at middle-class women were for small items such as covers for needle cases, slippers, pen wipers, antimacassars and doilies. Sewing of all kinds was presented as a demonstration of feminine industry and virtue, and to have sufficient leisure to make additional items was also no doubt seen as a sign of their gentility – after all, in previous centuries only wealthy women could spend their time in this way. The weight given to such craft production in print culture suggests their cultural importance, despite the way in which they have often been seen as peripheral by historians (Logan 1995: 213: Parker 1984).

By the 1880s, the Aesthetic Movement heralded a further dimension to homemaking and the symbolic expression of furnishings (Gere and Hoskins 2000; Aslin 1969). While for much of the nineteenth century homemaking advice revolved around establishing home as a haven for the family, and comfort – both physical and spiritual – was expressed in particular through the use of textiles, the choice of pictures and the inclusion of homemade crafts, the new and 'first proper interior-decorating craze' encouraged people to express their individual taste rather than merely showing that they had 'good' taste (Breward 2001: 420). The need to be original may have added to anxieties around home furnishing but the craze soon became commercialized, and manufacturers and retailers catered for the needs of homemakers with Japanese fans, peacock feathers, and blue and white china ornaments. By the early twentieth century, Art Nouveau was gaining in popularity for home decoration but was viewed with suspicion in some quarters, it being seen as a decadent style (Jennings 1902: 55). The link between homes and morality was also present in the interiors associated with the Arts and Crafts Movement, where 'honesty' to materials and methods of manufacture was celebrated, so that Ruskin's words on the link between taste and morality already quoted applied throughout the period 1800–1920.

THE REALITY OF HOMEMAKING, 1800–1920

The ideal meaning of home was reproduced in visual and literary examples and described in advice literature throughout the nineteenth century. These representations perhaps expressed the social and cultural ideals of homemaking that the producers of the image thought appropriate for families to create and experience. It must be acknowledged that it is impossible to gauge to what extent people sought to emulate the ideals portrayed in the representations or followed the advice literature. As Jane Lewis has argued, it is not 'clear how far women of any social class paid attention to the domestic ideal'. Instead, she suggests that many may have adjusted the ideals to 'fit more easily with the reality of women's lives, or that they were consciously resisted' (1986: 6). In any case, even where the ideal was desired, circumstances often prevented its realization. Large numbers of the working-class population lived in poor housing conditions that did not provide sufficient space to offer any of the segregation that was thought to be desirable, and the lack of running water and shared WC made even basic hygiene difficult, although many families tried to mitigate the difficulties, such as using a bowl in the scullery for personal washing (Hoskins 2014: 345). Middle-class families usually lived in rented accommodation where short leases and difficult landlords often prevented alterations and improvements to imperfect properties. In addition, changes in employment might require removing to a different location, while loss of employment or illness might result in the need for retrenchment (Muthesius 1982: 17–18; Burnett 1978). Though an advantage of rented properties was that a move to better accommodation could easily be facilitated as circumstances presented themselves.

There was a huge difference in the respectable rented accommodation of the middle classes and the lodgings inhabited by the working class. Lodgings suggested a more makeshift arrangement that might be acceptable for a young man still establishing his career but not for a family with aspirations of gentility and hopes of respectability (Davidoff and Hall 1997: 361). The worst lodging conditions were experienced by the poor who resorted to the night shelters with shared dormitory accommodation in common lodging houses. There were a huge number of these privately run establishments; in 1852, official statistics found that there were 3,300 alone in London (Hamlett 2015: 112; Glazier 1996). While the conditions no doubt varied, the general level of provision was basic and often squalid. The authorities thought that they would harbour criminals and that they would generally lead to a breakdown of morals with unpoliced sleeping arrangements and children accommodated alongside adults. In addition, it was feared they might become a breeding ground of disease, particularly during the 1840s during the cholera outbreaks. This was the kind of establishment that presumably Dickens was referring to when poor Jo the crossing sweeper in *Bleak House* was befriended by the mysterious Captain Hawden who took pity on his situation and 'gave him the price of a supper and a night's lodging' ([1853] 2003: 178). His readers would have comprehended the pathos of the situation; a child on his own in such a place and yet this was an improvement on his regular accommodation. Common lodging houses appeared to be the very opposite of what the ideal home should be, and the authorities tried to remedy the situation through legislation from 1851 with the Common Lodging House Act, which attempted to control the use of space and the level of hygiene and introduce a 'basic standard of domesticity' (Hamlett 2015: 112).

SINGLE PEOPLE AND HOMEMAKING

The idea of home revolved around the nuclear family of mother, father and children, therefore anyone not fitting this description was at a disadvantage in their homemaking. Many people, both male and female, remained unmarried throughout their lives. The unmarried state produced a variety of problems both practical and emotional, as well as a change in attitude by society as to the morality of the single state. In the seventeenth century, the celibate life was still commended but by the eighteenth century women in particular were castigated if they chose not to marry and might be ridiculed as 'old maids' if they failed to find a husband. In the nineteenth century, the census revealed that some 12 percent of women remained single in late middle age and this was seen as an economic drain on society (Wrigley and Schofield 1981: 426–28). The term 'surplus women' was used and recommendations were put forward for sending unmarried working-class women to the British colonies (Levitan 2008; Fedorowich 2008: 78). Middle-class women were particularly vulnerable to criticism since they had few methods available to them to earn a living that protected their respectability (Holloway 2005; Hill 1996). The impoverished gentlewoman working as a governess and living out an awkward existence in her employer's house where she was neither family nor servant is something of a cliché in Victorian novels but was a common enough experience, as testified in diaries from the period. Charlotte Brontë, for example, worked as a governess and drew on her experiences in her novels *Jane Eyre* and *Villette*. It should also be noted that the most common form of employment for women was as servants, the majority of whom were unmarried women who lived in the homes of wealthier people, varying from the single maid of all work in an attic room of a modest house to the vast armies of servants in large houses where segregation according to sex and hierarchy was preserved (Sambrook 1999; Horn 2004). Similarly, other forms of employment involved workers living on the premises, such as early department stores where dormitories were provided for the unmarried shop girls and boys (Lancaster 1995). The experience of home in these situations was far from ideal but must also have varied considerably according to the nature of the employer. On the whole, furnishings were provided and imposed on unmarried workers and their own contribution to homemaking was minimal in the form of a few small items brought from their parental home and to which some emotional attribution could be invested. For many of these workers the lack of a home was a temporary condition that ended when they married and set up home for themselves.

One solution for an unmarried middle-class woman was to live with relatives such as a brother where she could keep house for him until he married. However, when that happened she would often be side-lined by the new wife, though perhaps allowed to remain in residence earning her keep by helping with childcare and taking some of the work but little of the credit for running the household. This was the experience of Anne Boulton, who disliked her sister-in-law and eventually set up home on her own. Fortunately for Anne, she was financially secure and could afford furnishings from the top Birmingham suppliers and even items made by fashionable London cabinet-makers, though she had been reluctant to take what she saw as a momentous step to gain independence (Mason 2005; Hussey and Ponsonby 2012: 53–5-7).

Unmarried middle-class women might achieve independence through a limited number of occupations such as china painting, as careers for women in artistic decoration increased a little by the end of the century (Long 1993: 24). At the same time, some career options were emerging that stipulated women remain unmarried, such as teaching and the civil service, including working for the Post Office (Holloway 2005). Alternatively, some women inherited money or an annuity that allowed them to rent a few rooms or even a house. Some towns more than others seem to have attracted genteel unmarried women in the eighteenth century, and this practice of congregating in county and leisure towns such as Bath, Ludlow, Shrewsbury and Chichester continued in the nineteenth century (Sharpe 1999; Froide 2007). The small numbers of inventories that survive for this period, compared with the plentiful number for earlier periods, do still provide an indication that unmarried women with sufficient means to live a genteel life produced a home that mirrored to some extent family homes of the period albeit with some modifications. Rather than a formal dining room, these homes probably favoured a dining parlour, while libraries and studies were less usual than breakfast or morning rooms, both informal daytime sitting rooms, and therefore they followed the gendered nature of rooms in their decoration, furnishing and use (Hussey and Ponsonby 2012: 112–15; Ponsonby 2007: 138-149). A more common situation for less affluent unmarried women who had no family to provide for them was to take lodgings in another person's family home where they only had command over a small space in which to create home and which placed them in a precarious ethical position since young single women in lodgings were liable to be classified as prostitutes (Hamlett 2010: 164). The literature that advised on suitable furnishings was little help since furniture was provided. In such cases, the emotional content of the meaning of home would depend on small items brought from the family home, gifts and hand-made items which could recall the symbolic associations that the owner invested in them.

For men who remained single homemaking also had its difficulties, although they were somewhat different to those of their female counterparts. Men could still pursue their careers, some of which had openly encouraged or even insisted men remain single, such as when following a university career, although this was beginning to change in the nineteenth century. Single men could enjoy the same income as their married counterparts and indeed they could benefit from not having the expense of a wife, children and household.

Like single women, unmarried men could exercise some preferences in their use of rooms and choice of furnishings. Male homemakers were more likely to include a study or library as a second sitting room, especially if they worked from home, such as clergymen and doctors. Such rooms could employ more 'masculine' wooden furniture like bookcases, large desks and seating upholstered in leather, with textiles kept to a minimum (Hamlett 2010: 38–39). A minority of wealthy or eccentric single men went further and created highly individual homes that disturbed the accepted notions of the ideal home, with large collections of antiquarian artefacts or natural and geological specimens. Andrew Crosse made the ballroom of his country house into a laboratory while the artist Benjamin Robert Haydon allowed his huge canvases to take over his small lodging rooms. Single women were perhaps less likely to diverge from the standard arrangement whether due to finances, lack of career or the need to conform to society's expectations being greater, although there were exceptions to this rule such as the astrologer Caroline Herschel (Hussey and Ponsonby 2012: 129–47).

Single men could often draw on an unmarried female relative – a sister or niece – to keep house for them or they could employ an efficient housekeeper to ensure that their home ran along appropriate lines. Men might also sidestep the chore of homemaking by renting a few rooms where their housework and laundry were done for them and they could take their meals at an inn; for the wealthier members of the middle classes in London, there was the opportunity to spend time at their club where they could enjoy a high degree of comfort and hospitality (Milne-Smith 2006). However, while such measures overcame the practical aspects of homemaking, society might in some cases view them with suspicion, that the man without a family home was not quite respectable, as in the example of George Vavasor in Anthony Trollope's novel *Can You Forgive Her?* (1864). Single people could never achieve the same level of ideal homemaking that was possible for families because quite simply the ideal was a family home. However, the single state was experienced by many at some point in their lives whether before marriage, in widowhood or as life-long singles. The opportunity to create a close approximation to the ideal was often dependent on income; sufficient money ensured all the ingredients of home could be achieved and with them respectability was also a possibility.

MAKING A HOME IN AN INSTITUTION

Many people in the nineteenth century, including members of the middle classes, lived in institutions of one kind or another. Some were related to their employment, others were as punishment for misdeeds or simply due to poverty. As Jane Hamlett explains, this form of homemaking was on the increase in the nineteenth century when 'The expansion of the military, the relief of the poor, the punishment of criminals, the treatment of the mentally and physically ill, and the education of children all gave rise to an expansion in institution building on the part of the government and private and charitable bodies' (2015: 1). An example of a charitable institution that offered an alternative to private accommodation for a minority of homemakers was the almshouses. While these might seem to offer close approximations to independent homes, they were controlled in such a way as to confirm their institution status and thereby their compromised home conditions.

These institutions had been set up by endowments provided by wealthy individuals from medieval times, although they originated as hospitals associated with religious houses. Even as late as the nineteenth century, almshouses usually retained a religious aspect and their popularity gained a fresh impetus from the religious revivals of the century along with the middle class need to practise a religious life through philanthropy. Unfortunately, many of the older premises were under-funded and as a result were poorly maintained; for example, St. Mary's Almshouses in Shrewsbury were described in 1808 as 'wretched, filthy, and dangerously unwholesome' (Anon. 1808: 327). Like most institutions in the nineteenth century, they came under scrutiny and there was a call for tighter controls, in this case the Charitable Trusts Act of 1853 and several subsequent acts (Goose and Moden 2010: 65). The legislation was meant to tidy up the running of these institutions, as each had its own set of rules and financial arrangements; while some might be well run with adequate funds, others were the opposite. Scandals over the mismanagement of funds that were reported in the press gave rise to this topic being explored by Anthony Trollope in *The Warden*. It was hoped that with better legislation and the amalgamation of smaller institutions, almshouses would provide appropriate homely conditions for elderly and deserving individuals.

The image of almshouses as a safe haven for elderly women was portrayed in an article published in *Chambers Journal* by an anonymous writer in 1856 when recounting a visit to an almshouse in Shropshire. Although apparently based on a real institution near Wellington, the description idealizes the accommodation, making it appear an appropriate representation of homes within an institution that the readers of the paper would recognize. The writer mentions many key ingredients such as the 'air of comfort', the 'religious peace', 'tea tables and pleasant occupants', and one room in particular with its 'glowing hearth' and display of 'spotless' things 'all nicety and neatness with pretty landscapes round its walls' (Anon. 1856: 104). Thus the institution was represented as a collection of miniature homes inhabited by deserving inmates. However, almshouses were institutions that proclaimed their status in a great many ways.

The architecture of almshouses often stands out from that of other housing stock, since they mostly followed a particular pattern no matter the century they were founded. Small units of one or two rooms were arranged in blocks often around a quadrangle, one or two storeys high, sometimes with a chapel included. These units were intended to house a single person, sometimes with another family member to care for them, or a married couple. Many almshouses were intended for only single people and some stipulated they were only for men or for women, this being dependent on the wishes of the patron and the particular cause that they favoured. Some were specifically for people who had practised a particular trade. Gaining a place in an almshouse therefore depended on the person in need of a home fitting the requirements of the institution in their town; in addition, the committee or trustees who oversaw the running of the institution would vet all applicants and their character and morals would be assessed. Once admittance was gained, the inmate was then obliged to follow the rules; their homemaking was circumscribed by a host of regulations that varied from one almshouse to another. A few examples of such regulations governing the running of these institutions will provide an overview of how homemaking was a compromise that fell short of the nineteenth-century ideal home.

For example, the movement of inmates was controlled through gates and doors being locked at a set time at night, many stipulated that nights away from the building must first be sanctioned by the warden, and church attendance was either encouraged or enforced – at Coningsby Hospital in Hereford, for example, the elderly male residents were marched in line to the cathedral every Sunday (Beese 1971). These men would have stood out on the streets of the city due to their distinctive red uniform. Many almshouses provided uniforms, often of an old-fashioned style that set the inmates apart; even when uniforms were not provided, clothes were distributed once a year with the style and materials therefore being controlled by the warden or governors. Control over furniture was also imposed through some premises having built-in beds, cupboards and seats; while space-saving, these articles were common to all the dwellings and were of an outmoded style that distinguished them from what would have been considered desirable furnishings (Gilbert 1991). Perhaps more objectionable was the level of surveillance that some almshouses practised, along with enforced cleaning regimes. An example of an early twentieth century instance of this kind of surveillance is provided by the Bournville Almshouse in the village founded by the Cadbury family. In addition to providing Christmas gifts and an annual tea party, the Ladies' Visiting Committee also regularly inspected the properties, recording 551 visits to the 33 dwellings in 1904. Since many were felt to be insufficiently clean, tidy and well-aired, the Ladies instigated enforced Spring cleaning so that 'every house was thoroughly turned out and cleaned – bedding and carpets beaten etc.' every April and to encourage personal cleanliness a laundry was provided.[1]

Surveillance and attempts to govern cleanliness were not only an invasion of privacy but also a reminder to inmates that they resided in an institution. All institutions imposed rules and regulations about good behaviour. Common lodging houses and workhouses also enforced periodic whitewashing to keep disease under control and perhaps also to emphasize symbolic control over the inmates. The most stringent conditions were imposed by the new standardized workhouses and correctional prisons to deter dependency in the one and reoffending in the other. Rather than 'the chaotic, lawless abandon of the unreformed eighteenth-century prison', new penitentiaries introduced strict discipline that punished inmates and controlled behaviour, but also was designed to strip away individuality (Finn 1996: 205). Workhouses were often referred to as bastilles, since they were like prisons and split up families and couples into male, female and children wards (Fowler 2007: 41–64). One aspect in particular of both workhouses and prisons is pertinent here, that of depriving inmates of personal possessions and imposing basic but thoroughly institutional clothing and furniture (Gilbert 1991). While domestic and homely appurtenances in almshouses and common lodging houses and housing founded by charitable organisation were felt to give moral well-being to their inmates, in the case of prisons all associations with home were deliberately avoided. Workhouses were similarly stark in their provisions, although there was some softening in the regime by the later nineteenth century for their elderly inmates.

COLONIAL HOMEMAKING

During the nineteenth century, the British Empire was expanding and consolidating in various distant parts of the world, including South Africa, Canada, Australia and New Zealand, as well as the long established settlement in India, all of which presented a host of challenges for homemakers including climate, availability of goods and the difficulties associated with living in remote regions. Despite these difficulties, the strength of the meaning of home for the Victorians meant that the morality of homemaking and the desire for gentility was taken to the colonies by migrants and was translated into versions of the English model with the circumstances of each colony producing its individual response. In addition, the practices of homemaking in these various communities changed over time.

Just as in Britain, it was women who were at the heart of homemaking in the Empire; however, the permanence associated with each colony dictated whether British women relocated to distant parts of the world and established homes there. Single men working on a temporary basis as civil servants in India and East Africa probably made arrangements much as they would in England. Longer-term settlement occurred in India, particularly after the suppression of the Indian uprising of 1857–58, although the large population of India prevented permanent settlement and most British people returned home when they retired (Blunt 1999: 439, n. 10). In Australia and New Zealand where settlement was established by the 1830s, and in Canada after the fur trade was superseded by settlement in the 1850s, residence was on a permanent basis and these people knew they would probably never return to Britain (McPherson 2012: 222). Recreating the gentility of the Victorian home with its moral dimension through the material culture and use of space in the colonial setting was important in order to demonstrate control over difficult locales.

Acquiring appropriate furnishings presented a variety of challenges for colonists that varied according to location. The established communities in India could make use of local producers to make approximations of what was required. In newer ventures and expanding colonies in Australia and New Zealand, there was initially more reliance on goods taken from Britain. Newspaper advertisements carried listings of households to be sold by auction in much the same way as they did in England. However, there were the additional announcements of the arrival of shipments of goods of furniture and other household effects.[2] However, furnishings produced initially for consumption in the British climate were often inappropriate for the hot and humid conditions of Australia, especially the use of thin veneers which lifted to reveal poorly made furniture underneath. Tracey Avery (2007) has demonstrated that over time furniture makers became established in Australia to fulfil the requirements of the colonists using local timbers in solid wood construction. The production of furniture, rather than importing it from Britain, was in line with the colony becoming more self-sufficient and independent.

While acquiring suitable and appropriate furnishings was important, the meaning of home also needed to be preserved. Lawrence cites the numerous and detailed descriptions that women made to material culture in their letters and diaries (2012: 106). Items taken from England and those that were sent to them from family and friends were particularly prized, and the investment in the emotional meaning of home through material goods was especially strong among first-generation colonists who never expected to return to England.

Feeling 'at home' in a colony was important for individuals as well as the overall success of a settlement. Katherine Raine has demonstrated how this was achieved by female settlers in New Zealand through cultivating gardens. They favoured plants that were familiar and that would remind them of England, such as roses and lavender, so that 'ultimately for these women gardening was an important part of the psychological process of coming to feel at home in New Zealand' (Raine 2000: 83). While the cultivation of flowers might be partly nostalgic, the women were also using gardening to exert their dominance over the alien landscape. Through being responsible for vegetable growing as well as flowers and keeping hens, they not only helped supply the family with food and also traded produce with other women. In this way, they contributed to the success of the household and were perhaps able to exercise more power than they would have in England.

Rather than simply exporting a British way of life and imposing it on a variety of alien circumstances, the settlers were adapting the social and cultural uses of the physical space, which refashioned the meaning of home. Lawrence has shown how women adapted and reinterpreted refinements of lifestyle to suit the local situation and thereby reinforced their position as successful colonists. A prime example of this adaptation was the adoption of the veranda in tropical climates. This sheltered outdoor space was preferable to enclosed and stifling interiors. However, the veranda was open to observation by casual visitors and invasion by the local wildlife, thus undermining the privacy, protection and control that were desirable in a domestic setting. Civilizing this space became a key undertaking for many colonists and it emerged as an important part of the display of appropriate furnishings and genteel behaviour, such as immaculate tablecloths and extensive tableware for hosting dinner and tea parties (Lawrence 2012: 199–200).

However, in many 'bush' and frontier locations, houses were small and interiors were poorly furnished and did not provide the gentility and respectability that was expected in England. Women seem to have created a role for themselves that gained respect despite the shortcomings of their homes. In Canada, for example, Kathryn McPherson has traced this process through how the women interacted with local First Nation People. The women, recalling their experiences, cited their bravery, adaptability and use of domestic skills to show how they were 'authentic pioneers' (McPherson 2012: 232).

In some colonies such as Canada and Australia, there were fewer members of the servant class or at least fewer who had the appropriate experience to achieve middle-class standards of home maintenance, resulting in the mistress of the house being required to do more of her own housework. The opposite was the case in India, where even quite small households had ten to twelve servants, far more than was usual in Britain. This situation, which produced its own challenges, especially as many servants were male, is discussed in more detail in Chapter 2. Alison Blunt has studied the large number of advice books that were produced (Figure 1.6) specifically for women setting up home in India in the period 1880–1920, a period when the number of British women in India rose from almost 5,000 to around 42,000 (1999: 26). The advice books concentrated on the 'unequal relationship between British women and their Indian servants [which] reproduced imperial power relations on a domestic scale' (1999: 429). Blunt concludes that women through their homemaking played an important political role in spreading the imperial power of Britain in India, which was particularly important after the uprising of 1857–58.

Setting up and maintaining a home in one of Britain's colonies in the nineteenth century varied considerably across the Empire, involving the need to adapt to the local physical components, the use of space and the management of members of the household. However, the power of homemaking to unite

FIGURE 1.6: The prevalence of servants in the colonial home in India. 'Our Magistrate's Wife', by George Franklin Atkinson from *Curry and Rice*, India, c. 1860. © Victoria and Albert Museum.

and protect family life, to work as a civilizing force, and to maintain respectability was in evidence in the colonies as much as in England. The meaning of home throughout the nineteenth century was used for political purposes; in the colonies, domestic homemaking became a powerful component of empire-building.

CONCLUSION

The meaning of home in the nineteenth century was symbolic and emotional as well as the physical reality of houses and their contents. Homes were meant to convey a message about the family and their social, economic, moral and cultural standing. The image remained strong throughout the period 1800–1920, although it did evolve during that time. The earlier period encompassed the time when the newly emerging middle classes were becoming the dominant force in England and for them the idea of home expressed their love of sober domesticity rather than the extravagance of the aristocracy, and they incorporated their moral and religious views in the choice of 'correct' furnishings with gendered uses and the segregation of the household. The emphasis on cleanliness kept the family safe from disease and made clear their separation from the sordid living conditions of the working classes, while the inclusion of home-made items incorporated the symbolic message of sentiment for the members of the family. While the visual and literary representations were unified and unambiguous in their message, the lived experience of homemakers was messier. The ideal does not take account of the unhappy homes, or where the husband mistreated his family or where the wife was not a good manager. Loss of employment and sickness were constant threats to the well-being of the household. In addition, countless people did not fit the ideal image even within the middle classes where single people, for example, inhabited a compromised home.

Many members of the working classes were unable to afford most of the requisite elements of the Victorian home. Representations of poor homes such as the paintings by Hardy suggest that the industrious and moral members of the working classes wanted a similar ideal if on a different scale to the middle classes and would work hard to secure it. The reality was that many things prevented working-class people achieving a comfortable, clean and attractive home despite their hard work. The insanitary condition of slum housing was a particular concern throughout the nineteenth century and was only gradually addressed through legislation, with the 'by-laws' of the 1870s governing minimum requirements for housing and after the Great War the Addison Act forced local authorities to begin to provide social housing (Burnett 1978: 156–57, 221).

For the middle classes, the later nineteenth-century home was still a site of ideal family life but could also be a means of self-expression, with the purchase of goods increasingly seen as a way of expressing individuality. The middle classes in the early twentieth century were confident in their taste and pursued it through purpose-built housing, mostly in the suburbs. The ideology of domesticity was undermined by the growth of feminism and an increase in middle-class female employment. Although this gathered pace after the Second World War, even by the inter-war period the decrease in servant numbers had its effects on home furnishing and maintenance. Publications, particularly magazines, might feature fashionable interiors and advice on furnishing but it was with less condescension than in the early nineteenth century and most of the instruction was in the form of consumer advice with the Good Housekeeping Institute, for example, founded in 1900. In theory, the working-class home was more open to influence and it was to this that the critics such as the Design and Industries Association turned, but with mixed results. The rules and regulations of council housing were often undermined by their tenants who insisted on decorating and furnishing to their own idea of home just as the inmates of common lodging houses and other institutions had resisted regulations in the nineteenth century (Hamlett 2015: 10; Attfield and Kirkham 1995).

The period 1800–1920 established the home as a central concern for family life, as a potent image that could be made use of by politicians and social and artistic critics, but ultimately its meaning became a place of privacy, individual choice and expressions of personality.

CHAPTER TWO

Family and Household: Domestic Service in Colonial India[1]

FAE DUSSART

During the nineteenth century, the British Empire expanded to become the biggest territorial empire the world has ever seen. Across the Empire colonists and their families established new kinds of households, domestic units that were different from homes in Britain. In India, the so-called 'jewel' in the imperial crown, such households were emblems of imperial domesticity, often including a large contingent of domestic servants. This chapter focuses on these households and the relationship between Indian servants and their British employers in nineteenth-century British India, its structure and its emotional dimensions.[2]

By the 1830s, the joint-stock East India Company had expanded its reach from its initial base in Bengal to become the paramount authority in the Indian subcontinent. Ostensibly a trading company, its pursuit of India's riches led it, via conquest and treaty, to end up governing vast swathes of the region. The Company's rule was enforced by a huge private army of locally recruited Indian soldiers, administered by its own civil service, and supported, then eventually regulated, by British governmental sanction and subsidies. It was the epitome of corporate colonial power. In the eighteenth and early nineteenth centuries, British men who travelled to India under its aegis rarely intended to settle permanently, even though many of them established households and families there, often with Indian women, and adopted or interpreted local domestic practices. Put simply, Company men were in India to extract its wealth rather than transform its indigenous cultures.

By the early nineteenth century, technological change was improving communications within India and between the colony and the metropole. This allowed for the swifter movement of political, social, economic and cultural ideas across imperial space. In Britain, evangelical and utilitarian reform enthusiasms infused the rhetoric that framed British rule in India, and its governance was increasingly viewed as sorely in need of 'the benefit of men capable of applying the best ideas of their age to the arrangement of its important affairs' (Mill 1820: 402). Drawing on the scholarship of classical philologists, who had established Sanskrit as belonging to a common Indo-European family of languages, some early-nineteenth-century scholars suggested Europeans and Indians shared common origins, thus providing justification for the idea that with guidance Indians could become 'civilized' according to a definitive European standard (Sinha 1995: 20). Central to the early-nineteenth-century perception of India's need for reform was a representation of Indian society as in a state of barbarous immaturity, lacking in the 'civilization' that supposedly defined the culture of the metropole.

An important part of the British ideal of 'civilization' was the manifestation of domesticity that was realized through the household. As we saw in Chapter 1, in Britain, industrialization had entailed the expansion of a middle class whose distinctive culture articulated the home as a private, sanctified and feminized place of consumption and reproductive labour. According to this ideal, appropriately masculine middle-class men worked in the public world outside the home, while middle-class ladies' work constituted management of the household and family, cultivating 'accomplishments' and sometimes philanthropy. The labour of domestic servants released time for family members to pursue these other gendered and classed activities. Furthermore, through deference rituals, servants embodied and signalled status difference to household members and outsiders alike. Seebohm-Rowntree, in his study of York in the late nineteenth century, took the distinction between the working class and those above them in the social hierarchy to be marked by 'the keeping or not keeping of domestic servants' (1903: 14). This kind of domestic organization was key in the construction of middle-class respectability, as the index of gentility did not include cooking, cleaning or the messy dimensions of childcare. Servant-keeping thus became *de riguer* for anyone in Britain with aspirations to middle-class status. Of course, for many families this ideal did not reflect the reality of their lives. Nonetheless, it was powerful. Even while tighter boundaries were drawn around the private sphere of home and family in the nineteenth century, more and more of those who aspired to middle-class status were bringing strangers into their homes to cook their food, nurse their children, clean their homes and deal with the most intimate aspects of their daily lives, if necessary hiring servants cheaply from workhouses, or taking on impoverished kin. It is perhaps unsurprising that in nineteenth-century Britain, domestic servants were the largest occupational group of working women; indeed, they were the largest occupational group in the economy after agricultural labourers (Davidoff 1995: 21–22).

In colonial India, domestic servants were predominantly drawn from the Indian people. The ways in which they were viewed were inseperable from colonial understandings of racial difference. As Indira Ghose has written: 'the later generation of East India Company rulers was anything but enamoured of Indian arts and culture' (1998: 4). As the nineteenth century progressed, Indian society was discussed in ways that stressed socio-cultural decline, signified by the putative effeminacy, sensuality and feebleness of Indian people. As the reform enthusiasm of the 1840s waned, the development of 'scientific' theories of racial difference allowed many mid-century British observers to perceive Indians as a totally different, and inferior, race from the British:

> In point of race the Hindoos have been regarded by naturalists as belonging to what they call the Caucasian, and even to the same family of that race as the white man of Europe! But this is a fantastical notion, for which there is hardly even so much as the shadow of a foundation.
> —McCullock 1858: 81

The discursive construction of Indian character as inherently debased was 'proved' by the so-called 'Sepoy Mutiny' of 1857. This rebellion was sparked in May in Meerut, when rumours spread amongst Indian Army soldiers – *sepoys* – that pig and cow fat had been used to grease cartridges for new Lee Enfield rifles. The use of such animal products was offensive to both Hindu and Muslim soldiers, who were already disaffected by the negative effects of Company rule on their own and their communities' lives. The soldiers' rebellion spread rapidly across North India, encompassing civilian populations, with atrocities committed on all sides. After the rebellion had been brutally repressed by the British, control of India was removed from the hands of the East India Company and taken over by the Crown in 1858. The shift to Crown control saw the establishment of a government in India that was directly responsible, via the Viceroy in India and a Secretary of State for India in the India Office in London, to Parliament. Though nationalist movements emerged towards the end of the nineteenth century, India was to remain a Crown colony until its independence in 1947.

After the establishment of Crown control and the beginning of the Raj in 1858, the numbers of Europeans in India expanded, particularly as more women travelled to the subcontinental colony. Nonetheless, by the time the first comprehensive Census of India was taken in 1881, the British population in India was still a tiny, if supremely powerful minority, scattered across rural areas and concentrated in towns in the north and northeast of the region.

According to the census returns, amongst the British born residents, the population was overwhelmingly male, young, and even if not single, it would appear that around half the married men had travelled to India without their wives (Plowden 1883). As Mary Procida's research has demonstrated, unless a husband had achieved a certain status in his official or army career, 'there was no place for wives in the Raj' (2002: 31). For the unmarried man, as Alice Perrin wrote, 'India could be a very Paradise; to a married man it might easily become the reverse, what with anxieties about health and money and children, and the everlasting self-sacrifice that a family must needs entail' (1912: 164). The testimony of Anglo-Indians, who recorded their experiences of colonial life in letters, journals, memoirs, advice books and interviews, also confirms the lack of a place in India for children or the elderly. Anne Wilson wrote in a letter that 'no one is old in Calcutta; everybody is of the same age and that is about twenty five' (1911: 292), while Mrs Murray Mitchell noted 'two points of difference between Indian and home society [which] strike the eye at once; here there are hardly any old people, and very few boys and girls' (1876: 71).

Pejorative attitudes to Indian people amongst Anglo-Indians pre-existed the events of 1857, but were hardened by it. This impacted on the social existence of Britons in Raj India. Vastly outnumbered, the Anglo-Indian community grew ever more insular, rejecting interaction with Indians in favour of 'the compulsory sociability of the English nation' as the missionary Edward Thompson termed it. Anglo-Indian society came to be almost exclusively white, and servants appear to be the Indians with whom the colonizers had the most quotidian contact. This chapter will explore this relationship in detail, considering the structure of service, the various roles servants took on, the problems of their intimate knowledge of their employers' lives and the characteristics consequently attributed to them.

The varied character of the climate and environment in India, as well as the mobility of the Anglo-Indian community who, if they could afford to, moved between the hills and the plains with the shift of seasons, meant that Anglo-Indian houses in India were quite different from those in metropolitan Britain. Eliza Fay claimed the banks of the river in Calcutta were 'absolutely studded with elegant mansions' (1925: 171), while J.H. Stocqueler described Anglo-Indian residences in that city as 'surrounded by extensive grounds, laid out in miniature representations of the beautiful parks of England' (1844: 257). Of course, there were plenty of English people in India who did not live in quite such comfort, residing in colour washed mud-brick bungalows or, if they lived in the cities, in boarding houses or flats. The spouses of ordinary British soldiers certainly enjoyed little luxury; for many, throughout the nineteenth century, their living arrangements constituted a 'screened-off corner in the barracks' (Macmillan 1988: 75–76). Nevertheless, the writers of popular domestic advice manuals directed at novice memsahibs recommended that Anglo-Indians gentrify their domestic environment according to familiar domestic tropes

FIGURE 2.1: Planter's bungalow, Allahabad, India, 1877. Photograph, 1877. © Photo by SSPL / Getty Images.

inasmuch as circumstances would allow. 'By dint of hanging up photographs, pictures, brackets for odds and ends of china, Japanese scrolls, having books and papers about, and a piano' suggested the author of *Indian Outfits and Establishment*, 'a room can be made fairly pretty' (An Anglo-Indian 1882: 63).

Setting up the household in the right way was key in the formation of Anglo-Indian identity. Advice manuals such as that quoted above recommended structures both practical and psychological: routines, recipes, modes of thought and behaviour, economies of trust and punishments for when those failed. After all, 'the end and object is not merely personal comfort, but the formation of a home ... that unit of civilisation' wrote Steel and Gardiner, famously (1898: 7). In manuals such as *The Complete Indian Housekeeper and Cook*, the organization of the domestic sphere was posited as intrinsic to the imperial civilizing project. In the colonial context, colonizers invested new meaning in domesticity as they saw it doing the work of colonization. The domestic sphere ideally was the place where the values of British civilization were displayed to servants and visitors, with Anglo-Indian employers insisting on cleanliness, order and respect for the ruling race. However, though advice manual writers imagined domesticating India through rigorous household management, the everyday experience of British women in India was rather different. Far more than the climate and the transience, Indian domestic servants complicated visions such as that of Steel and Gardiner. In reality, the home was a place in which, in the minutiae of everyday life, servants were agents in the creation of colonial domesticity and the identities it framed. This chapter, in exploring the organization of colonial households, will demonstrate the centrality of domesticity to the making of Empire and the relations of power it entailed.

THE IMPERIAL HOUSEHOLD AS A SYMBOL OF POWER

The class categories by which society in nineteenth-century England was increasingly stratified were transformed in the Indian colonial context. For the British in India, social rank depended largely on occupation, and military families ranked below those in which the husband held an official position. Status in the metropole was of relatively little consequence in determining social ranking in early-nineteenth-century India, but the signifiers of high rank were similar nonetheless. As one commentator put it, India provided 'the opportunity for "clerks" and "pedlars" to sit on "the thrones of Aurangzebe"' (Collingham 2001: 21). Early-nineteenth-century images of Anglo-Indians attended by retinues of servants display references to stereotypes of the indulged European aristocrat and the court of the 'oriental' prince. Englishness was re-defined in India, as a uniquely Anglo-Indian way of life endorsed European power in an 'Indian idiom' (Majeed 1992: 22). Eliza Fay described Madras society as characterized by 'Asiatic splendour, combined with European taste exhibited around you on every side, under the forms of flowing drapery, stately palanquins, elegant carriages, innumerable servants, and all the pomp and circumstance of luxurious ease and unbounded wealth' (1925: 162). Under Company rule, the large numbers of servants employed by the British were an important status symbol, assisting Englishmen, mostly of modest beginnings, in usurping and mimicking the lives of elites both Indian and English in an effort to gain political and cultural legitimacy (Collingham 2001: 18–20). But as the nineteenth century progressed, the nabob gave way to the sahib. The orientalism of 'Company men' fell into disfavour as utilitarian and evangelical ideas gained purchase across imperial space. From the 1830s, the language of reform echoed through the corridors of power, conflating ideas about what defined Britishness and concepts of what constituted a civilized society, codified in the writings of men such as Bentinck, Macaulay and Mill who advocated educational, judicial and moral reform according to a British liberal agenda as necessary for India's future stability and prosperity (Collingham 2001: 51–52). Colonial governance was thus increasingly organized towards the goal of transforming Indian society and culture according to values defined as central to British 'civilization'.

As a part of this shift, more conscious efforts were made by Anglo-Indians to distinguish 'British' social practices from those of earlier colonists and of indigenous Indians. The home remained an important site for the expression of imperial authority, but the rhetoric surrounding it altered in character, in correspondence with a similar shift in metropolitan Britain. The perceived need to maintain prestige in Indian eyes remained an important factor structuring the relationship between servants and employers and their relation to Indian and English identities. But increasingly, the home was defined in a range of texts as the heart of civilization and the place 'where father and children, master and servant, employer and employed, can learn their several duties' (Steel and Gardiner 1898: 7). This idea of the household as a place of cultural pedagogy had been translated from the metropole to the colony, and was given imperial significance in the translation. In Britain, people learned their social place through their relation to service. In India, where domestic workers were relatively cheap and plentiful, ruling Indian servants became a part of the way in which the colonizers displayed the racial and social hierarchies underpinning British notions of civilization both to colonial subjects and to themselves.

Maintaining households in an appropriately imperial fashion necessitated the work of many servants. Anglo-Indians required servants to sweep verandas and clean floors and furniture, keeping the constant barrage of dust at bay in the hot

FIGURE 2.2: A British family celebrating Christmas in India, *c*. 1900. 'Indian Christmas', by E.K. Johnson, Rischgitz Collection. © Rischgitz / Getty Images.

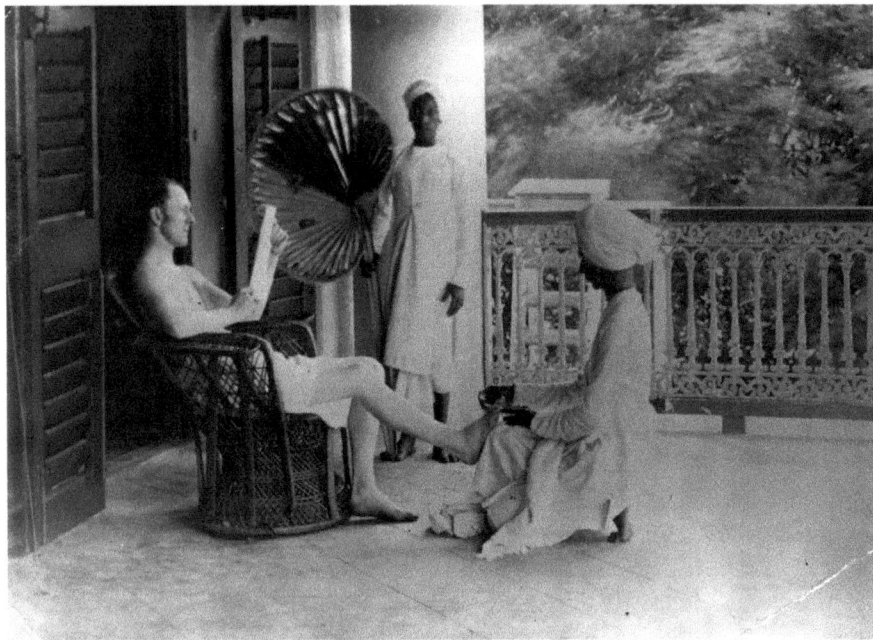

FIGURE 2.3: A British officer in India receives a pedicure from an Indian servant. 'Indian Pedicure', photograph, undated. © Hulton Archive / Getty Images.

months and later in the year removing the stains caused by monsoon damp. Various servants were needed to cook elaborate western and Indian meals on basic stoves, fetch water and wait at tables at both family and social events (in India, Anglo-Indians took their own servants with them to other people's houses to serve them at dinner parties). Servants were needed to do laundry, beating their employers' calico dresses and cotton undergarments against heavy river stones to get them clean. Servants were required to admit callers and deliver cards, assisting their white employers' application of the rituals of 'Society' to the colonial setting. Liveried servants were needed to carry the heavy *jhampannies* in which wealthier Anglo-Indians reclined while travelling. Servants were required to sit on the veranda and pull the great fans that cooled houses in hot weather. Servants performed intimate personal services for their employers; they washed their employers' bodies and dressed their hair. Servants were required to care for, and even breastfeed children, while the children learned to exercise authority not only over the servants, but over the Indian populace they were seen to represent. The work of servants facilitated the domestic civilizing project, and as the Indians with whom Anglo-Indians had the most contact, they were its primary recipients.

Anglo-Indian households employed large numbers of servants, often many more than they would have been able to afford in England. In Edward Braddon's words: 'The active and handy housemaid who cleans the house, washes a child or two, does the marketing, cooks the dinner, waits at table, and performs other offices, is represented in India by some ten individual specimens of menial humanity' (1872: 113). In the 1830s, Julia Maitland wrote that she kept 'fewer than many people . . . altogether twenty seven' (1846: 51), while Emma Walter recorded in her journal in 1839 that she had nineteen servants, not more than she needed. Julia Maitland poked fun at the extravagance:

> I have an ayah (or lady's maid), and a tailor (for the ayah cannot work); and A- has a boy: also two muddles – one to sweep my room and another to bring water. There is one man to lay the cloth, another to bring in dinner, another to light the candles, and others to wait at table. Every horse has a man and a maid to himself – the maid cuts grass for him; and every dog has a boy. I inquired whether the cat had any servants, but I found that she was allowed to wait upon herself; and as she seemed the only person in the establishment capable of doing I respected her accordingly.
> —1846: 18

The numbers of servants employed in Anglo-Indian households do appear to have declined somewhat as the century progressed, but still remained far higher than in the English counterparts. Servants remained as important an indicator of racial and social status for the sahib as they had been for the nabob. In 1873, Lady Mary Hobhouse had around thirty servants to cater for her and her husband's daily requirements, while most manuals recommended approximately thirteen servants to cater for a household in India, with extra servants to care for children as required. Even those Anglo-Indians who were of the large number classed by David Arnold as 'poor whites', and who lived alongside indigenous Indians in mixed neighbourhoods in the bigger cities, would often keep servants (1979: 104–5). For example, the probate of Elizabeth Tilyard, a midwife who died in 1859, indicates that her small house in Calcutta was part of a neighbourhood inhabited by Indians as well as Anglo-Indians. Nevertheless, Elizabeth employed three servants.[3] As one author claimed in 1882, it was 'one of the social follies of Indian life . . . that you must keep three [servants] to do the work of one' (An Anglo-Indian 1882: 49).

THE ROLES OF SERVANTS IN THE COLONIAL HOUSEHOLD

The races of servants are very different at the three Presidencies; at Bombay there is a large proportion of Native Portuguese, Parsees, Mussulmans, and Hindoos, besides Eurasians; at Madras Native Christians take the place of Parsees at Bombay; and at Calcutta there is a mixture of every caste and grade in India. There are some among these who speak English, and who generally bear but very indifferent characters.

—Riddell 1871: 3

Within the category 'servant', Anglo-Indians perceived many variations. Some of this variation was believed by Anglo-Indians to be a result of the effect of caste on service: the majority of domestic servants were Hindu and specialized service roles were often associated with particular caste designations (Plowden 1883: 376). Caste was often given as the reason why Anglo-Indians needed to employ more servants than they would have in Britain. As Minnie Wood wrote to her mother in 1857: 'Each department has a Servant of a caste which does not permit them to do anything else consequently it obliges one to keep more than one would wish' (1857a). It was not in servants' interest to challenge the British belief that caste restrictions were fixed, because the decline of the Mughal aristocracy meant that many servants needed work, and the differentiation of tasks ensured employment for the greatest number (Collingham 2001: 18). Also, the assertion of caste arguably provided a way for servants to resist the absolutism of their employers' authority. Indeed, many writers appear to have felt that servants asserted caste restrictions simply to irritate their employers, as Edward Braddon's words suggest: 'Caste or custom forbids that the Indian servant should make himself generally useful and live in the esteem of his fellow men, and so he is generally useless' (1872: 113).

There were also geographical variations in the way domestic service occupations were defined, as Steel and Gardiner claimed in *The Complete Indian Housekeeper and Cook*: 'In Bombay, Madras, Ceylon, and Burmah the manner of life is so different, that residents in these Presidencies will find it necessary to piece the duties of the various servants together into a new classification' (1898: 54). Steel and Gardiner also suggested that there was one similarity between all Indian servants, which was that 'the majority of servants, from Himalaya to Cape Comorin, are absolutely ignorant of the first principles of their various duties' (1898: 54). In fact, the hidden script of texts such as this was that Indian servants' knowledge was key to Anglo-Indian survival in India. As Cecilia Leong-Salobir has argued, 'domestic chores, in food purchasing, preparation and serving, were relegated to the local people . . . it was the servants' local knowledge that procured food' (2011: 60–61). Newly arrived British women might have had little or no experience of employing servants, or indeed household management, before their migration to India, and even if they had, that experience might be of little use to them in the Indian context. The proliferation of household manuals across the nineteenth century catered to a market uncertain about, rather than confident in, the expression of imperial authority in matters domestic.

In their explanations of servant hierarchy, Anglo-Indian employers mapped the familiar structures of British households onto domestic organization in India.

The indoor servants were generally regarded as 'upper' servants and the bearer was the head of the Indian servant hierarchy in Anglo-Indian households. His role was an important one, more or less equivalent to that of the housekeeper in English households. It was important to engage the right man, as the author of *A Guide to Indian Household Management* advised: 'On your head servant or bearer depends much of your comfort; be, therefore, very particular in your choice, and do not engage too young a man' (James 1879: 44). As well as discharging 'all the functions of a valet for the sahib' the bearer was, according to most accounts, also responsible for dusting furniture and looking after the lamps (An Anglo-Indian 1882: 50). He would receive guests or their cards and as a measure of his responsibility, was usually 'entrusted articles of value – money, jewels, clothes, &c' and was responsible for 'the general good behaviour of the staff' (1882: 50). The bearer could act as an intermediary between employer and staff. As Elizabeth Garrett wrote of the bearer, 'his master and mistress should be able to look to him in case of any dispute in the compound' (1887: 20). Bearers were valued for their loyalty and trustworthiness and their employers often appreciated and reciprocated their bearer's attachment to them. The Hobhouses intended to bring their bearer to England with them when they left India and Bertie Maynard wrote of his bearer, Khuda Buksh, that he

> was one of those Indians who for thirty rupees a month or thereabouts – shall we say eighteen pence a day – and a little 'cherishing' . . . will serve with whole-hearted devotion a strange being of another complexion, of different religion and different thoughts; put up with his tantrums; bring meals into existence for him in the wilderness, wait for him for months, even for years, when he withdraws himself to that distant and mysterious 'home' of his; love and guard his children; risk disease and death for his sake and under his protection, and most effectively thwart the machinations of others like himself to get other employers served first and served best; putting affection before justice and before self.
> —Lethbridge 1990: 158

Bertie's fantasy of servant devotion, figured as the kind of love an ideal parent has for its child (though crucially, and unlike most Anglo-Indians, he acknowledged its paid-for nature), resonates with the writings of other employers. After her bearer supported her when her mother died, Lady Wilson wrote to a friend: 'Of the sympathy shown us in times of sickness and sorrow by those of our own household, most Memsahibs can speak with feeling . . . sometimes such things mean a great deal to us' (1911: 284–85).

Another key servant role, and one of the few household roles occupied by a woman, was that of the ayah. The ayah would act as a lady's maid for the mistress of the household and as carer for small children. Many wealthy households employed more than one ayah, particularly when there were children to be catered for. A good ayah was highly valued, as the author of *Indian Outfits* attested: 'a better maid I never wish to have; gentle, quiet, attentive, careful and trustworthy – in fact, a domestic treasure' (An Anglo-Indian 1882: 47). Her role was one that entailed considerable access to the intimate areas of her employers' lives and memsahibs often expressed fondness

FIGURE 2.4: A European Lady and Her Family Attended by an Ayah, or Nurse. This hand-coloured aquatint was made from a drawing by Charles D'Oyly and published in *The European in India* by Charles D'Oyly and Thomas Williamson.
© Stapleton Collection / Corbis / Corbis via Getty Images.

for their ayahs, while the gentle brown hand and jangling bracelets of a soft-footed ayah are recurrent images in the rememberings of Anglo-Indian children held in the British Library's oral archive. The combination of warmth and stereotype in such memories indicates the way in which the peculiar intimacy of the relationship between servants and employers, its emotional dimension, was framed by the servant's 'Indian-ness'. It speaks of the way in which the servant might have acted as a medium through which India could flow into the most private recesses of Anglo-Indians' material and psychological existence, no matter how much they tried overtly to prevent it from doing so.

Cooks were also important within the Anglo-Indian household, and Steel and Gardiner advised Memsahibs who had found a good one to 'do anything to keep him – short of letting him know that you are anxious to do so' (1898: 72). Memsahibs were advised to avoid the kitchen, or at least give notice before they went into it because, according to Elizabeth Garrett, '[a]n Indian cook-room is so painfully unlike a kitchen at home that a visit to it affords little pleasure to the English matron' (1887: 19). Steel and Gardiner did not mince their words, in their estimation the Indian kitchen was 'a black hole, the pantry a sink' (1898: ix). Nevertheless, good cooks could work apparent miracles with limited equipment, as Anne Wilson discovered: 'As for the cook, all that he seems to need is two bricks or a hole in the ground. He takes the pots out of the panier ... lights his fire of wood or charcoal, and gives us dinner as good as he ever prepared in his kitchen at home' (1911: 15). A cook's boy, or *masalchee*, who would do the washing up, assisted the cook. The *khansamah* was also a servant of significant responsibility. He oversaw 'the concerns of the table and of the servants attached to it', who were called *kitmutgars*, and would also go to the bazaar and do the marketing for the household (Riddell 1871: 6).

Servants in India, who were mostly male, did not live in the house as their counterparts in England did, but usually occupied huts on the compound where they lived with their families. The kitchen was also usually sited apart from the main house. Employers preferred that the external servants of the household did not enter the house beyond coming to the verandah to receive instructions or wages. Even indoor servants would ideally wait on the verandah until summoned by their employers with a call of '*Qui hye?*', though such restrictions were hard to place on servants who worked indoors. Bathrooms had doors opening onto the compound so that the servants who cleaned them would not have to walk through the house (Collingham 2001: 103). External servants included punkah pullers, employed during the hot season to pull the great fans used to cool houses, who would do their monotonous work from the verandah and who apparently tended to fall asleep while on the job. Most households also employed a *bheestie* to fetch and carry water for the house. In a household with horses, a *syce* was required to look after each horse, while grasscuts would cut grass for them. Similarly, if cows were kept, a cow-man was hired, if fowls, a fowl-man. *Malis* cared for the garden. Better off establishments also hired *jhampannies*, footmen who carried sedan chairs for their employers, *chuprassies*, who acted as messengers and *chowkidars*, who were watchmen. The *dhobie* was the washerman and was the source of much complaint and the butt of many jokes for his brutal treatment of his employer's clothes. E.H. Aitken provided a mocking sketch of this servant:

> Day after day he has stood before that great black stone and wreaked his rage upon shirt and trouser and coat, and coat and trouser and shirt. Then he has wrung them as if he were wringing the necks of poultry, and fixed them on his drying line with thorns and spikes, and finally he has taken the battered garments to his torture chamber and ploughed them with his iron, longwise and crosswise and slantwise, and dropped glowing cinders on their tenderest places. Son has succeeded father through countless generations in cultivating his passion for destruction, until it has become the monstrous growth we see and shudder at in the *Dhobie*.
>
> —1897: 81

At the bottom of the servant hierarchy in Anglo-Indian households was the *mehter*, or sweeper, described by Steel and Gardiner as 'a savage with a reed broom' (1898: ix). The sweeper was invariably of very low caste, or was Untouchable. It was his task to sweep and perform 'other menial offices, which no other servant will, on any consideration, put his hand to' such as emptying and cleaning the thunderbox and dealing with refuse (Braddon 1872: 114).

THE PROBLEM OF PROXIMITY

Although the uprising of 1857 does not seem to have resulted in a major shift in employer/servant relations in India, attitudes towards servants reflected growing ambivalence amongst Anglo-Indians about the difference of Indians from English people that pre-dated and appeared to be confirmed by the events of 1857. Throughout the century, Anglo-Indians claimed the barbarity of 'the Indian' was manifest in their servants, both before and after the uprising of 1857. The fact that there does not seem to have been any great shift in attitudes towards servants before and after 1857 may be due to the particular intimacy and ambivalence of the servant/employer relationship. Some servants were loyal to their employers during the uprising, risking their own lives for those of the families they served; others turned on their employers. Since servants were already mistrusted by many employers, perhaps those who betrayed their employers simply confirmed pre-existing ideas about the untrustworthiness of servants and facilitated the mapping of those ideas onto the character of 'the native'. As for those who were loyal to their employers, their loyalty could be seen in the context of ties to the family, developed through service, which overrode other allegiances to native community or kin.

As Anglo-Indians moved towards developing a more self-consciously distinctive domestic life, they expressed more frequently discontent with the proximity of Indian servants to individuals and families in Anglo-Indian households. This apparent increase in anxiety about servants' presence may be due to the fact that as the century progressed, more women travelled to India and produced texts that focused on Indian domestic life. Frederick Shore took measures to assuage his discomfort, writing that he had 'had bells hung in all the rooms in the house, after the English fashion' in order to ensure some kind of privacy for his wife and himself. Shore described the servant as a 'sort of spy, and by no means an inattentive observer of all that passes in the private apartment of his mistress' (Shore 1883).

As Frederick Shore's words indicate, some Anglo-Indians felt uneasy with their servants' necessary presence in their households. Anglo-Indian discomfort with servants' proximity appears to have become understandably intense during the uprising of 1857. Minnie Wood, in a letter to her mother written during the uprising, wrote that '[o]ne has to put up with so much now from one's servants. They are most insolent, and think nothing of telling you that soon we shall all be in the service of the King of Delhi' (1857d). The construction of the household as a place where a memsahib should 'govern and rule as well as train her domestics to greater perfection' (An Anglo-Indian 1883, preface), which emerged in the second half of the nineteenth century, was perhaps a response to anxiety produced by this crisis and a tacit acknowledgement of servants' power. It subverted the idea that employers were under observation by dangerous employees: by constructing the home as a place of domestic pedagogy, the servant's watchfulness was controlled and utilized in the service of civilizational development and imperial authority, in theory at least.

RELATIONSHIPS BETWEEN SERVANTS AND CHILDREN

In advice manuals and letters, Indian servants were recommended for their devotedness to, and 'unwearying patience and gentleness' with, children (A Lady Resident 1864: 61). Nonetheless, the trust that Anglo-Indians put in their Indian servants' tenderness towards children was marked by ambivalence. The danger tended to be articulated in terms of a threat to children's moral, rather than physical, well-being. The author of *A Domestic Guide to Mothers in India* warned mothers to beware of their 'native servants' who, if allowed too much contact with English children, would 'instil all kinds of poisonous ideas into their young minds. Being heathens themselves, they see no harm in teaching them all the dogmas and obscenity of their religion' (A Medical Practitioner

1848: 49). Furthermore, according to this author, the 'native servants are very fond of [deception]; and if children are left much to them, we see them grow cunning, deceitful and tellers of falsehoods' (1848: 62). Similarly, Elizabeth Garrett advised that, in India 'great patience is needed in training our children in habits of truthfulness. Their surroundings, alas! are generally a hindrance, rather than a help in such lessons' (1887: 112). According to Florence Marryat, 'the conversation of the natives, as a rule, is too filthy to be imagined, which always gave me a great horror of permitting my children to pick up the Tamil language from their ayahs' (1868: 55). Nevertheless, despite disquiet about English children's contact with 'heathens', employers were often reluctant to hire Christian servants. Several employers seem to have thought Christian servants were opportunistic, professing Christianity only to gain some advantage. 'A Lady Resident' recommended that her readers should 'as much as possible, secure for your servants a set of unmitigated heathens. Converts are usually arrant humbugs; Catholics little better; indeed, the domestics who have robbed and cheated us during our sojourn in India, have with one exception been Christians and I have resolved never to engage another knowing him to be "master's caste"' (1864: 55). This response to Christian servants may have been due to the fact that sharing a common faith may have brought servants too close to their employers for comfort (Chaudhuri 1994: 552). Although many employers seem to have been irritated by their servants' difference, difference was perhaps more comfortable than similarity, particularly in matters of faith, as Mrs Murray Mitchell's comment in one of her letters indicates: 'The bearer is a Christian, and an old servant of Mr D.; a small, keen-eyed, dark Madrassi, with a towering mass of white turban, and full of springy activity. It is nice to have a Christian servant; but this man looks perhaps rather too clever' (1876: 69).

Often male bearers would undertake the duties of childcare, indeed, it was widely seen as a part of their duties to look after the children once they had reached a certain age. The relationship between memsahibs and their male servants was complex. Male servants' gender and racial difference to English female servants was problematic for mistresses, and this problem was not resolved by their being 'placed on a level with British female servants' as one historian has argued (Chaudhuri 1994: 553). As lower class male Indians who had access to the private lives of their employers, their maleness added to the threat of their 'otherness', as Emma Roberts' words indicate:

> None of the inferior domestics keep themselves, as in England, in the background . . . and in Bengal, where the lower orders of palanquin-bearers wear very little clothing, it is not very agreeable to a female stranger to see them walk into drawing-rooms, and employ themselves in dusting books or other occupations of like nature.
> —1835: 9–10

Male servants' resistance to the authority of Anglo-Indian women is a recurrent theme in their letters and published writings. It is often stated by women that they have problems being understood by their servants and that they needed their husbands to dictate their orders to ensure they were obeyed. Minnie Wood wrote in a letter to her mother that 'I quite dread book-keeping as I have no power over the servants . . . & the accounts I have to get my husband to translate every morning' (1857a), while 'A Lady Resident' claimed that 'One bad trait . . . is the frequency with which they disregard the comfort and convenience of ladies, often their express orders, unless most directly enforced by the master' (1864: 60).

GENDER, AGE AND SERVANT CHARACTERIZATIONS

While it does seem to be case that servants were frequently characterized as childishly immature, servile, stupid, dirty, indolent, dishonest and likened to animals, they do not appear to have been feminized or described as effeminate in the same way as middle-class so-called *'baboos'* were. Elizabeth Garrett, in her advice book *Morning Hours in India*, wrote:

> After the child is three or four months old he should be carried by the bearer. The child will feel much safer than in a woman's arms . . . Hindoo bearers become much attached to the children of whom they have care, and take a great pride in their young charges. For boys, after they are six or eight months old, they are undoubtedly the best nurses.
>
> —1887: 80

The reference to the strength of the male, as opposed to the female servant, and the implication that male children are better cared for by one of their own sex suggests that the male servant can bring usefully masculine qualities to the role of 'nurse', rather than that he is feminized by it.

As Ann Laura Stoler has written, the representation of racialized Others as like children was one that 'conveniently provided a moral justification for imperial policies of tutelage, discipline and specific paternalistic and materialistic strategies of custodial control' (1995: 150). The idea that Indian servants were effectively children endured throughout the nineteenth century; in the bible of Indian housekeeping, *The Complete Indian Housekeeper and Cook* (1898), Steel and Gardiner claimed that '[t]he Indian servant is a child in everything save age' (1898: 2). They went beyond simply describing the Indian servant as a child and suggested he or she 'should be treated as a child' (1898: 2). To this end, the authors claimed that in training their servants, they 'adopted castor oil as an ultimatum in all obstinate cases, on the ground that there must be some physical cause for inability to learn or remember' (1898: 3). The description of Indian servants as children resonated with the idea that the servant/employer relationship should be organized along paternalistically pedagogical lines. Advice manual writers recommended caring for one's Indian servants in a paternalistic way in order to inspire loyalty. Provided one was kind they would 'prove in many little ways, by many little actions, many little attentions, that they fully appreciate your kindness, and endeavour, in their way, to repay it' (James 1879: 43). However, like a teacher with unruly children, it was always important that employers of Indian servants be authoritative: 'In being kind, draw the line, do not overdo it . . . do not allow them to mistake kindness for weakness' (James 1879: 43).

The idea that Indian servants were dependents within Anglo-Indian households was problematic. While styled as children in their attitudes and behaviour, they were not dependent within the household in the same way as English servants were. First, they were mostly male. Second, they were often married with families of their own, who often lived within the compound and who were dependent on them. Third, they were culturally different to the English in so many ways. As Minnie Wood described to her mother:

> Your servants with their families live in your compound in mud houses & pens, but that is all, you do not feed them or have anything to do with them, only allow 1 hour & a half each day for their Khana or dinner which is the only meal of which they ever partake & as to touching anything from off our table, that is unheard of, they generally have the same thing, rice or lentils, over & over again each year.
>
> —1857b

Nevertheless, the Indian servants were repeatedly referred to both angrily and with affection as children in texts ranging from household manuals to missionary writings and personal letters and diaries. Such a construction provided a way in which Anglo-Indians, and especially Anglo-Indian women, could reassure themselves that they were not only superior to, but also authoritative over, their Indian servants. It was a way of denying their dependence on the servants, which was certainly a source of frustration for many mistresses.

JUSTIFICATIONS OF VIOLENCE AND COLONIALISM

Throughout the nineteenth century, colonial governmentalities sought to anglicize mainly high caste Indians, redefining their identities as 'native gentlemen', differentiated from lower class Indians by their respectable 'English' education and collaboration with the ruling bureaucracy. Despite this project, most Anglo-Indians also saw all Indians through a similar lens: racially inferior to the British and yet in constant need of reminding of their inferiority. Julia Maitland bemoaned the 'rudeness and contempt' (1846: 20) with which Indians were treated by their British rulers, writing that '[t]hese natives are a cringing set, and behave to us English as if they were the dirt under our feet; and indeed we give them reason to suppose we consider them as such' (1846: 20). Similarly, Mary Hobhouse described Indians as 'slavish people, all whose habits and instincts, good or bad, seem of a servile nature' (1906: 64). Some Anglo-Indians sanctioned violence as a means to keeping the native servants in line. 'Of course', stated an editorial in *The Pioneer*, 'cuffs and stripes, and all kinds of corporeal maltreatment are recognised in India by Indians as well as Europeans, as more in accordance with the natural fitness of things than such phenomena would be thought in Europe' (Anon. 1876). Admittedly, many Anglo-Indians, such as Mary Hobhouse, found the use of violence unnecessary and offensive:

> This behaviour to natives is one of the things that make one a little sick here sometimes. I read quite a commonplace report of an officer the other day, whose servant had not filled up his lamp sufficiently with oil. He sent for the man, who was unwilling to come, and then twice threw a knife at him, and the man was severely wounded and taken to hospital – the officer fined fifteen rupees. In the very same paper was a letter saying, 'India was going to the dogs since the enactment by which servants were allowed to bring actions against their masters'.
>
> —1906: 129

In July 1876, a case took place in which a *syce* (a groom/footman – a lower servant), having failed to bring a carriage to the front door of his English employer's house on time, was beaten by his employer and subsequently died. The employer, Mr Fuller, was sentenced to a fine of thirty rupees. Concerned by the leniency of the sentence, Lord Lytton, then Viceroy, issued a Minute in which he expressed disapproval of Anglo-Indians' inclination to control their servants with violence, and at the Courts' tendency to punish such offenders lightly. According to Mary Hobhouse, this raised

> a howl of indignation from the Anglo-Indian press, who all look upon beating as the right and proper way of treating servants. One man writes this morning to say, 'I wish Lord Lytton would tell me what I am to do when my servants bring breakfast a quarter of an hour late'. We, Arthur and myself, always say 'what would you do if an English servant was at fault?' but this is considered a ludicrous and inappropriate sentiment.
>
> —1906: 252

Although beating servants was generally frowned upon in Anglo-Indian society, many Anglo-Indians believed it occasionally unavoidable, and certainly understandable. The fact that Indian servants, as well as being Indian, were also usually male was probably relevant to their employers' belief that they sometimes needed physical chastisement in order to show them who was in charge. As an editorial in the *Pioneer* stated in response to Lytton's Minute: 'the truth is . . . that there is hardly a large household in India which could be kept in decent order by strictly legal means' and advised 'every European here' to 'take care that he never strikes a servant in a way that can possibly have more than a superficial effect' (Anon. 1876). Florence Marryat suggested that Anglo-Indian employers were driven to violence by their servants' lack of appreciation of how lucky they were:

> their usual behaviour is so aggravating that, however much I may condemn, I cannot wonder at any one losing control of their temper when with them; but in general they serve you well as long as it suits their convenience to do so, and when it does not no amount of past kindness and indulgence will secure you from the effects of their ingratitude.
> —1868: 31–32

Furthermore, those people (including the government) who did disapprove of violence tended to do so not because beating servants was bad for the servants as much as because it brutalized the employer and so was 'injurious to the honour of British rule, and so damaging to the reputation of British justice in this country' (Moffusilite 1876).

AMBIGUOUS CHARACTERIZATIONS

Certain characteristics were associated with some of the different servant roles with degrees of negativity reflecting the hierarchy of service. For example, the *khansamah* (table servant) was seen as a cheat, who 'carries on an avowed system of plunder' (Anon. 1883b) and whose dishonesty was incurable. '[I]t is manifestly hopeless to attempt to reform the khansamah' wrote one correspondent to *The Englishman*, 'He has been spoilt beyond redemption by a long and undisturbed career of plunder and must be lopped off from our household establishments like a rotten branch' (Anon. 1883a). Bearers, however, were generally characterized as 'a hardworking and very trusty class of people' (Riddell 1871: 8).

Where in Britain certain failures of character were associated specifically with domestic servants, such as tendencies to dishonesty and to taking illicit perquisites, in India, rather than being confined to servants, they were cited as evidence of inherent defects in Indian native character. For example, Dr Riddell generalized from a discussion of servant character, claiming that '[c]unning and double-dealing characterise the Native and are some of his principal faults' (1871: 9). Florence Marryat went further, claiming that '[b]oth men and women are inveterate liars and it is impossible to place dependence on anything that they say' (1868: 36).

At the same time, many employers testified in letters and manuals to servants' loyalty and in particular, to their kindness when their employers fell ill. Dr Riddell wrote that '[i]n sickness they will take the greatest care of you, doing for you services that a European seldom ever will' (1871: 8), while 'A Lady Resident' claimed the 'extreme lightness and delicacy of touch which characterizes the native, makes the ayah often a very great comfort' (1864: 53). Bertie Maynard wrote in a letter home that he found 'the servants very good when one is at all unwell' (Lethbridge 1990: 24). Some writers even spoke out against Indian servants' poor reputation. The author of *Indian Outfits* suggested that 'grumbling against servants is a national fault amongst us' (An Anglo-Indian 1882: 49) and claimed that new arrivals in India 'will be told that natives are everything that is bad and cannot be trusted' (1882: 46). However, she advised that she had 'seen a good deal of native servants, and I know no reason why, from my experience of them, they should not be trusted quite as much as others of their class' (1882: 47).

By generalizing pejoratively about Indian character from their experience as mistresses of Indian servants, Anglo-Indian women could make a claim to personal authority over their households. They could also claim agency in the imperial venture, implicitly endorsing the moral legitimacy of British colonialism as progress towards civilization. However, alongside generalizations, there were variations in attitudes towards Indians. Although generalized and negative ideas abounded and experience interacted with public discourse to reinforce them, encounters with Indian servants being part of this experience, it is simplistic to suggest that a widely disseminated and effective idea of 'the Indian in general' was drawn from memsahibs' relationship with their servants. Certainly, there were general ideas about Indian servants that interacted with ideas about 'native character', but the one did not necessarily produce the other.

The relationship between servants and employers was strikingly ambivalent. For example, writers of manuals and letters often testified to the general dishonesty of Indian servants and then recommended some of them for their trustworthiness. Anglo-Indians were aware of the confusing nature of such variable attitudes. Mary Hobhouse wrote in a letter that 'Mr C's dictum as to these servants is "Trust them entirely and look into nothing yourself"; and the same evening Mr W. said to me, "look into everything; be firm and patient – never indulgent"' (1906: 49). Shortly after her arrival in India, Anne Wilson also noted the range of opinion, and tentatively drew her own general conclusion: 'Servants differ greatly in different parts of the country, and their employers' opinions of them as a class vary as widely, ranging from enthusiasm to despair. Take them as a whole, I think I find them as yet distinctly trying' (1911: 10–11).

The dependence of Anglo-Indians, particularly those white women living isolated lives in the *mofussil*, on their Indian servants, and the inscrutability of the culture to which those servants belonged was a source of confusion for employers in India. Despite the derogatory reductionism which writers employed to justify putative English superiority, the ambivalence of their writings bears witness to such uncertainty. The profound difference of Indian servants, and the India their employers saw them as representing, from what Anglo-Indians remembered or imagined of their distant Home produced mixed feelings. 'I realise that I am face to face with a sphinx who is not dumb, but who remains an eternal enigma' (1911: 87) wrote Anne Wilson in one of her letters home. The writers of letters and manuals interpreted what they saw of their servants in a place that mystified, alienated, delighted and terrified them, and they thus produced ambivalent, racialized notions of Indian character for their readers.

CONCLUSION

What Anglo-Indians seem less conscious of was the way in which their colonial setting had moulded their own identities. Despite their effort to remain separate, and to construct a British domestic ideal in the Indian context for the sake of both their own authority and their native servants' edification, the climate and culture of the subcontinent nevertheless shaped Anglo-Indian domestic life. In nineteenth-century India, a specifically Anglo-Indian way of domestic life emerged that was peculiar to its Indian context but was also connected to metropolitan discourses constructing 'Englishness'. As Elizabeth Buettner has shown, on return to Britain Anglo-Indians frequently suffered disappointment that things were not as they felt they should be. No longer part of a powerful white minority, many Anglo-Indians found they could not afford the numbers of servants they were used to or the domestic lifestyle they had envisaged themselves leading. Somewhat estranged from metropolitan society, Anglo-Indian returnee communities developed, with their own domestic cultures (Buettner 2004, ch. 5). Beryl Irving remembered of the Anglo-Indian community of Bedford, in which she grew up, that 'the houses were crammed with Benares tables, strings of little carved elephants, placid buddhas and malevolent Gods', while 'our mothers made good curries' (Buettner 2004: 235).

The difference of those Englishmen and women who had permanently or temporarily made the outposts of empire their homes, signified by their development of a different kind of domesticity, strained simple links between whiteness and metropolitan national belonging. As an advice manual written for returnees from India suggested, Anglo-Indians were a different kind of English people, who understood 'each other's language' requiring 'no aid from a dictionary to understand the meaning of *'Durzee'* or *Ghorawallah*, and they do not want an explanation if you should happen to speak of a *pucka* house!' (Waring 1866: 62–63). Though servants did mark the difference between colonizer and colonized, the specificities of servant/employer relationships across imperial space also marked differences within those categories. The variability of the master/mistress/servant relationship across metropole and colony helped produce different kinds of Englishness, as the way people conducted their domestic lives shaped their position on a spectrum of imperial belonging. For example, on return to England, rumours of Anglo-Indians' allegedly harsh treatment of their servants in Bedford marked them as different from their metropolitan neighbours. According to the *Bedfordshire Times* in 1891, there were 'tales about "kitchen hunger" in some houses, where the servants have not enough to eat . . . this is what happens with some of the rulers of our "great dependency", their ideas of what is necessary to keep up the strength and physique of an English servant being derived from their experience with natives who live on rice and wear scanty raiment' (Buettner 2004: 236).

Structures of domesticity were key in the making of colonial identities. In the nineteenth century, across metropole and colony and in a range of literature, the home was constructed as a place of cultural pedagogy where characters were formed and the relations through which society was structured were organized and managed. In India, this cultural imaginary of domesticity intersected with the notion of an imperial civilizing project to inform raced, classed and gendered ideas about duty and service across imperial space. A specifically Anglo-Indian way of domestic life emerged that was peculiar to its Indian context but was also shaped by Anglo-Indians' sense of their relation to Britain, the Homeland and the values they associated with it. Though Anglo-Indians used the language of rule to describe their household authority with the progression of the nineteenth century, this was a project in which colonized people had some agency. Anglo-Indian authority was dependent on the labour of domestic servants, who as a result of their uniquely intimate position in the homes of their colonial employers, shaped the character of the place understood by many to be at the very heart of imperial society: the family in the home.

CHAPTER THREE

The House: Inside and Outside Villas and Terraces in England

LESLEY HOSKINS AND REBECCA PRESTON

The nineteenth century saw a transformation in housing in England as rapid demographic, economic, social and technological changes contributed to shifting ideas of what new dwellings and their environment should provide – what kind of residential life they should facilitate. Between 1801 and 1911, the population of England and Wales rose from nearly nine million to just over 36 million (Mitchell and Deane 1971: 6). Estimates suggest that the relative increase in the housing stock was even more rapid; something like six million new dwellings were built in this period, the majority after 1850 (Mitchell and Deane 1971: 239; Muthesius 1982: 17, 20). England – more so than much of Western Europe and indeed other parts of the UK – experienced rapid urbanization with the result that its population and its housing stock became increasingly urban or suburban (Burnett 1980: 7, 13). Residential conditions, especially the crowded environments of the poorer inhabitants of large towns, became a focus of social, moral and health concern and intervention (Driver 1988). Early urbanization, large- and small-scale industrialization, and growing commerce led to an expansion of England's managerial, clerical and small trading sectors and a smaller group of wealthy entrepreneurs and rentiers (Rubinstein 1988; Higgs 2005: 159–64). From the 1870s onwards, real wages for many workers also rose overall (Boyer 2004: 280–313; Humphries 2004: 257–66). This general, relative, if personally precarious, prosperity fuelled a demand for improved housing, although the exact nature of the dwellings and their facilities varied according to matters such as time period, geography, social and economic position, and cultural norms (Burnett 1980; Hoskins 2013; Muthesius 1982).

The majority of nineteenth- and early-twentieth-century dwellings were erected, for profit, by builders or developers. Some were owner-occupied, but the vast majority were rented. More expensive dwellings were let for six months, or longer. Dwellings for those with insecure or low incomes were let by the week. Privately run common lodging houses and, by mid-century, philanthropic 'model' lodgings, offered beds costing a few pennies a night (Hamlett 2015, chs. 5 and 6). Philanthropic capitalism was responsible for a number of other model housing schemes, as were local authorities from the 1890s, but, overall, these contributed less than one percent of the total housing stock before 1914 (Daunton 1983: 194).

Most of the new dwellings in England and Wales were built as houses. Flats comprised only about three percent of the housing stock in 1911 (Muthesius 1982: 1). A tiny proportion of these were mansion flats for well-to-do occupants. Rather more were improved tenement blocks designed for the working classes but they were considered barrack-like and expensive and were not well liked (Dennis 2008, ch. 9). More common, and more popular, were flats or tenements that looked from the outside like terraced houses (discussed further below).

In 1911, the majority of English houses, catering for a broad range of economic and social groups, from the elite squares of London's West End to the working-class courts of Bradford, were built in rows or terraces – a format that had been common since at least the eighteenth century (Muthesius 1982: 1). Although frontages varied in width, internal layouts were similar, with rooms ranged one behind the other. In the early Victorian years, the bulk of urban working-class housing comprised mainly dwellings of between two and four rooms, variously arranged (Thompson 1988: 183). Many of these, especially in the north, were densely laid out, sometimes back-to-back, and often with a separately inhabited cellar (Pooley 2001: 447). Considered to be both unhealthy and lacking the basic amenities of decent domestic life, building byelaws from the 1860s onwards attempted to outlaw back-to-backs in favour of through-houses with their own back space and facilities (Burnett 1980: 156–57).

Detached or semi-detached houses in gardens, often known as villas, began to gain currency in the early part of the nineteenth century. They were intended for the well-to-do or middle classes. This group is notoriously difficult to define but, using the payment of income tax as a proxy, in 1861 about a third of Londoners fell into this category whereas the proportion was less than ten percent in many northern industrial cities (Rubinstein 1988). Villas were generally erected on the edges of towns, benefitting from access to urban amenities as well as a healthier and leafier environment. By the early 1900s, these accounted for about ten percent of English dwellings (Muthesius 1982: 1).

While many people, at all social and economic levels, occupied older dwellings, this chapter focuses on two of the new and common forms of housing – villas for the well-to-do in the first half of the nineteenth century and small terraced through-houses for working people from about 1865 to 1914 – in order to explore the ideals and realities of the living environments of a large number of people. As the Introduction to this book and Chapter 1 have shown, the nineteenth century saw an increased emphasis on the value of the home as a private space away from the world of work, which was often reflected in its spatial organization. We find that, although privacy certainly was an important concept in structuring dwellings intended for both well-off and working people, in practice this apparently guiding principle co-existed with different impulses. When viewed as a composite whole, the house, garden and setting of the villa opened up the home to the broader imperial world, while the relative privacy of the small terraced house was contingent upon the numbers and relationships of the residents, the proximity of neighbours, and the streets outside.

VILLAS FOR THE WELL-TO-DO

While there was a long history in London of permanent or intermittent retirement to villas on the metropolitan outskirts (McKellar 2013), from the turn of the nineteenth century, villas – the substantial, detached, residences of the business and professional classes – became a common feature of the fringes of English towns and cities (Slater 1978: 130; English Heritage 2011: 5). Some of the earlier nineteenth-century houses were huge, with a sweep up to the house, pleasure grounds, walled kitchen garden, stabling and service buildings. But many smaller, sometimes semi-detached, villas, often in Italianate or neo-Gothic style, were built from the 1820s onwards (Figure 3.1). Newspaper advertisements of the early 1800s show that even some modest versions had kitchen gardens as well as pleasure grounds and it is clear that, whatever the scale, a villa meant both house and garden. The smaller villa has been described as displacing the urban terraced house as the new dominant mid-nineteenth-century middle-class dwelling (Muthesius 1982: 26).

Although it is difficult to be precise about who lived in these houses, they fall into the category described by the architect Robert Kerr as 'the gentleman's house', which he took to be a commonly understood term applying to people whose incomes and occupations might differ but who shared a domestic culture. He wrote in 1864 that 'there is indicated an entire class of dwellings, in which it will be found, notwithstanding infinite variety of scale, that the elements of accommodation and arrangement are always the same; being based, in fact, upon what is in a certain sense unvarying throughout the British Islands, namely,

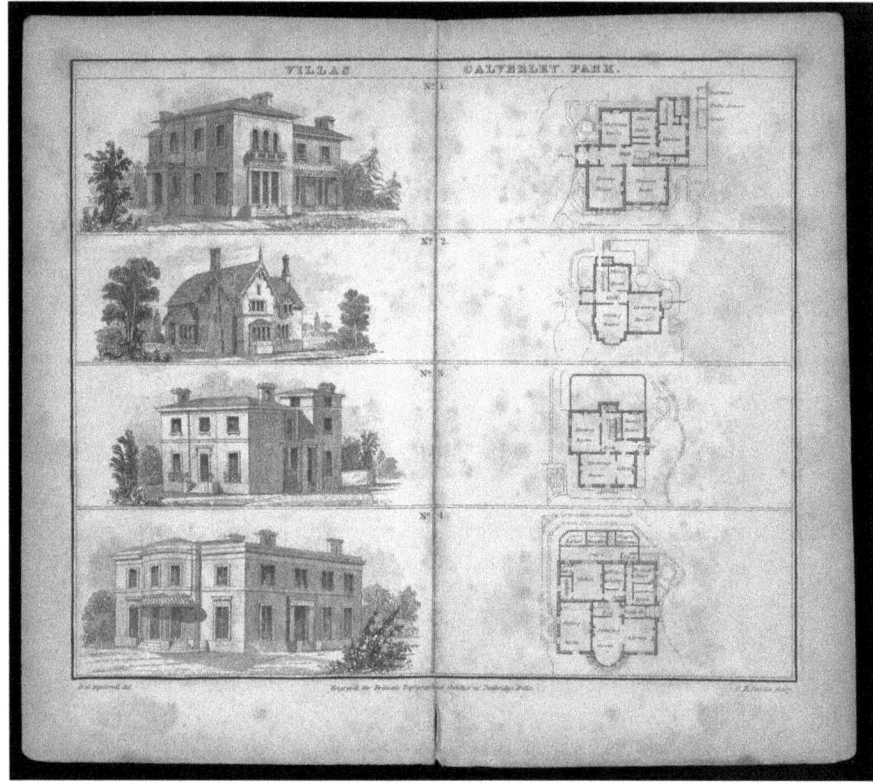

FIGURE 3.1: Detached villas 'suited for families of moderate extent' at the exclusive Calverley Estate, Tunbridge Wells, 1820s and 1830s, designed by Decimus Burton. From John Britton, *Descriptive Sketches of Tunbridge Wells and the Calverley Estate* (London: John Britton, 1832). © Wellcome Library, London.

the domestic habits of refined persons' (1864: 70). His book is useful because it is so explicit about the social intentions of the residential layout.

Larger villas required significant economic resources. Heath House in Stepney, east London, in place by about 1810, was a 'substantial freehold brick built mansion with stabling, coach house, large garden and forecourt'. In 1864 it was valued at £2,000 and let for almost £100 a year.[1] But there was great variation in costs; a villa in the exclusive Rock Park estate near Liverpool was let for £50 at mid-century.[2] A growing number of people were able to afford such houses, which were often built on the edges of towns, where land was cheaper than in the centre (Slater 1978: 131; Daunton 1990: 202). Ideas about health and amenity also encouraged an outwards move. Central districts, because of high land costs, tended to become densely built up, while intensifying industrialization often increased noise and dirt. Areas upwind from industry and town centres, ideally on higher ground, were understood as salubrious

(George 2000: 5–8). The gardens that were an essential component of villas were spaces of pleasure but they also fostered good ventilation, which was increasingly considered vital for domestic health.

Until the introduction of cheap transport later in the century, poorer working people needed to remain close to employment possibilities, usually in built-up areas. Urban fringes therefore promised a residential location relieved of indiscriminate and unsolicited contact with people of different social groups. In the growing manufacturing town of Birmingham in the early 1800s, for example, the new, socially homogeneous, suburb of Edgbaston appealed to the clergy, professionals and businessmen. Here, as in similar settlements, the owners of the land under development specified the size and type of houses to be built, with the – not always successful – intention of social exclusivity (Davidoff and Hall [1987] 2002: 368–9). Nonetheless, shops and trades would follow, making these areas more mixed than is often assumed (White 2007: 82).

Informed by a Picturesque aesthetic, which placed a value on irregularity and individuality in architecture and scenery, the villa was favoured for upmarket suburban residences in the early 1800s (Slater 1978: 132; English Heritage 2011: 5–6). The large villas of the Broom Hall estate on the edge of Sheffield, built between about 1830 and 1850, were individual in style and picturesquely detailed, set in miniature parks that disregarded the building line (Tarn 1977: 184). A view *from* the house was advantageous too. John Claudius Loudon, a prolific and influential architectural and gardening authority of the first half of the nineteenth century, wrote that without a prospect 'a villa may be beautiful, picturesque, or romantic; but it never can be dignified or grand, and scarcely even elegant or graceful' (1842: 764). If the prospect could include water – sea, lake or river – so much the better (Nicol 1809: 2–3). Views of shipping were also desirable. David Lambert (2002: 129) argues for a distinct 'Bristol picturesque' in the late eighteenth century, with 'views of the rivers Avon and Severn, filled with merchant shipping and personal association of those benefitting financially from maritime trade and naval power . . .'. Early-nineteenth-century seaside developments took advantage of similar associations. The new villa colonies and upmarket resorts on the Wirral peninsula, across the River Mersey from Liverpool, for example, were economically dependent upon Liverpool and Atlantic trade and writers observed their relationship to the city with interest. One of these colonies was Rock Park, a settlement and upmarket seaside resort designed in 1837, facilitated by the new steam ferry from Liverpool (Figure 3.2); here some forty semi-detached and detached villas were intended to produce 'a fine picturesque effect, superior, although on a smaller scale, to any part of the Regent's Park, London . . .'.[3] The principal windows and gardens of the prime villas above the esplanade, owned and occupied by wealthy merchants and financiers, looked out, not on Rock Park's leafy grounds, but on the docks, shipyards and town of Liverpool – a panorama that reflected

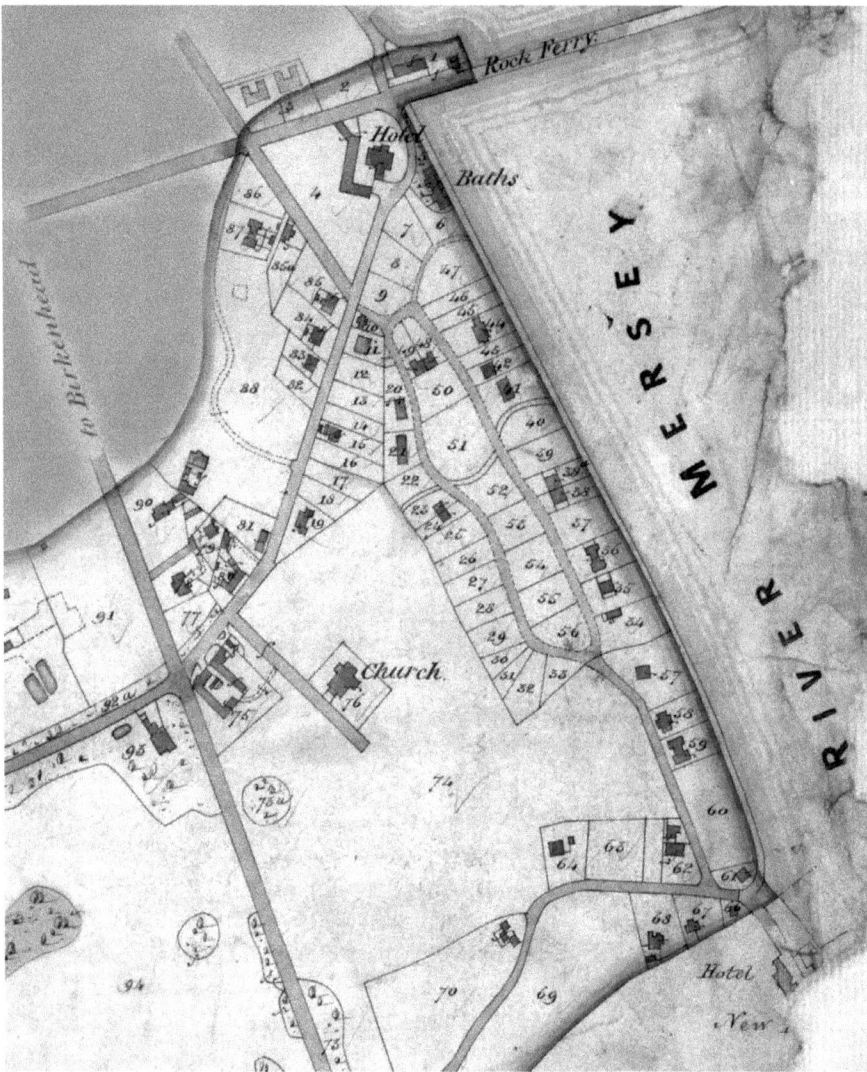

FIGURE 3.2: Rock Park, Cheshire, a development of select villas built in the late 1830s and 1840s, across the River Mersey from Liverpool. Detail of tithe map of the Township of Higher Bebington, Cheshire, 1844. © Cheshire Record Office, EDT 200/2. Records in the Cheshire Record Office are reproduced with the permission of Cheshire Archives & Local Studies and the owner / depositor to whom copyright is reserved.

the residents' position and influence in the second city of empire, and thus their wider colonial interests. Elsewhere, villa views embraced aspects of the modern landscape, such as canals, aqueducts, suspension bridges and railways while the villas were themselves described as part of the same improved scene; Loudon, for example, was 'much struck with the effect of the carriages passing along the line of the Manchester railway, as seen from the beautiful villas' (1838: 30). Many villas, of course, did not enjoy fine prospects. In such cases, shrubberies could screen disagreeable views (McIntosh 1828: 805).

Historians (e.g. Kay 2008) have paid more attention to the siting of villas and their architectural development than to the rationale of the organization of space inside. This is perhaps because villas had to meet much the same broad essential needs as other kinds of dwellings for middling incomes. Kerr (1864) used the general term 'house' in his discussions. By the nineteenth century, many (but not all) villas were built as permanent homes, rather than as alternatives to a town residence, and so had to meet the requirements of full-time accommodation. However, the villa form itself had some effect. Unlike the urban terrace, which was constrained in width (Muthesius 1982: 6), a villa outside the town could spread horizontally. Picturesque irregularity, on a large building plot, allowed for flexibility in the plan and, at least in theory, for a favourable orientation towards the sunlight – what Kerr called 'aspect' (1864: 79–83). A garden was an essential component of a villa and access, or at least a view of it, was desirable from the day rooms, which partly for that reason were often now at ground level, rather than, as in the urban terrace, on the first floor.

We now discuss the internal arrangements of villas with reference to contemporary and historiographical literature, using an unusually detailed inventory to consider how, in this case, rooms and spaces were differentiated and used and whether the arrangements correspond to those discussed in advice manuals. The inventory relates to Heath House in Stepney, east London, near the River Thames – a villa in form though not in name – which was built in about 1810 and owned and occupied by Mr Thomas Ward until his death in 1847, when the inventory was taken as part of the death-duty process. Ward was an enormously wealthy man, having built up his fortune from a family-owned mast-making business in the area. He became a property owner, ship-owner and merchant. Active in local affairs, he was a Justice of the Peace and in 1829 held the prestigious position of Sheriff of the City of London. He married in 1820 and had one child, a daughter born in 1831.[4]

When it was first built, Heath House was sited amongst fields on the urban fringe but it can never have been intended as part of an exclusive enclave because it fronted Commercial Road, one of the busiest thoroughfares in the world, built shortly before to funnel trading traffic from the docks in the east of London into the City. Mr Ward was one of the trustees of this enterprise. By the time of his death, Heath House was surrounded by houses and businesses, some of them owned by Ward. Nor was there an impressive view, since the house was on low-lying land, with commercial buildings obscuring any sight of the nearby River Thames. Heath House, then, had neither the prospect nor the exclusive setting of the ideal villa, but it was buffered from the surrounding hustle and bustle by shrubberies and boundary trees.

There were at least twenty-six rooms in the house, similar in number and name to those set down by Kerr as the minimum required for the domestic habits of refined persons (1864: 413–14). Kerr wrote that social relations precede the organization of domestic space but the thrust of his book was actually that the differentiation and specialization of space manages social relations. Such specialization was by no means new and has been much discussed by historians (e.g. McKeon 2005) but it is generally agreed that it was more widely adopted in the nineteenth century, at least for people who could afford the space to make it feasible (Muthesius 1982: 45; Daunton 1990: 207, 211). For Kerr, specialization served the main principle of domestic planning – privacy, in which the separation of the family from the servants was the most important element (1864: 74–75). He reckoned that at least three live-in servants were necessary (Kerr 1864: 400) and privacy required that they be accommodated in specialized quarters. The very wealthy Ward family is likely to have employed several servants and the inventory suggests that, at Heath House, there was indeed a basic spatial separation of the two groups. The service areas were distinct from the family rooms, either in a wing and outhouses or perhaps a basement. One bedroom at the top of the house, named as the man-servants room, was equipped for two people. But the inventory does not list any other rooms or beds for servants and it is possible that some slept on the same story as the family.

Privacy also dictated that the main part of the house should be 'relieved from the immediate occupation of the children' (Kerr 1864: 159). By the 1850s and 1860s, and perhaps earlier, it was common for well-to-do families to dedicate specialized nurseries or schoolrooms to children and their servants, allowing parents to maintain a physical and emotional distance, in keeping with current ideas about childrearing, but to modify the distance, if desired, in daily practice (Hamlett 2010: 111–12). Usually on the bedroom floor, these rooms were adapted to this specialized use only for as long as needed. No room was named as a nursery or schoolroom at Heath House, perhaps because, at the date of the inventory, the Wards' only child was almost sixteen years old. However, the presence of a child's chair, a nursery bason stand and fittings, and a second, inferior, bedstead in one of the two smaller bedrooms on the first floor indicates that it had been a child's room, which had probably been shared with her nursemaid or nanny.

By the late eighteenth century, bedrooms for the middling and upper sorts largely excluded cooking, dining and formal socializing (Cruickshank and Burton 1990) and by the mid-nineteenth century their functions were taken for granted: sleeping, sickness, marital intimacy, washing, excreting, dressing and clothes storage. They were perhaps also a place for personal privacy. Heath House had four bedrooms on the first floor. One was the small child's room, just mentioned. Another, a large, handsomely furnished, 'spare front bed chamber' contained up-to-date bedroom equipment but also a sofa, sofa table, inkstand and chess box, which made it usable as a space for personal withdrawal and perhaps private sociability. The other front chamber was also well-equipped as a bedroom though with rather less 'sitting furniture'. In addition to the large mahogany four-post bedstead there was a single bedstead. This was likely the bedroom of either or both Mr Ward and Mrs Ward. Why was there an extra bed? One of them, judging from items in the house, was an invalid. Perhaps the single bed allowed them to share a room without disturbing each other; or perhaps it was for a servant or nurse. The final, smaller, bedroom was more simply equipped but nonetheless included a bookshelf, ornaments and hand-screens. All these bedrooms were more than respectably and comfortably furnished for the usual bedroom purposes but they also offered the possibility of personal space, away from the more public dayrooms downstairs. It was common for bedrooms to be shared – either by spouses, siblings, children, or servants – and it is interesting to see that even here, in a very wealthy household, two of the four family bedrooms contained more than one bedstead.

Historians agree that, by the nineteenth century, rooms earmarked for formal hospitable purposes had become an important element in the design of new houses for the well-to-do (e.g. Muthesius 1982: 43, 45; Young 2003: 180). Leonore Davidoff (1973: 13–21, 47) argued that from about the 1820s, certainly amongst the elite and increasingly amongst the broader middle classes, complicated rituals of hospitality helped to manage social exclusivity at a time of expanding social mobility. An important tool in this etiquette was a pair of entertaining rooms – the drawing room and the dining room. Like other villas, Heath House had these rooms, decorated and furnished in the conventional gendered manner, discussed by Margaret Ponsonby in Chapter 1. Approached, as suggested in advice literature (Young 2003: 176), through an impressive entrance hall, the drawing room was enormous, containing, amongst other furniture, eight tables, eighteen chairs, two couches, three settees, a pair of what-nots and a grand piano. The furniture allowed for light refreshments, talking in groups, music, games and perhaps for other quieter, maybe even solitary, activities. The dining room was large enough for an expanding dining table, a set of fourteen dining chairs, a sideboard, and numerous pictures and ornaments. The stores were crammed with the cutlery, glasses, dinner and tea services, napkins and tablecloths that would have enabled Mr Ward, a prominent member of City and local mercantile society, to host large formal entertainments. But a bagatelle board and a child's chair and stand in the dining room suggest that it was also used informally. In smaller homes it was common (Hamlett 2009: 583) and quite acceptable, even to Kerr (1864: 111), to use the dining room as a family sitting room. Heath House also had a third day room. This often appeared in building patterns for villas (e.g. Brooks 1839) and in more general advice literature, especially later in the century (Hamlett 2009: 580–4). Its function was variable – a morning room, a breakfast room, a study or, as in this case, a library. Here it was smaller than the drawing room, with less grand furnishings than those in the other two day rooms. But items such as a ladies' work table, a toasting fork and a coffee table suggest that it was a room for the family or for informal hospitality and was therefore in some ways a more privileged room. Heath House, with its three day rooms, certainly met the requirement for a 'gentleman's house'. Empirical evidence suggests that, at mid-century, the possession of both a drawing room and a dining room was largely limited to the wealthy or the professional and upper middle classes (Hoskins 2013: 103; Muthesius 1982: 38–48) and that, although a library often appeared in advice literature, it was, in practice, only a feature of particularly well-to-do homes (Hoskins 2013: 99).

The internal arrangements of the house do, then, appear to have been geared towards the construction of privacy – for the household as a whole, for family members and their guests, and for individual household members – as demanded by Kerr and other domestic authorities. Yet, if we view the contents of the villa and its exterior and situation as a whole, we see an outward-facing as well as inward-looking world. Liverpool merchants left town counting-houses for quiet villas in the exclusive and salubrious Rock Park but their chosen views were of the docks and shipping that were the source of their wealth and power. People leaving Heath House would have immediately found themselves on one of the biggest and busiest trade traffic routes in the world, which was an immediate reminder of the owner's position as one of the wealthiest ship-owners and merchants in London. And Mr Ward was proud of the source of his fortune; when he was elected a Sheriff of the City of London, his official carriage bore among other things the shipwrights' arms.[5]

Inside the house some items, such as deed boxes and secretaires, allowed Mr Ward to attend to business at home as well as at his offices, which were some minutes away. More widespread within the villa – on the stairs and landings, in the library, the dining room, the drawing room and, perhaps more unexpectedly, in several of the bedrooms – were many decorative objects, including several models of ships, a glazed case of insects, several display collections of shells, a canoe and 'a portion of a vessel', which clearly derived from and celebrated his shipping and trading businesses. In the 1820s and 1830s, Exeter's new villas, many of whose occupants were retired members of the East India Company, contained trophies such as 'foreign shells and minerals, stuffed crocodiles, birds of paradise and natural curiosities' (Newton 1977: 19). Nor was it only well-to-do traders who showed this interest. A local historian later wrote about the ordinary residents of the Commercial Road:

> In many a home hereabouts the picture of a fine, tall vessel in full sail, the coral in the case, the curious shells, the vases from India and the Far East told their story to the folk in mid-Victorian days, who daily saw conveyed along the road the great bulk of merchandise from distant ports . . .
> —Maddocks 1932

A garden, as already discussed, was an essential element of a villa. It provided an area of private space around the house, sometimes enclosed, as at Heath House, or sometimes celebrating external views, as at Rock Park. But in either case it also provided a place for the acquisition and display of plants, especially 'exotics'. In part a response to the array of 'new' species introduced from abroad, the Gardenesque style – in which specimen plants were scientifically arranged to accentuate their natural forms – was pioneered by Loudon in the 1830s, and was particularly associated with the gardens of suburban villas (Daniels 1981: 394). Tender plants could be protected in glasshouses, which from the 1850s, with the repeal of glass tax and the popularity of the Crystal Palace, became common for even modest villas. In 1847, the conservatories at Heath House held more than five hundred potted plants. While some collectors of exotics were directly involved with overseas trade or were travellers, this was never a prerequisite for their enjoyment. Rather, their collection reflected a general interest in the unknown and for obtaining global artefacts, which helped familiarize foreign lands (Preston 1999). At a time, then, when British trading activities were riding high, the settings, outward views, internal decoration and garden planting of villas give a sense, not so much of their inward-looking seclusion, as of their place in a wider urban panorama – one that celebrated British industrial, commercial and maritime success.

SMALL TERRACED HOUSES, C. 1865–1914

From around the mid-century in England, speculatively built housing increasingly provided ordinary working people with decent dwellings that were cheaper and better equipped than in the rest of Europe (Thompson 1988: 191). The public health movement of the early part of the nineteenth century responded to urbanization, overcrowding, lack of sanitation, and cholera with a series of increasingly effective and standardized controls that sought to govern the width and arrangement of streets, the amount and nature of the open space around a dwelling, and how houses were to be constructed and organized internally. These regulations, intended to bring about an improvement in the living conditions and morals of the working classes, were many, varied around the country, were often permissive rather than compulsory, and were frequently evaded (Harper 1985; Burnett 1980: 154–63).

Nonetheless, and with important regional variations (Muthesius 1982, ch. 12; Daunton 1983, ch. 3), from the 1840s, sanitary ideas promoted the through-house, with both a front and back entrance and an open space behind, 'as the essential vehicle of cleanliness, hygiene, and better health' because it allowed for through ventilation and because each back yard would contain its own convenience (Thompson 1988: 185). This was intended as a significant improvement on the back-to-back arrangement, whereby each house was built up against its neighbour at the rear and on either side; an individual house therefore had no through ventilation, and frequently shared sanitary and water provision with its neighbours. Although plenty of people continued to live in back-to-backs throughout our period (Daunton 1983), by 1908 *The Report of the Enquiry . . . into Working-Class Rents, Housing and Retail Prices* noted that 'self-contained two-storeyed dwellings, possessing four or five rooms and a separate scullery . . . may be taken as the typical dwellings of the English working classes' (Board of Trade 1908: vii) (Figure 3.3). These new small houses – often called byelaw housing – were built as speculative developments in repeat terraces of four or more units. Designed for, and occupied by, middling and better-off working people between about 1865 and 1914, they were also a response to falling land prices and increased incomes, which created the right conditions for improved, affordable, housing on a large scale (Daunton 2001b: 31). The majority of these houses were erected in new suburban areas, usually as small-scale speculations by builders or minor capitalists (Barson 1999: 65). An assessment would be made of the house type best suited to the social standing of the area to be developed and then a scheme would be devised to accommodate the maximum number of houses, constrained by local topography and byelaws (for the case of Liverpool, see Menuge 2008: 31–36). Regular grid layouts were generally chosen because of their efficient use of space. These densely built streets did not offer the leafy seclusion of those for the well-to-do but they did offer relatively spacious, adaptable, houses with modern facilities. Supported by inexpensive transport links to workplaces and urban amenities, many people were evidently willing to spend a greater proportion of their income on suburban living conditions (Pooley 2001: 436).

Building regulations, byelaws, street layouts, floorplans and the facilities inside the dwelling were all – like advice literature and builders' pattern books – intended to support or promote a particular way of life. We now go on to consider some of the intentions embedded in these small terraced houses while bringing forward evidence for how they were actually inhabited to draw conclusions about their occupants' own preferences.

Building economically led to standardization of design and much contemporary commentary focused on the monotony of the new streets (e.g. Muthesius [1904–5] 2007: 146). Yet even the smallest terraces boasted some decorative architectural features (Menuge 2008: 36–39). It was claimed that one of the advantages of separate dwelling houses was that each could 'have that touch of individuality . . . so important in the construction of a home' (Alden and Hayward 1907: 108–9). Forecourts, together with wider streets, were sanitary measures, designed to increase air circulation and light. But their size usually corresponded to the houses' size and rent and, 'if kept in good order', improved their appearance and added to their privacy (Maitland 1910: 33). Bay-windows at the front, on one or both stories, also denoted the status of the street. Charles Booth observed that, in London, the front space of 'little four- and five-roomed houses' was

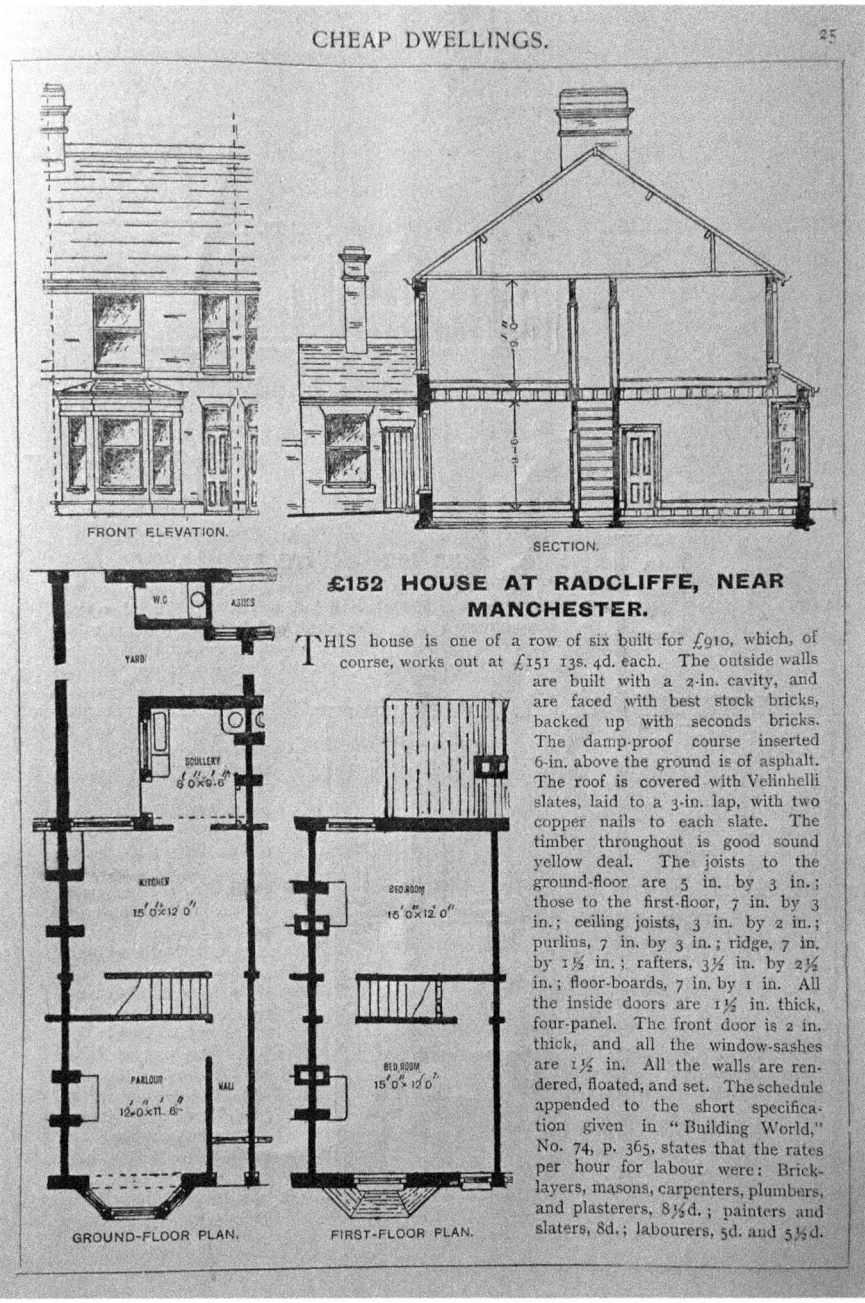

FIGURE 3.3: A typical four-roomed 'through-house' with small yard, built near Manchester, c. 1900. From Paul N. Hasluck, *Cheap Dwellings Actually Built Costing from £75 to £300 Each and Upwards* (London: Cassell, [c. 1900] 1908).

between one to three yards deep: 'In some quiet nooks this place is made really a garden, filled with carefully tended plants and decorated with rockery or "grotto" of shining stones and shells – in other places the hard beaten earth is without ornament and puts forth no green life'; but whatever its planting, this space was 'useful in giving some privacy to the front room, the window of which is otherwise too close to the eyes and hands of every passer-by' (1891: 235). Frances M. Jones argued that tenants' work in maintaining the fronts of their homes rendered the terraces of industrial towns 'uniform' but not 'monotonous' and that these acts represented statements of choice, however restricted (1968: 176, 178). Immaculate doorsteps and windows (Kelley 2009a: 729) and tidy forecourts (Preston 2014: 212–14) were crucial to the performance of 'respectability' and neighbourhood propriety in the byelaw home.

One very important element of these through-houses was the requirement that they should have an area of open space behind – usually interpreted to mean an exclusive back yard. Its length related to the height and width of the house, depending on byelaws and available land. It was usually reached from the kitchen or scullery at the back of the house (Daunton 1983, ch. 3), and, especially where water-closets were not provided, there was often a back alley for the removal of night-soil. The yard usually contained the coal-shed, the ash-heap and the convenience. The water closet was the most sanitary and inoffensive type of convenience but it required a good supply of water and did not become the most common sort until the early twentieth century (Daunton 1983: 247–62). By the end of the 1800s, water-borne sanitation allowed the closet to be incorporated inside some new houses, usually as part of the scullery annexe (Burnett 1980: 158).

The provision of a yard was, wrote Stefan Muthesius, 'probably the most decisive regulation of all'; it became 'an extension to the house, its main purpose being to keep the house clean' (1982: 137). The sanitary facilities and the light and ventilation it provided were understood as a health issue and as ministering to the comfort of the occupants. But its use as a *garden* (as opposed to an open space) was rather little addressed in the sanitary literature on urban terraced housing (e.g. Murphy 1883). Turn-of-the-century commentary on improved housing, informed by garden city planning, was usually pitched against the 'byelaw method' because its grid layout hindered light and left little room for gardens (e.g. Unwin 1912). Some terraced gardens were however relatively large (Figure 3.4), and it is clear that many people living in small terraced houses *did* garden (Preston 2014).

Memoirs and contemporary photographs record a preference for annuals and fast-growing, often scented, perennials in back gardens. This kind of house was usually rented by the week, which probably contributed to the desire for speedy garden-making. Climbers, often grown over trellis, helped to screen out neighbours, as the gardening press recommended. Leasehold laws, which stipulated that trees and shrubs became landlords' property and so could not be

FIGURE 3.4: Postcard view of part of Cranford Park, Ilford, Essex, completed in the early 1900s, with smaller terraced houses in the foreground, c. 1918.

removed on quitting, probably discouraged major garden overhauls. But owner-occupiers also seem to have adopted the same kind of practical gardening, using seeds and cheap and easily replaceable plants. Richard Church's family bought their semi-detached house in turn-of-the-century Battersea, south London; his mother, a schoolteacher, grew jasmine around the French window of the kitchen extension, sunflowers in a tile-bordered bed down the side, and a 'forest of annuals' beneath the sycamore tree at the end (1955: 62, 169). A growing number of gardening books catered for the 'migratory' tenants of small houses (e.g. Havart 1912: 25). The correspondence and legal columns of *Amateur Gardening* magazine from 1884 onwards indicate a large readership of amateurs gardening in small, overlooked, urban spaces, who required advice on their rights as tenants, and on how to deal with the authorities and their neighbours.

Children, at least when younger, played at the back. Richard Church set out his toy soldiers and railway in the concrete yard (1955: 90, 169, 202). Harry Burton remembered the gardens behind the southwest London terraces where he lived as a child in the early 1900s as being 'reasonably long, though very narrow' (1958: 17). In at least two upstairs flats he had access to a shared garden. He recalled playing in one of them and the wooden fences, tobacco plants and nasturtiums of the other; there was a shrub at the end into which the child of a 'superior family' over the fence threw books and worse (1958: 23,

51). In a subsequent, larger and more self-contained, first-floor flat, there was only a 'veranda' opening from the back door, with corrugated iron roof and sides, on which were the dustbin, wringer, baths, flowerpots and cat-litter tray: 'It was all the garden we had, but at least it gave a sweeping prospect of other people's gardens' (1958: 51). In addition to children's play and sheds for storage, this space had to survive 'the traffic of washing day' (Willis 1960: 155–56); the provision of self-contained back-garden space may therefore have been intended – and valued – as a means of keeping personal items private, as well as to prevent disease (Crisp 2012: 18).

Fenced or walled back spaces were thus important because, ideally, they allowed an individual household access to its own outside space, convenience and washing facilities, without having to go out into the street or share with others, as was necessary in back-to-back or court housing. Whereas courts and shared facilities had involved a communal way of life, these back yards were intended to foster a more insular or 'encapsulated' style of living that focused on the conjugal family and the domestic life of an individual household (Daunton 1983, ch. 2). However, very often, the yard and facilities were used by more than one family since individual terraced houses were frequently occupied by two or more households. Maud Pember Reeves found that in Lambeth, when two families shared this type of house, 'the landlady of the two probably chooses the ground floor, with command over the yard and washing arrangements', which often led to disagreements ([1913] 1979: 33). Nor were the back yards and gardens actually 'private', for they were overlooked from the adjoining houses and Cecil Hewitt recalled how children played ball games across neighbouring plots. However, he did not remember much else about the back gardens of his Edwardian childhood – probably because 'children of all ages used the road as a playground' (Rolph 1982: 61–62, 92). Autobiographical accounts, recalling a seemingly endless stream of activity in the residential streets, including football crowds, funeral processions, street sellers, beggars, photographers and musicians, make it clear that, while the back yard offered a partially encapsulated space for each house, a great deal of communal life continued to take place in the shared open environment at the front (Davin 1996: 64–66).

Within the house, the amount of space and its layout affected how occupants lived. By the 1870s and 1880s, many byelaw terraces were no more than two storeys because that required only a single-brick nine-inch wall, making them cheap to build (Muthesius 1982: 4, 6). Their widths varied from 16 to 25 feet (Muthesius [1904–5] 2007: 146–47), with corresponding variations in room dimensions. The basic layout of a single-fronted terraced house was similar for the range of rents. The cheapest four-roomed houses were arranged as a sitting room at the front, with a kitchen behind and two bedrooms upstairs. Bigger houses usually had a single- or double-height back extension, which projected into the yard. Five-roomed houses typically comprised a parlour at the front, a kitchen behind and a scullery in the back extension, with three small bedrooms above. Six-roomed houses were deeper and contained two living rooms or parlours downstairs (often separated by folding doors, allowing the space to be used flexibly) with a separate kitchen and scullery in the back extension (Daunton 1983: 51), and three bedrooms upstairs. Ideally, bedrooms were zoned by age and gender: 'one for the parents, one for the boys and one for the girls' (Kelley 2009a: 724).

Differences in the number of rooms and, especially, the availability of space for a hall or passage, influenced how the rooms were apportioned. In Liverpool, the front doors of the smallest houses opened directly from the street into the kitchen or general living room; there was a scullery behind but no back extension (Menuge 2008: 36). This cut down the possibilities of differentiating space although, where there was a back lane, it was possible to make a distinction between the front and back entrances (Daunton 1983: 280–81). A larger house footprint allowed for a passage entry, so that access to different rooms could be controlled and their functions more easily specialized.

The sources of energy also contributed to the use of space (Daunton 1983: 237–46). In dwellings with only two rooms downstairs, the kitchen or living room was where most of the daily activities took place (Kelley 2009a: 724). This room was warm because cooking was done on the range. However, from the 1890s, with the introduction of payment by slot meters in some areas, gas cookers became a more convenient alternative to the range and facilitated moving cooking to the scullery, leaving the kitchen as more of a single-function living room (Daunton 1983, ch. 10). The front room or parlour was usually reserved for best, opened up – and heated – only on special occasions. The small wash-house, scullery or back kitchen was the location of the home's only water supply and the copper for heating the water (Muthesius 1982: 61–62; Daunton 1983: 246–47; Kelley 2009a: 724). It was the place for wet or dirty work such as laundry, washing up, preparing food and personal washing.

However, the number of occupants and their relationship to each other complicated the ideal arrangements. In theory, the more rooms, the more the differentiation (Faire 1998: 42) but, in practice, multi-occupancy was frequent, even in new, apparently single-family, houses. The 1908 Board of Trade *Report . . . into Working-Class Rents, Housing and Retail Prices* shows that it was not unusual for two families to occupy a house originally intended for a single household or for there to be lodgers. This did not only apply to those in irregular manual occupations. In 1871, lodgers were present in one in three of the houses in Liverpool's suburban terraces, tenanted mostly by the lower ranks of 'white-collar' occupations (Menuge 2008: 31). This also appears to have been the case in many of London's late-nineteenth-century byelaw suburbs, where lodgers and sharing between two families were common (Johansen 2006: 73–74, 176). Family income, regional house type, the life course and composition of the household, as well as the cost of accommodation arguably had as much an effect on how a dwelling was organized as the intentions of the builder or the authorities (Faire 1998: 43). The remainder of this chapter considers how some of London's small terraced houses were actually arranged and lived in.[6]

Cecil Hewitt, born in 1901, was the son of a City of London Police sergeant who rose to chief inspector by 1911. With wages of 31 shillings a week in around 1908, father was 'rich' (Rolph 1982: 23). Cecil remembered that between 1906 and 1910, the family (three boys, their parents and an unpaid maid-of-all-work) lived in a terrace (built around 1870) in Islington, north London (Figure 3.5). Their house had a 'small front garden' (where the baby slept in his pram), a downstairs bay-window, a small back 'garden' and six rooms inside. Unusually, the Hewitts' house had two lavatories, one upstairs and one outside and, before they moved in, father had the smallest bedroom on the half landing converted into a bathroom (hot water being carried up from the kitchen). The 1911 census shows many of the houses on the Hewitts' side of the road in multi-occupancy; Hewitt recalled that the street's back parlours were often used as extra bedrooms, and that upstairs rooms usually had to accommodate 'grannies, lonely aunts and lodgers' (Rolph 1982: 42). Daily life took place in the 'living-room-cum-kitchen' where the family ate, wrote letters, did homework and ironing, and pursued winter hobbies by gaslight. Here was the sink and 'a kitchen range with an oven, a whitened hearth stone, and a hob' – details he believed to be identical in similar houses throughout the country (1982: 41). In 1910, the Hewitt family moved to an almost exactly similar

FIGURE 3.5: Recent view of Corbyn Street, Islington, London, a terrace built *c.* 1870.

house in Fulham, near the River Thames in southwest London, where they stayed until 1916, paying 16 shillings a week in rent (1982: 68–71).

Between 1901 and 1916, the young Harry McGuire Burton and his family lived in the same area as the Hewitts. Burton recalled that the recently built houses 'were designed for just the type of people who inhabited them; most of them, in fact, were designed for occupation by two families, although few had two front doors to them' (1958: 117). The *Report . . . into Working Class Rents, Housing, and Retail Prices* recorded of Fulham that:

> The commonest type of working-class dwelling is a six-roomed house let in two flats of three rooms [plus scullery] . . . The more highly rented tenements are those which have been built as separate flats and contain a kitchen and a scullery and have water laid on both floors. In these flats there is frequently a staircase from the upper tenement to the yard, and in some cases there are separate front entrances.
> —Board of Trade 1908: 34

Harry Burton's father was a housepainter, whose income seldom reached £2 a week and who was often unemployed. The Burtons lived in several subdivided houses and, latterly, in one of the 'separate flats' noted in the Board of Trade report. The family always took the upper floor, though Burton was unsure if this was because it was cheaper, 'more superior' or if the family preferred not to hear another family overhead. They 'lived almost entirely in the kitchen', washing in the scullery; the toilet was 'out the back' (Burton 1958: 22–23, 43, 45).

For both of these turn-of-the-century households, the ownership of a parlour was important. The Burtons' 'front-room (never the "parlour")' was well-furnished, with 'a carpet of sorts, brass fire-irons, an "arty" table-cloth concealing a cheap deal table, a book-case for prizes and superior books, and a "suite"' of furniture (1958: 42). But it was used only on Sundays, for special occasions or when the kitchen grew too hot for comfort. Illnesses aside, it was definitely not for sleeping: 'There was no spare room and no spare bed, so we never had a visitor to stay the night' (Burton 1958: 43). In 1911–13, the family rented a purpose-built five-roomed flat. With a front room and a kitchen, the eight members of the household – comprising his parents, five children and their grandmother – slept in three bedrooms. They chose this somewhat cramped sleeping arrangement for the sake of maintaining a best room in the manner that contemporary social commentators and housing reformers considered a showy waste of space (Burnett 1980: 169). The relatively and securely well-off Hewitts had a superior whole house in their Islington terrace, with two parlours; the back parlour held comfortable furniture, and an ornate mantelpiece with ornaments. But Hewitt remembered the *front* parlours in the street as 'little used', and that his own remained empty until they could afford furnishings (Rolph 1982: 42–44).

Thomas Wright wrote journalistic pieces about working-class life from the inside; his contemporary description of a Sunday in the home of a fictional skilled working man in late-1860s London presents an idealized view of complicated differentiations of space, managed in cramped conditions (1868: 205–48). The parlour, kitchen and wash-house on the ground floor were functionally differentiated, with additional specialization achieved by opening them to different groups of people at different times and by using special equipment. The kitchen housed most of the family's everyday activities and eating but Sunday dinner was a formal event, which took place in 'the best room, and on the best table, covered with the best table-cloth, and the family plate'; only invited guests participated. After dinner, the women retired to the kitchen – 'a movement equivalent to the "society" one of ladies retiring to the drawing-room . . .' – to chat and clear up; the men remained in the parlour. Sunday tea was also in the parlour, but with a group of friends and family who might just 'drop in'. Wright's description suggests that the rooms were gendered: the parlour, where the male head of household read his paper and smoked while dinner was cooked and where he remained with his male guests afterwards was more 'masculine'; the kitchen was where women and children congregated, both for work and informal sociability.

Recalling the houses (built in the 1870s) in his terrace in Bermondsey, south London, around 1900, Frederick Willis, successively a printer's boy and a hatter, considered that 'their aesthetics were not discussed. But they were snug, warm, and sound, and what more could you expect for eighteen shillings a week? Each house was, of course, a replica of its neighbour, with iron railings, tiled forecourt, and nothing green growing about it, presented an austere appearance' (1960: 13). Although critical, Hermann Muthesius in his survey, *The English House*, applauded the 'measure of independence and quiet' afforded, considering that even the smallest of these 'miniature' homes reflected their occupants' preferences: 'a real house, as befits those in England known as respectable people' ([1904–5] 2007: 146–47). As Menuge writes of late-nineteenth-century Liverpool, 'for thousands, single-family occupancy of a house enjoying its own sanitation and a constant water supply – even if that meant a single tap in the kitchen or scullery – became an achievable goal' (2008: 45).

CONCLUSION

Of the millions of new houses that were erected in England during the nineteenth and early twentieth centuries, villas and small terraced houses were the most common. By the end of the 1800s, groups of small terraced houses were not uncommonly designated as 'villas' while many middle-class suburbs featured terraces similar in layout to those for working people but with more and bigger rooms, better sanitary facilities, more architectural detailing and larger gardens. Although on different timescales, both villas and small terraced houses came to include increasingly sophisticated and convenient utilities. The self-contained house, with attached open space, had been a desirable form of residential accommodation for the English well-to-do from the beginning of the period. As the century progressed, supported by ideas about improving public health and morality, it was also increasingly presented as an ideal for the less well-off. Speculative builders, working for the market, provided them in their hundreds of thousands. Harry McGuire Burton wrote about his working-class family's 'progress' from small to larger flats in subdivided houses, 'mostly away from the poorest streets', until, in 1913, they experienced 'the neat luxury' of their first full 'villa' (1958: 54, 51); his wording offers evidence of the desire for an individual self-contained house but indicates that people were constrained by their economic situation and life-stage.

A self-contained house did not necessarily equate to a nuclear family living on its own. Lodgers and extended family were common in working households; even villas provided smart lodgings or apartments in high-rent areas. Live-in servants were not unknown in small terraced homes and were an absolute necessity in better-off households. In many cases, more than one household shared an individual house.

Internal specialization can be seen in both villas and terraces, although the specific differentiations varied according to economic ability, space, the number and relationship of occupants, but also according to different priorities. Small terraced houses did not have, for example, rooms designated as drawing rooms or dining rooms; their parlours were more multifunctional. But it is evident that the maintenance of a 'best' room could be so important that people would tolerate apparently crowded bedrooms. Housing reformers advocated the segregation of sleeping by sex, age and relationship, but in practice, even in larger houses, sharing bedrooms was not uncommon.

Self-contained open space outside was an important element of both kinds of house. The ornamental and sometimes productive gardens of villas provided all-important ventilation as well as the pleasure and active leisure increasingly attached to gardening. Aesthetics and health were thus combined in the new villa landscape. Initially, on the other hand, health and hygiene were predominant motives behind the requirement for external spaces associated with urban byelaw housing; stipulated distances between buildings and self-contained rear space were intended to maximize light and air in areas of relative high density, and to provide for better waste removal. But, as the century progressed, there was ample advice for, and by, the occupants of the new terraced homes who were willing and able to treat these spaces as gardens. Even so, tight budgets and short tenancies favoured an aesthetic of quick-growing, cheap, plants rather different from that of the specimen planting of villa gardens. By the end of the century, with the growing influence of the garden city movement, gardens for healthy and productive leisure became part of the repertoire of demands for working-class housing.

This period saw the predominance of individual self-contained houses, erected in informally – and incompletely – socially 'zoned' neighbourhoods. This has been understood as demonstrating the widespread adoption of the ideal of private, familial, domestic life distinct from the workplace – an ideal that was crucial to the development of the middle classes from the end of the 1700s, and which was increasingly adopted amongst working people as their living and working conditions improved in the second half of the nineteenth century. However, at the same time, we can see an engagement with the wider world and community. The occupants of villas, with multiple rooms and big gardens, could aim for privacy by segregating servants, and by shutting out unwelcome sights, smells and persons. But simultaneously they welcomed in views of industry and enterprise and displayed the fruits of work, trade and empire in their rooms and gardens. The occupants of small terraces could enjoy privacy behind their own front doors – even if their homes were shared with another household, and were cheek-by-jowl with neighbours in busy streets, which continued to be a rich source of communal life.

CHAPTER FOUR

Furniture and Furnishings: Transnational Production and Consumption Networks in East Africa

BRITTA SCHILLING

Images of 'colonial style' are everywhere around us: from the Ralph Lauren Safari and Cape Lodge Home Collection of Spring 2008 to popular coffee-table books and frequent evocations in blogs, interior design publications and fashion magazines (Foley 1993; Beddow and Burns 2002; Jordan 2000, 2007; Algotsson 2000; Fraser and Allen 2007; Reiter and von Schaewen 2007; Jafferji and Pitcher 2003). The popular image of 'colonial style' today – as produced by publishers usually based in the United States or Europe – evokes sentiments of exoticism, romance, virility, mystery and nostalgia. Sometimes, it is a fanciful composition of elements from Africa, India and the Far East, a compendium of 'otherness' embodied in home furnishings. More often than not, these reawakened colonial fantasies of 'Safari Style' and 'Swahili Chic' are meant to be located in Africa, and East Africa in particular.

'Colonial style' furnishings have a long history which stretches back to the age of Empire, particularly from the 1850s onward. This was a period of increased mobility and transoceanic connections between far-flung empires and European metropoles, networks facilitated by the opening of the Suez Canal in 1869 used by travelling people and travelling goods, including furniture and furnishings. Many historians now see this age as the beginning of modern globalization

(Stearns 2010; Magee and Thompson 2010; Dejung and Petersson 2013; Conrad 2010; Huber 2013), an age in which millions of Europeans made their homes in the Empire, at the same time as images and ideologies of empire made their way 'home' (Hall and Rose 2006; Cooper and Stoler 1997; Mackenzie 1986).

As much as a 'colonial style' today calls forth dreams of the exotic 'other', during colonial times themselves, the colonial home was often seen as an idealized version of the European self. Whether implicitly or explicitly, contemporary advice books and manuals proposed the home to be a building block of 'Britishness'. Consider the idealized home which Mary Aline Buxton sketches out in her account of a Kenyan interior in the 1920s:

> The outside, whitewashed and thatched, was as picturesque as any cottage in an old village in England, and inside it was even better. On the floor were Persian rugs, the deep window-seat was gay with a most attractive cretonne. In the centre of the room was a lovely old gate-legged table and Jacobean chairs. Some carnations in a cut-glass vase lit up the dark Welsh dresser. On the low mantelshelf was some rare old china. Near the door, on a seventeenth-century chest, a bowl of big dark violets scented the whole room. The simple artistic room carried my thoughts miles away, till they were abruptly brought back to Kenya by a native in a long white *khanzu* who came in with a shovel of burning charcoal. . .
> —1927: 178–79

The outside appearance and the interior furnishings of the home Buxton visits seem to be copied directly out of a picturesque English village. In fact, the author suggests that the home indeed has the ability to mentally transport its inhabitants back 'home' to England, were it not for the abrupt intrusion of the African domestic servant onto the scene.

Buxton, like many of her contemporaries, seems obsessed with staking out Britishness in an unfamiliar world. This was all the more important in an environment carefully constructed to underline the racial 'rule of difference' (Hall 2002; Stoler 2002; Kennedy 1987). As the doyenne of African home-making manuals, Emily Bradley, declares well into the later stages of empire: 'Your home is a microcosm of the world in which you live, and your attitude to the whole race will be determined, or at least affected, by your contact with it at first hand' (1950: 67). In this sense, the ideal home in Africa was not wholly unlike the ideal suggested in advice books for Britons travelling to India, where, as Thomas Metcalf has remarked, bungalows were 'islands of Englishness' (Metcalf 1995: 178; Steel and Gardiner [1890] 2010). And yet, as Robin Jones has also found in the South Asian context, there is a danger of taking this advice too literally (2007: 15).

Both the images of the colonial home propagated through advice books of the nineteenth and twentieth centuries, as well as the image of the colonial home circulating in popular culture today, are more dream than reality. The disjunction between ideal and real homes has been the subject of diverse recent histories of home, including Amanda Vickery's (2008) work on eighteenth-century London houses or Jane Hamlett's (2010) work on Victorian homes in England. Several studies of colonial homes and architecture, particularly in South Asia, also draw a distinction between desired representations of (colonial) power in domestic spaces and the realities of everyday life (Jones 2007; Chattopadhyay 2000, 2002, 2005; Glover 2004; also Lawrence 2012).

But we need to look in more detail at the material culture of the home in what was a crucial hub of empire, colonial East Africa, in order to see why there was such a discrepancy. How was it resolved? What impact did colonialism really have on the home, both economically and culturally? What role did indigenous people play in the construction of the colonial home? We can only begin to uncover these issues if we use sources which approximate the reality of lived experience in the home; if, for example, we consider colonial home furnishings, the cornerstone of 'colonial style', not just as ornament but, using the framework of material culture studies, as active objects interacting meaningfully with people in the processes of production, circulation and consumption (cf. Appadurai 1986). This chapter therefore goes back to the construction and furnishing of colonial homes in British East Africa and situates these homes within the globalizing context of the time in order to deconstruct a mythical colonial style, a myth propagated as zealously in the twenty-first century as in the nineteenth. It uses archival material, memoirs, often read against the grain, and a growing database of information garnered from former colonial families themselves.[1]

East Africa was one of the most active arenas of empire in the late nineteenth and early twentieth centuries. British possessions included Kenya Colony (under Company rule from 1888, declared a Protectorate from 1895 and a Colony from 1920), the Uganda Protectorate (from 1894–95) and Tanganyika Territory, a mandate taken over from Germany after the end of the First World War. By 1947, British East Africa encompassed 750,649 square miles and a population of 14.8 million (Kirk-Greene 2006: 3–4). It was governed according to 'indirect rule', meaning that a small number of Europeans ruled a much larger indigenous population through a local elite. Britons in East Africa included missionaries, civil servants and settlers. The latter were mostly members of the upper and middle classes who settled above all in the Kenyan highlands between 1907 and 1909; numbers rose again particularly with the Soldier Settlement Scheme after the First World War (Kennedy 1987: 6, 42). Civil servants, also mostly from the middle classes, stayed for a tour of duty from two to four years at a time, returning 'home' to Britain for leave intermittently. Missionaries included thirteen British societies, foremost of which was the Church Missionary Society (CMS), who were active in Kenya since 1844, and Uganda and to a lesser extent Tanganyika since 1876. By the mid-1920s, 359 missionaries working for British societies were living and working in these three territories, 202 of whom were CMS missionaries, who came largely from middle-class backgrounds (Beach and Fahs 1925: 90; Keen, n.d.). In 1901, there were a total of 528 whites living in the East African Protectorate and 1.22 million 'colored' people (British Foreign and Commonwealth Office 1901–2: R1–R2); by 1931 there were 16,812 'Europeans', 57,135 'Asiatics' and 2,966,993 'natives', and numbers continued to rise (British Foreign and Commonwealth Office 1931: 242–43). Although the furnishing of their homes displayed some differences, for all of these diverse groups, the home was a key site for the production of empire. For Europeans, its furnishings were a symbol of refinement and civilization in what many still saw as the 'dark continent'.

In spite of the relatively wealthy background of many Europeans who chose to come to East Africa, their homes were fairly simple structures by European standards. With the exception of the rare mansion built by renowned architects Ernest George & Yates in the interwar period, most houses were made out of either local or inexpensive imported material. Along the coast, settlers and sojourners often rented or built dwellings made of coral rag and lime in the local Arab-inspired *tembe* style. Further inland, the railway and military built houses made of wood and corrugated iron which were eventually improved and standardized. Moving towards the interior, though, most Europeans lived in 'wattle-and-daub', mud-and-thatch or mud-and-bamboo houses with a compacted earth or cowdung floor, homes which drew on local building traditions. In British East Africa, this was called a *banda* and consisted of a round or rectangular framework of poles onto which a double layer of sticks were tied with strips of green bark. This would then be plastered with mud and decked out with a roof made of grass or dry banana bark. Eventually, access to more hardwearing material such as cement improved, but the basic structure remained the same.

The plan drew on a proven model: the bungalow, a product from another realm of the British Empire, India. Seventeenth-century Bengali peasant huts, made with thatched roofs and extensive verandas, were relatively inexpensive to build and provided effective shelter from the elements. Their design was thus adapted by the British East India Company and exported across the Empire, becoming, in the words of Anthony King, a 'global' phenomenon (King 1995; Desai, Desai and Lang 2012). Knowledge of the relatively easily built bungalow model thus greatly facilitated home design for ordinary British settlers in East Africa. But of course the exterior architecture was only the starting point for the development of a particular colonial style in East Africa. Much of this style was determined by the furniture and furnishings in the interior or on the veranda – these included three types of items: objects imported directly from Europe, non-European objects from the wider Indian Ocean World, and European-looking objects produced locally. This chapter will trace the object histories of these furnishings as they travel from Europe to the Indian Ocean, are purchased from regional markets, produced by Asian and African craftsmen, and consumed by European and non-European elites.

TRAVELLING OBJECTS

Items such as beds, china, linen and plate were all recommended and usually actually brought out from Britain, though they could also increasingly be bought in urban centres such as Nairobi (Gurdon 1919: 115). Transporting larger items such as furniture from Europe was an expensive undertaking, however. Not only shipping costs, but also railway charges and/or porter fees for moving heavier items inland had to be considered, and porters could only be tasked with carrying up to 25 kilograms each. This created a situation whereby the wealth of a household could be read off of the number of larger items which had been imported from Britain. Certainly among civil servants, the number of things of European manufacture was directly linked to rank: as we can see from the *Notes for Officers Appointed to East Africa* from 1914, heads of departments and other high-ranking officials received six chairs, junior officials only two (Table 4.1).

In addition to items furnished by the British government or more treasured smaller items brought from home, such as clocks, books, table linens or paintings, settlers and sojourners could try to purchase furniture through a

TABLE 4.1: Government allowance of furniture in East Africa. From Colonial Office (1914), *Notes for officers appointed to East Africa and Uganda* (London: Waterlow & Sons), 60–1

I. Heads of Departments, Provincial Commissioners, 1st and 2nd Secretaries	Bed with spring mattress 2 pillows and mosquito net	2
	Washstands	2
	Dressing table	2
	Chest of drawers	1
	Wardrobe	1
	Dining table	1
	Sideboard	1
	Chairs, dining room	6
	Chairs, bedroom	2
	Chairs, lounge	3
	Filter	1
	Commode	2
	Set of bedroom crockery	1
II. All other gazetted officers	Bed with spring mattress 2 pillows and mosquito net	1
	Washstand	1
	Dressing table	1
	Chest of drawers	1
	Dining table	1
	Chairs, dining room	4
	Chairs, lounge	2
	Filter	1
	Commode	1
	Set of bedroom crockery	1

(continued)

TABLE 4.1: *Continued*

III. European junior officials	Bed with spring mattress	1
	~~2 pillows and~~ mosquito net	1
	Chest of drawers	1
	Dining table	1
	Chairs, dining room	2
	Commode	1
	Set of bedroom crockery	1 enamel

Enamelled iron toilet sets, and not crockery ones, are issued to all Government stations off the Railway. Mosquito nets are renewable in April every year.

In Uganda, the scale of furniture is laid down according to the class of house allotted to the Officer as follows:

First Class

1 wardrobe	1 dressing table
*2 bedsteads	3 tables
4 arm chairs	2 commodes
6 table chairs	2 sanitary pans
	1 filter

Second Class

1 wardrobe	3 tables
*1 bedstead	2 commodes
2 arm chairs	2 sanitary pans
6 table chairs	1 filter

Third Class

*1 bedstead	3 tables
2 arm chairs	1 commode
4 table chairs	1 sanitary pan
	1 filter

Fourth Class

*1 bedstead	2 tables
1 arm chair	1 commode
4 table chairs	1 sanitary pan
	1 filter

Fifth Class

*1 bedstead	1 commode
2 table chairs	1 sanitary pan
1 table	1 filter

* Includes mattresses, 2 pillows and mosquito net.

growing second-hand market. There were, however, certain items which were usually considered worth buying in Europe. These included the versatile folding chair – useful not only for the decks of shipping liners, but also for verandas and even living rooms. Camp furniture was also multifunctional and a smart choice to furnish the 'first home'. Both could be bought in Army and Navy stores (Cohen 2006: 53) as well as specialist tropical outfitters. Together with makeshift furniture made out of packing crates, these sorts of furnishings embodied the ideals of what many expatriates considered an unmistakably

British quality of 'making do', inventiveness in adverse circumstances (Lawrence 2012: 108), and sometimes also a certain sense of understatement.

Another popular chair imported to Africa was the Thonet model, designed using revolutionary wood-bending techniques in the mid-1830s by Michael Thonet and perfected and mass-produced by his sons from the 1860s onwards. Thonet was a company set up by a German in Austria, but the company did have offices in London. Thonet and his competitors produced some of the first chairs for a mass market and their enterprise was booming all throughout the late nineteenth and early twentieth centuries. Their 1912 catalogue featured over 12,000 different pieces of furniture, and in 1913 their factories were producing 1.8 million articles of furniture per year, mostly chairs, the most famous being the least expensive No. 14 and later No. 18 (Wilk 1980: 43, 70, 75). These were also the most popular models amongst Europeans going overseas. The advantages of the Thonet chair to colonialists were that it could be taken apart into six pieces and later reassembled (the very early days of flat-packed furniture), and that it was light, thus reducing shipping costs. It was also held together by screws rather than glue, the latter being an attractive food for insects.

Thonet's overseas exports amounted to almost 30 percent of their total sales by 1913 (Wilk 1980: 75). Most of these items went to the United States, Brazil and Argentina, but many also found their way to East Africa. In contrast to Europe, where the less expensive models were initially only meant for public spaces such as cafés (Wilk 1980: 33), in Africa they were deemed appropriate for the home long before they were included in the interior designs of the likes of Mies van der Rohe in the 1920s and 1930s. Sir Harry Johnston's dining room in Entebbe, Uganda, which combined the traditional white tablecloth with the common café chair, was thus inadvertently avant-garde (Figure 4.1).

The Thonet chair and its numerous copies were made with an eye to a globalizing market and a pan-European clientele, but there were also other furnishings industries which were even more particularly tailored to colonialists and travellers going overseas. These included well-known names in the colonies, for example, Tilley lamps (Kirk-Greene 2006: 57) and Dover stoves, originally manufactured in Dover, New Jersey but essential items for expatriates into the mid-twentieth century.[2] Piano and harmonium manufacturers also offered portable designs (cf. Lawrence 2012: 115) that were of particular value to missionaries seeking to underscore their Christian message with song. Others, such as civil servant Alexander Gilchrist Gibb, were able to buy a piano 'by private treaty' from a captain in the King's African Rifles, allowing him to play the 1920s hit *Coal Black Mammy* in his Dar es Salaam residence loud enough for all the neighbourhood to hear (Gilchrist Gibb 1936: 34).

Furnishings brought from Europe were expensive in terms of their commodity value, determined in part by transport costs, but also because of their rarity and the difficulties involved in replacing them. Sets of objects were valued in

FIGURE 4.1: Sir Harry Johnston's dining room in Entebbe, Uganda, c. 1902. From Sir Harry Johnston, *The Uganda Protectorate* (London: Hutchinson, 1902), Plate 199. Reproduced by kind permission of the Syndics of Cambridge University Library.

particular for their completeness, in Jean Baudrillard's terms, each one being prized in its relationship to a system 'on the basis of which the subject seeks to piece together his world, his personal microcosm' (1994: 7). The value of a teacup in this context, then, lies not merely in its utility, but in its ability to be possessed, and some members of the expatriate community appear to have been passionate, if not obsessive, collectors and keepers of a complete set of porcelain. Baudrillard's ideal type is the male collector, but in the colonial home, women seem to have been particularly concerned with their own and their neighbours' ability to produce the complete set at social occasions. Consider the following extract from Miss E.M. Furley's journal during her stay in Uganda, which was included in a Church Missionary Society publication in 1895:

> In the evening, by special request, we all went over to the Mission-house to dinner. I should think the annals of Kibwezi never knew such a dinner party. For twenty Europeans to sit down to a meal together at one table, so far in the interior of Africa, is most unusual. How they managed to supply us with cups, saucers, plates, &c., was an astonishment.
>
> —Furley 1895: 187

Completeness was not just a source of wonder but also of envy: in her memoirs of life in Kenya, Mary Aline Buxton laments her own dingy appearance at a dinner party, but:

> I did not recover from feeling as dispirited as the Queen of Sheba before Solomon's glory until soup was on the table. Then, to my joy, I noticed my host drinking his portion of soup out of an enamel mug – there were not enough plates to go round! That put me on my feet again, with the glad memory of my own 'dozen of each' sitting as yet unscathed in the pantry cupboards.
>
> —Buxton 1927: 16

Again, here we see Baudrillard's theory at work, as an object – in this case, a soup bowl –'acquires its exceptional value *by dint of being absent*' (Baudrillard 1994: 13, original emphasis). Unbeknownst to many colonial homeowners, at least in urban areas, the 'dozen of each' was often assembled through a system of borrowing amongst domestic servants (Gilchrist Gibb 1936: 156–57), further usurping the ideal of personal ownership which underpins the collector's very sense of self, according to Baudrillard.

Porcelain itself, however, was not new to East Africa, nor exclusive to Europeans. Archaeologists have dated its first probable use in Swahili culture to somewhere between the eleventh and fifteenth centuries (Zhao 2012: 64). Rather than being used as tableware, however, porcelain objects such as plates were displayed by wealthy 'cosmopolitans' as ornaments in special plaster wall niches in the home. This practice continued amongst the Zanzibar elite into the nineteenth century and, indeed, also formed part of a culture of collecting and Baudrillardian object systems, as Jeremy Presthold argues (2008: 96–97; also Zhao 2012). What made European porcelain unique amongst the expatriate community, then, was its origin and to some extent its form, both of which reminded one of 'home', but above all its use. The use of porcelain to distance the body from food remained a symbol of European refinement and culture.

LOCAL GLOBAL MARKETS

Another option for obtaining home furnishings was to buy 'local', which meant tapping in to this very Indian Ocean trade system which had been flourishing since the seventh century (LaViolette 2008; Presthold 2008; Sheriff 2010; Moorthy and Jamal 2010; Machado 2014; Ghosh and Muecke 2007; Chandra 1987; Chaudhuri 1990). Buying local made above all economic sense, as expatriates had to pay an import duty of five percent, in addition to harbour dues, on all foreign goods (e.g. goods from Europe); from 1904–5 this was raised to ten per cent (British Foreign and Commonwealth Office 1901–31).

Furnishings obtainable in coastal East Africa as well as South Asian *dukas*, or shops, dotted along the way inland included things like Persian carpets, a favourite for colonial homes despite discouragement from advice books because they could potentially harbour insects.

Another popular home furnishing item among expatriates were small wooden octagonal tables. A surviving example, now housed in the Victoria and Albert Museum, was made in Hoshiarpur in Punjab, India around 1880 from hisham wood and inlaid with ivory and ebony. The design, according to museum researchers, originated in Turkey but flourished in India, as it was produced increasingly for a European market for oriental furnishings. European retailers included the renowned department store Liberty.[3] In Britain, these sorts of tables were used to decorate 'cosy corners' and add to the allure of having a room, often the men's smoking room, in an 'oriental' or 'Moorish' style (Girouard 1978: 297; Neiswander 2008). Appropriating one of the most recognizable signs of Islamic art and architecture, the octagon, these tables were part of a larger Orientalist craze in the art and cultural world (Said 1978; Nochlin 1989). Deborah Cohen interprets these furnishings as part of a wider trend to invest the home with a sense of individuality (2006: 126–30), but, unlike previous fads for luxury goods produced in India and China and imitated in Britain (Berg 2004), these sorts of furnishings were actually made available to large portions of the middle-class population. Not just in Britain, but also in the United States, housewives were urged to emulate this fashion to demonstrate their 'cosmopolitanism' (Hoganson 2002; Schuyler Matthews 1894).

In East Africa itself, the inclusion of octagonal tables in European rooms was usually much more limited and practically motivated than in the interiors promoted for fashionable European and American parlours. Rarely do we see a full-blown orientalist fantasy. Much more likely is the subtle punctuation of a European-looking interior by an octagonal table; for example, consider the living room of the head of the Public Works Department in the East Africa Protectorate, William McGregor Ross, in his family home in Nairobi around 1916 (Figure 4.2). The table here appears to be simpler than its counterpart in the V&A, entirely made of wood but with intricate carving along the sides. Similar types can be found circulating in auction houses today; these are usually made of teak and some can even be taken apart by removing the top and folding the side panels together. Particularly for civil servants and their families, this potential for mobility, if not always fulfilled (William McGregor Ross stayed in East Africa for over twenty years), was no doubt also an attractive feature, and may have been designed by Indian joiners to suit this very purpose. There thus appears to have been a multidirectional movement of certain types of orientalist furnishings between Europe, Asia, the Middle East and the United States between the 1870s and early 1900s, so perhaps it is no surprise that many also ended up in East African colonial homes. Were British expatriates also trying to

FIGURE 4.2: Dining room of William McGregor and Isabel Ross in Nairobi, *c.* 1909–16. Papers of William McGregor and Isabel Ross, Oxford, Bodleian Library, MSS. Afr. s. 1876/17/19/11: Nairobi House *c.* 1909, text on back: 'N.W. corner of drawing room with Somail. Aug 7, 1916'. © Bodleian Library.

recreate orientalist fantasies in their drawing rooms? Or were they simply attracted to the fact that they could obtain such objects at a much lower price than in Europe?

To answer these questions it is perhaps useful to investigate another non-Western type of furnishing in colonial homes in East Africa: Arab or Zanzibar chests. In contrast to what their name suggests, these chests were not usually made in Zanzibar and were not made by Arabs, but instead imported from Persia, or Surat and Bombay in India to cater to the European market (Huxley 1985: 6). They were, however, historically imported to Arabia and indeed arrived in Zanzibar via Arab traders' dhows, which explains their name (Adie 1949: 104). Commonly made of teak, the chests are covered with brass studs and plates, and are complete with all the trappings of imaginative 'treasure chests' including lock-and-key drawers, partitions, a padlock, sometimes even a secret compartment (Adie 1949: 104). During the British colonial period, one could find antique chests which had been refashioned, but might also fall prey to a market of imitations. A real chest, however, was deemed a good investment not least because of its usefulness (Adie 1949: 106–7).

Zanzibar chests also fuelled the colonial imagination, as the following passage from Elspeth Huxley's memoirs suggests:

> [N]ow and again you could find one that had been used for its proper purpose, to stow the clothing and possessions of the sailors. My father had managed to find one such and had bought it for me as a wedding present. It was a Lamu chest, smaller and simpler than the Zanzibar ones and more roughly carpentered. Sometimes I wish I could tell of its experiences, of the creaking dhows in which it had traversed the Indian ocean, of the ports at which its crew had whiled away the furnace days, drinking endless cups of sweet thick coffee poured from those tall, thin, swan-necked pitchers of the Arab world, while waiting for the monsoon to blow their vessel back to Lamu.
> —Huxley 1985: 6–7

Huxley's chest is not merely a wooden box; it is an object of memory, both real and imagined. It evokes all the symbols of the Indian Ocean World: dhows, heat, ports, sailors, coffee, monsoon winds. Her description also reveals a certain quest to find an 'authentic' chest, one which had indeed been used by sailors rather than one which had been made explicitly for an expatriate or tourist market. These were the opportunities which living in East Africa afforded the discerning buyer, a chance to try their hand at connoisseurship, and to possess an 'original'.

In a detailed study of Arab chests, Sheila Unwin, herself a British expatriate, presents a typology based on origin, and suggests that they are actually an amalgam of European and Eastern (Indian/Arab) influences from the fifteenth century onwards. Some were brought over by Arab traders from India to the Gulf area and afterwards many were manufactured in the Gulf itself, where people stored their most valued possessions in the chests; some were painted red and given as dowry chests. They stem not only from traditional furniture-making centres on the Malabar coast but as far afield as Gujarat, which Unwin suggests is because they were essentially a trade item, one which could be modified, adapted and ornamented in different ways to please different audiences (Unwin 2006: 60). Chests were indeed also used by sailors in dhows but these were not likely to be highly decorated (Unwin 2006: 22); therefore it is unlikely that Huxley would indeed have been attracted to an 'original' chest. Decorated ones, however, were among the possessions of the Sultan of Zanzibar, and one in particular is still displayed in the museum on the island, a chest which belonged to the Sultan's sister, Sayyida Salme, Princess of Zanzibar and Oman (Unwin 2006: 117).

Sayyida Salme, born in 1844, fell in love with the German merchant Rudolf Heinrich Ruete and eloped with him to Germany, where she died in 1924 under the name of Emily Ruete. In 1888, she first published her memoirs in German, which were received with great curiosity and fascination by the German public and translated into English in 1907. While describing her surroundings growing up in Zanzibar, Ruete also mentions Arab chests:

> In the gentlemen's rooms the walls are decorated with trophies of valuable weapons from Arabia, Persia, and Turkey, with which every Arab embellishes his abode in the measure of his rank and riches . . . Wardrobes, cupboards, and the like are unfamiliar furniture, but you find a sort of chest with two or three drawers and a secret place besides for money and jeweler. These coffers – several of them to each room – are large and massive, and studded with hundreds of small brass-headed nails by way of ornaments.
> —Said Ruete [1888] 1907: 24–25

Ruete, someone who quite literally crossed both Arab and European upper-class societies, may well have helped the popularity of Arab chests amongst the European colonial elite. Her daughter, Antonie, also wrote a popular book on homemaking in the tropics; her advice, however, only extends to kitchen furnishings (Brandeis 1907).

By 1922, Zanzibar chests were once again given as wedding presents, for example as a gift to Princess Mary from the East African Women's League.[4] Their utility was thus paramount, but no doubt their romantic qualities also played a role in this choice. I have interviewed several families active in the former British colonies who now keep these Zanzibar chests in their homes as family heirlooms (Figure 4.3). Similarly, several examples of teakwood

FIGURE 4.3: Zanzibar chest in the home of David LeBreton, England, 2014. Photograph © Britta Schilling. Reproduced with kind permission from David LeBreton.

octagonal tables can still be found in auction houses, perhaps a trace of a European design trend, but also a material legacy of empire left by expatriates returning to Britain.

In their association with Zanzibar and other Indian Ocean ports, these chests touched upon what Sarah Longair has described as quintessentially exotic: 'the word itself epitomized mysterious otherness' (2015: 41–42). A large part of this romance was the notion of cross-oceanic trade. The Indian Ocean World system, regulated by the monsoon winds blowing alternately from the northeast and southwest depending on the season, had been used for trade for hundreds of years before Europeans arrived. Indian, Goan, Arab and, eventually in the fifteenth century, Portuguese merchants all exchanged goods in coastal hubs such as Zanzibar. Along the Indian Ocean, trade was governed by dhows long before it was governed by steamships, and, as Erik Gilbert has shown, the two continued in uneasy co-existence under the colonial regime (Gilbert 2004). From the coast, trading routes extended inland which had traditionally been used by Arab traders for the slave trade. Once the Uganda railway was built in the late nineteenth century, this route was increasingly used by South Asians (Oonk 2013: 83). They set up small shops called *dukas*, both admired and detested by the expatriate community for their ability to undercut the competition. As the travel guide author Linda Leigh wrote in 1901:

> The Indians' industry is a tropical marvel. These little shops are open very early in the morning, long before most of us are awake. Their store of baskets filled with oddment and their exhibits of fancy soaps and mirrors, knives and glasses, cottons, fabrics and ribbons, fruits and vegetables are displayed, and line the narrow streets. They do not leave their shops to others but sit hour after hour cross-legged in the open front, sheltered from the sun.
>
> —1901: 6

South Asians were also making a mark on the furniture trade. Around 1900, two major furniture dealers on Zanzibar's Main Street were Navroji Metha & Co. and Rustomjie Nowroji Talati (Leigh 1901: 43–44). Coastal hubs were the place to order furniture from Bombay (Younghusband 1910: 219–21) or, as was more frequently the case, to buy furniture which was made by Asian craftsmen, or *fundis*, in East Africa itself. Anne Dundas, wife of the District Commissioner of Moshi in Tanzania in the 1920s, for example, mentions furniture 'picked up from an Indian bazaar' in Tanga (Dundas 1924: 51–52). But in a colonial world steeped in unequal power relations based on race, how could it have been acceptable to bring Asian-made furniture into British households?

PRODUCTION AND LABOUR

According to Blue Book statistics collected and published annually by the British government, furniture imports to British East Africa between 1902 and 1916 appear at first glance to come overwhelmingly from Britain. However, around 1910 imports from India and Burma increased, followed by a sharp decline (British Foreign and Commonwealth Office 1901–16). This may have to do with one of several developments: the growth of competitive exports from Germany, a saturation of the market and the increasing success of a second-hand trade, and the growth of a native industry. The authors of the 1912 *Handbook of British East Africa* attribute this change exclusively to the latter (Ward and Milligan 1912: 203). This 'native industry' was to a great extent in the hands of Indian migrants to East Africa.

Customers included, for example, the Powys-Cobbs of Kerenget, a settler family living in the 'white highlands'. As Dorothy Powys-Cobb remembers:

> After the house was built the Indian in charge of the Saw Mill began to make furniture. Daddy had taken out a lot of Chippendale furniture patterns and using this, they made some good chairs. A bit heavier than real Chippendale, but quite good. The seats were leather from our own beasts. I still have two arm chairs and two singles. The Indian 'fundees' were very good craftsmen.[5]

The Indian *fundi* working on the Powys Cobb estate, who unfortunately remains unnamed in the Powys Cobb papers, eventually started his own sawmill and employed several Kavirondo in his service.[6]

Asian craftsmen were popular because they were adept at copying European styles. According to Lady Cranworth, Indian carpenters are 'cheap and excellent at imitation, but there their merits end. For anything of decent workmanship and which has any last in it, it is always best and cheapest in the long run to go to British workmen' (Gurdon 1919: 116). But British workmen in East Africa were few and far between. According to statistics cited by Robert Gregory, by 1948 there was not a single European cabinet-maker in Kenya (Gregory 1993: 165). Many South Asians arrived as indentured labourers working on the railways between 1896 and 1922, but some who had been resident in the Persian Gulf had already accompanied Sultan Seyyid Said when he moved the capital of the sultanate from Oman to Zanzibar in 1832 (Oonk 2013: 76–78). By 1922, 40,000 South Asians had migrated to East Africa, a combination of skilled workers, usually recruited from Bombay, and unskilled ones, usually coming from Karachi (Gregory 1993: 159–60). South Asians were employed by the Public Works Department and other government agencies in Kenya and Uganda, but they were also over time self-employed. Because they were considered more reliable and more skilled than Africans, South Asians were paid higher wages, and this caused considerable resentment particularly among the Kenyan settler community (Gregory 1993: 172–73).

In 1922, the Devonshire Declaration set the primary goal of the colonial administration as the 'development' of Africans in the British colonies and protectorates, which came to the detriment of Asian businessmen. Asian immigration was halted, and the European and African Trade Organization of 1923 campaigned against Asian businesses, organizing boycotts, which ultimately failed, however (Gregory 1993: 172). In Uganda, the Public Works Department had already replaced Asian carpenters, masons and blacksmiths with Africans as early as 1910 (Gregory 1993: 173). The increasing animosity towards Asian workers among some sectors of white society can be seen in an advertisement that appeared in an East African newspaper in 1911, promoting 'European' labour: 'Jas K. Watson, Builder & Contractor. First Class European Supervision Guaranteed ... Executed by European Labour'.[7] This was not unlike the situation in Australia in the late nineteenth century, where, as Tracey Avery points out, a British hegemony on furniture-making for settlers was disturbed by less expensive Chinese manufacture of European-looking furniture. In Australia, European-made furniture was eventually distinguishable from non-European-made items through obvious branding (Avery 2007: 81–85); this, to my knowledge, did not occur in East Africa.

Informal training through apprenticeships in Asian businesses thus remained among the foremost sources of European skills transfer to indigenous Africans in the construction and carpentry industry at least into the 1940s. The other major sources were missionary work and, eventually, government initiatives. In 1900, an industrial mission run by the Church Missionary Society (CMS) was opened at Mengo under the direction of K.E. Borup. Boys between fourteen and twenty were accepted as apprentices and regularly indentured by agreement 'for training in handicrafts of civilized nations'. This included building as well as printing work (Anon. 1900b). Generally, the CMS credo was that Biblical teaching came before industry, but this attitude changed over time with the increasing success of industrial missions. Alexander Mackay, Scottish master builder, engineer and teacher working for the CMS in Uganda noted, 'We must have houses and furniture if we are to live like civilized beings, and show the Natives how to use their hands and heads' (letter from Mackay, 22 January 1883, quoted in Anon. 1890).

As Keletso Atkins (1988) has shown in her work on 'kafir time' in the South African context, producing new material goods of course also entailed a new way of life for trainees. Borup was above all struck by the slow pace of work and the seeming inability of workers to judge a product's value in European terms. 'They are slow workers, and they do not seem to grasp the idea that the time consumed in finishing a given piece of work is a factor in determining its value. That we have to teach them, as well as to do their work rightly' (Borup 1902:

138). By 1920, the school at Maseno, Kenya, which was providing industrial training to fifty-one young men, received a government grant of £130; this did not cover all expenses but they were still able to make a half-year profit of £70 by selling objects made in the workshops (White 1920). Buyers from a similar school in Kako, Uganda, included above all government officials (Anon. 1920).

This industrial work soon shifted focus to include an increasing number of indigenous crafts in institutions which may be seen as the precursors to Makerere College in Uganda. Kyagwe Central School, Mukono was opened in November 1909 by T.F. Victor Buxton 'with a view to fostering and encouraging industrial work, and also of keeping alive and improving native handicrafts so much in danger of dying out'. The original departments of instruction included blacksmithing, pottery-making, carpentry, bark-cloth-making, rope-walk, weaving, sewing-class, basket-making and mat-making (Anon. 1911). Here we see an effort to preserve indigenous skills which became central to British-led domestic education in East Africa until well into the transition to independence (cf. Schilling 2014). The products featured in arts and crafts exhibitions such as in Hoima in 1912, an exhibition which included tables, chairs, baskets, writing tables, window shutters and carved bowls (Anon. 1912) – and a European audience which incorporated these into their homes. In homes such as that of Mrs Millington at English Point in British East Africa, not only orientalist items but also African products, such as baskets hanging on the *banda* wall, made their way into European expatriate homes.[8] Rather than being used for their original purposes, however, they were redeployed and used as decorative elements.

By 1914, the Public Works Department employed both missionary-trained Africans and South Asian *fundis* in their workshops. They produced standardized furniture that was into the 1940s, according to one expatriate, 'instantly recognizable. The entitlement was: 2 khaki colored armchairs and a sofa, a bookcase, a desk, a dining table and 6–8 chairs, a glass-fronted sideboard, beds, and bedside tables' (Tugendhat 2011: 65–66). The furniture would be passed from one family to the next, not always matching, prone to wear and tear. Perhaps because of its lack of individuality, women like Anne Dundas thought it was best covered up entirely with fabric (Dundas 1924: 52). Covering up no doubt had its practical applications, but there is no denying that this was also a way of covering over and making invisible the 'native' hands which had constructed the furniture.

In any case, as Mary Buxton, cited earlier, admires the gate-legged table and Jacobean chairs, Welsh dresser, rare old china and a seventeenth-century chest, we have to wonder. It may well be that this family had quite literally imported the fashion for antiques and historicity to East Africa. But it could just as well have been that these were copies, completely acceptable in Britain at the time after all (Thornton 1984: 358), and even more so in Africa, where there was a sizeable labour force on hand who could copy European designs and manufacture them for a fraction of their original price.

CONSUMING ELITES

Furnishings – imported from Europe, bought in an Indian Ocean port or manufactured locally – thus contributed to the development of a colonial style, a style which became the marker of an elite, whether European or African. This elite was governed by career more than class, a career in which it was important to display a certain level of interaction with the 'other'. The degree to which other 'hands', that is, non-European manufacturers, were visibly acknowledged or actively incorporated in the home, for example, reflects this career division. In East Africa from around 1914, settlers, missionaries and civil servants all came largely from a similar middle- or upper-class background. Yet it was above all civil servants and especially colonial administrators who openly displayed indigenous artefacts and furnishings in the home. Missionary homes, sparsely furnished in accordance with Christian ideals of thrift and modesty, generally displayed the fewest visibly non-European adornments, although in practice most of their European-looking furniture would have been made by Africans working in missionary workshops.

The patterns of this elite were not just British, but pan-European. Consider the drawing room of Kurt Freiherr von Schleinitz and his family in Dar es Salaam (Figure 4.4). Von Schleinitz was the group commander and eventually lieutenant-colonel of the German army in East Africa between 1907 and 1914. His home furnishings included a Chinese vase, Chinese wall scrolls, Bombay blackwood chairs, African cloth, a Persian carpet and, in the very centre of the photograph, an octagonal wood table. All of these accoutrements point to the location of this home at the heart of the Indian Ocean trade network and in inhabitants who embrace this alterity as part of a global identity.

At the same time, the East African elite increasingly incorporated European furnishings into their domestic consumption patterns. King Daudi Kasagama, King of Toro in Uganda (r. 1891–1928), continued to live in an indigenous-built home, but also made use of European-style chairs (Anon. 1901). King Daudi Chwa II of the Baganda (r. 1896–1939), who was raised exclusively by Christian regents, received visitors 'in the approved style in a comfortable sitting-room tastefully furnished, with carpets, curtains, English lamps and pictures, conspicuous among the latter being handsome portraits of King Edward VII and our Queen' (Hattersley 1908: 7). The missionary Charles Hattersley includes a photograph of Daudi Chwa and his regents in front of his palace (Figure 4.5), all apart from the king, or *kabaka*, sitting in chairs of European manufacture; we also see two Thonet models in the background. Above hangs a gas lamp, possibly manufactured by Tilley or another European company catering to the colonial market. Below the *kabaka*'s throne lies a

FIGURE 4.4: Sitting room in the home of Kurt von Schleinitz, Dar es Salaam, German East Africa, c. 1907–14. © Koloniales Bildarchiv, Universitätsbibliothek Frankfurt am Main, Bild-Nr 004-1052-19.

Persian carpet, a tradition which had already been in use by Daudi Chwa's father, King Mwanga II (Anon. 1894). Mwanga indeed courted Arab traders at the same as he negotiated with British missionaries and political representatives. In the 1890s, Baganda emissaries travelled to Zanzibar to trade with the Sultan, encouraging Arab traders to cross Lake Victoria and bring their wares to the Baganda (Walker 1893: 37–39).

The Baganda ruling elite, then, like the European expatriate community, selectively used elements of 'other' design, at least in representative semi-domestic spaces. A kind of colonial connoisseurship, this incorporation of the foreign stood for knowledge and skills transfer, but also extensive travel. In 1880, three of King Mtesa's envoys, Namkaddi, Kataruba and Sawaddu, paid a visit to Queen Victoria; in the early twentieth century both King Daudi Chwa and the prime minister, or *katikiro*, Apolo Kagwa visited England and toured the centres of the furniture industry in Buckinghamshire. Amongst these circles, gifts, for example a chair given to King Mukasa in 1888 by CMS missionaries, also became part of the inventory of the home. The result was an identity which was truly global in scope, an identity not unlike the 'imperial careering' identity which also characterized British administrators in Zanzibar (Longair 2015).

FIGURE 4.5: Daudi Chwa II with Regents, Uganda, *c.* 1908. From Charles Hattersley, *The Baganda at Home* (London: Religious Tract Society, 1908). Reproduced by kind permission of the Syndics of Cambridge University Library.

Importantly, though, this identity, as displayed through home furnishings, was characterized not by straightforward European imposition and African adoption of 'other' materials in their original context. John and Jean Comaroff have already alluded to this art of 'bricolage' in their study of the Tswana in South Africa (Comaroff and Comaroff 1997: 303). What is significant, following Appadurai's concept of an object's 'social life', is the ability to divert objects from their usual commodity path and thus change their value (Appadurai 1986: 22–29). Objects which were obviously 'other' were never used for their original purpose, but appropriated for another function, usually for display. The regent Zakaria Kisingiri used his European chair as a symbol of authority in public meetings; Mrs Millington used a grain basket as a wall adornment. This process of contextualization is not unlike how Nicholas Thomas analyses objects traded and consumed in the Pacific in the first half of the nineteenth century. Thomas urges us to consider the appropriation of European goods as a selective process, one in which indigenous peoples, in his case Pacific Islanders, exert a great deal of agency. In Thomas's case study of muskets traded in the Southern Marquesas, for example, he claims that 'what begins as a commodity is transformed, not exactly into a gift, but into a historicized artefact, the sign of a former owner and his works' (1991: 100). The islanders appropriate the 'new' European muskets, by making them familiar, literally inscribing them with the same inlaid shell decoration they traditionally used to decorate indigenous iron axes. Following Thomas's angle, what characterizes the colonial style – both for Europeans and Africans – is not merely the possession of foreign objects themselves, but the ability to re-contextualize them in a way that gives them a powerful new, yet 'readable' meaning. This may occur through physical adaptation, but also through a different use or arrangement.

CONCLUSION

This chapter has shown in what ways an understanding of furniture and furnishings in the Age of Empire needs to be embedded within pre-colonial and pre-modern trade networks, and within both Western and non-Western manufacturing processes and consumption trends. But we cannot forget that colonialism also changed global relationships. What difference did empire make? What was unique about the colonial home?

Colonialism undeniably impacted the economic relationships underpinning the furnishings of the colonial home. In their study of empire markets, Andrew Thompson and Gary Magee argue that the success of British businesses in the dominions was not because the colonial market was a so-called 'soft market' but because British exporters exploited a particularly 'patriotic sentiment' among colonial buyers; and indeed that they had to do so because they were not otherwise sheltered from the competition (Magee and Thompson 2003). Looking back at the statistics of furniture imports to East Africa, we see again that most imports come from Britain. But in the material culture of the home, we also see to what extent East Africa was an 'Indian frontier' not only initially (Kennedy 1987: 11); it continued to be part of a pre-colonial network reaching across the Indian Ocean. Home designers certainly drew on items manufactured in Britain, but we also continually see settlers and sojourners breaking through what Magee and Thompson have called the 'British World economy' (2010: 117–69) in favour of an even more diverse one (cf. Avery 2007: 79–80).

Culturally, colonialism facilitated the development of a colonial style, both real and imagined. As part of this new style, furniture and furnishings were never a direct replica of British trends, but moderated to suit new circumstances. This holds true for East Africa, but also for other realms of empire, as Robin Jones, Swati Chattopadhyay, Dianne Lawrence and Tracy Avery have found (Jones 2007; Chattopadhyay 2002; Lawrence 2012; Avery 2007). All of this resulted in a potential for hybridity, a hybridity which is remarkably similar to the spatial and material hybridity of colonial homes in India and, as John Potvin has recently argued, also for Oriental interiors in Europe (Potvin 2015: 5–6) – and of course in some cases even involves the same furniture. Scholars of India have labelled this 'problematic' (Lawrence 2012: 83), 'unsettling' (Jones 2007: 26) or producing 'anxiety' (Glover 2004: 61) – in the words of Swati Chattopadhyay, 'underwritten by a deep anxiety of loss and lack of control'. She argues that this brought forth 'a new set of values about material culture' emphasizing cleanliness and order (Chattopadhyay 2002: 244). But this, again, as in the African case, is assuming that people followed household guides.

Hybridity in the case of East Africa, however, seems to be much less unsettling; in fact, it is something which is celebrated as part of a distinguished colonial identity. Civil servants, settlers and missionaries were all, to different degrees, at ease with hybridity in the home in East Africa. Recent critics of the concept of hybridity claim it ignores the essential inequality in colonial power relations (Ashcroft, Griffiths and Tiffin 2013: 135–39). In this case, we also have to remember that hybridity for Europeans in this region was a conscious choice which often had to do with career as well as class; all Europeans may thus be considered part of an elite. For most Africans, whose access to European goods was limited by economic circumstances, the potential for furnishing a hybrid colonial home was dictated by a lack of choice. Yet that does not take away from the fact that there was a certain entanglement of people and things in the making of the colonial home in East Africa.

Perhaps a more appropriate term to describe this colonial style than 'hybrid', then, is as a 'diverted cosmopolitanism'. 'Cosmopolitanism' is a term that has gained particular valence in recent historiography (Neiswander 2008; Sluga and Horne 2010; Gestrich and Beerbühl 2011) and which has been used by historians researching pre-colonial trade in the region (LaViolette 2008; Presthold 2008); it therefore acknowledges a certain degree of continuity with these trends in the colonial era. But the addition of 'diverted' acknowledges the power relations inherent in the colonial encounter. The power to divert commodities from their intended path, whether exerted by European, African or Asian, old or new elites, is at the heart of the colonial encounter. It is why there was less anxiety about incorporating 'otherness' in the home: because it could be covered, inscribed, juxtaposed – rarely used in exactly the same way as intended by the original makers – at least not until those original makers started to cater explicitly to the colonial market. Diverted cosmopolitanism allowed Europeans to play upon colonial fantasies nurtured at home with furnishings produced by Africans and Asians for a much smaller price. But it also allowed East Africans to accept the material culture of Europe piecemeal, as one of many non-African influences in the region.

CHAPTER FIVE

Home and Work: Housework and Paid Work in British Homes

VICTORIA KELLEY

One way of thinking about the nineteenth-century home is to consider what it was not, materially or ideologically. The home was private, not public, it was the site of family relations more than professional ones, and it was the dominion of leisure, not work. Yet just as today the world of work constantly invades the home, so in the nineteenth and early twentieth centuries the division between leisure and labour in the home was not a straightforward one. Despite the idea of home as 'not work', there are many instances of home and work becoming entangled. Many professional men (clergy, for instance) used their homes as the base from which to organize and execute their work. The notion of the home as a place of leisure could only be supported by the intensive labour of those who provisioned, cooked, tidied and cleaned (in middle- and upper-class homes, this was usually servants, in working-class homes, wives and mothers). And in many working-class homes paid work was done, often by women who had no alternative but to combine domestic and childcare duties with some sort of piece-work, often very poorly paid. Clearly, it is not possible to ignore work within the Victorian home: there was a great deal of it going on. But neither can we straightforwardly accept its presence without asking how work sat within the definition of the home as a place that was distinct from the wider world of productive labour.

If the home was in fact a site of work, *what was being produced*? Paid work in the working-class home was an extension of the manufacturing economy: the assembling of cardboard boxes or the hand-seaming of machine-knitted stockings were part of an economic system that had not, with industrialization, separated home from the manufacture of things as thoroughly as we might think. But aside from paid work, what was being produced in housework? Unlike the things made by paid home working (standardized products churned out at so much the dozen, score or gross), housework created less straightforwardly quantifiable outputs. They included food, cleanliness and the ease facilitated by comfortably furnished rooms, so that one way of looking at the home as a site of productive labour is to see it as the place where *bodies* were made, not just in terms of procreation and the formation of families but also in terms of health. By extension, home was the private place where the public self was prepared, in ways that circled beyond health to encompass notions of correct presentation, beauty and fashion. In much historical analysis, the world of the home and the world of fashion are seen as being very far apart (fashion history and the history of the home are two distinct historical disciplines) but in fact the home was where the fashionable self originated, in the making and particularly in the maintenance of clothing. Fashion (as a quality that is additional to clothing) is rather an abstract thing, but this was by no means the most abstract product made in the home. Both status and respectability were qualities that were largely determined by home circumstances, and by the results of the work that went on there. Finally, we should ask about the reciprocal relationships between home and the world outside it. If the home was a productive mechanism, it was necessarily interconnected with the wider environment: it relied upon the circulation, in and out, of goods, people and ideas.

This chapter offers an overview of the extent and nature of work within the home in nineteenth-century Britain, arguing that the complicated and contested boundaries between home and work made work within the home a fraught and difficult issue. It will look at both housework and paid work, in both middle-class and working-class homes, drawing on British evidence. The long nineteenth century between 1800 and 1920 saw the latter stages of the transformation of Britain to an industrial economy (Floud, Humphries and Johnson 2014a: 1–16). It saw huge population growth, from around nine million (England only) in 1800 to around 43 million (Great Britain) at the 1921 census (Floud et al. 2014a: 75; Floud, Humphries and Johnson 2014b: 96). Large-scale urbanization occurred, so that by 1870 Britain was 'far and away the most heavily urbanised country in Europe' (Floud et al. 2014a: 16). Technological innovation transformed many areas of life, including domesticity, where amenities such as gas, electricity, piped water and sewerage all made a marked impact. Rising living standards at first predominantly benefited the growing middle class, but from the mid-nineteenth century significant sections of the working classes too began to see the rewards of industrialization and economic growth (Floud et al. 2014a: 10–11, 260–61). Finally, the period saw important developments in social thinking on gender roles, not least due to the impact of feminism. All of these changes affected both home and work, and the relationship between the two.

It is in the realm of gendered roles and ideals that we should place the discussion of home and work. By the middle decades of the nineteenth century, the idea that work and home were categorically separate was firmly founded, in the context of a wider redefinition and separation of public and private (Davidoff 2003). One of the most important effects of this idea was to establish that the categories of work and home should map onto gender categories of male and female – men were associated with the world of work (although they had an important stake in the home too), and women were organized into the sphere of the home (Davidoff and Hall [1987] 2002; Davidoff 2003). This can be seen, for instance, in Coventry Patmore's (in)famous poem 'The Angel in the House' (1860) and John Ruskin's essay *Sesame and Lilies* (1865) both frequently cited as evidence of the Victorian idealization of women in the role of mother and homemaker, sequestered from the wider public world, a phenomenon known to historians as *separate spheres*. Many historians (including Leonore Davidoff and Catherine Hall, authors of *Family Fortunes*, the classic account of the emergence of gendered domesticity) have recognized that to take the idea of separate spheres entirely at face value can obscure understanding of the ways in which many women were able to negotiate with its constraints (Davidoff and Hall [1987] 2002), living lives that encompassed considerable public, or even professional, activities, and demonstrating quite clearly the extent to which Patmore's idea of the 'Angel in the House' was just that – an idea, that may not have reflected reality as it was always lived (Gordon and Nair 2003; Gleadle 2009; Smitley 2009). However, compared with middle-class women, women of the working classes had relatively little room for manoeuvre: they crossed the public/private, work/home divide more frequently, motivated by sheer force of economic necessity, but as they did so they were subject to gendered judgements around public and private. Separate spheres may be the best tool we have for naming a complex range of ways in which men's and women's roles were routinely conceptualized as *different*, and remains useful in understanding the relationship of work and home, especially if we adopt a cross-class perspective. Work was fundamental to the functioning of the home, yet it was often difficult to accommodate the idea of work within the idea of home. Why would this be so unless there was some sort of very real antagonism between notions of work and home? Separate spheres goes some way to describing this antagonism, if only crudely.

HOUSEWORK: INCONSPICUOUS LABOUR

If the distinction between home and the external world of work was an important one, the boundary at which these two strongly contrasting categories met takes on particular significance. The doorstep and front door of the nineteenth-century home were treated in ways that made their symbolic boundary power very clear, and that demanded a great deal of work. Domestic advice writer Phillis Browne recommended that the front door be subject to a weekly routine of dusting, washing and polishing, with brass doorknockers 'thoroughly polished every day in damp weather, three times a week in dry weather' (1883: 872). For working-class homes, the front doorstep was a proud and potent symbol of the home. Maud Pember Reeves (1913: 4) described how in the south London community in which she worked on a study of maternity, it was the custom of the women to scrub their front doorstep and a portion of the pavement beyond defined by the arc of the woman's arm as she knelt on the step, working outwards and projecting a regime of housewifely care into the street, making it publicly visible. Failure to join in the laborious ritual was to break a powerful norm in which the home was defined by the work of women.

Historian Ruth Schwartz Cowan, in her classic book *More Work for Mother* notes that the term 'housework' first appeared in England in the mid-nineteenth century, and in the USA slightly later ([1983] 1989: 17–18). The compounding of the two nouns qualifies the idea of work by associating it with the idea of house or home, suggesting that as work in general moved out of the home with the development of the industrial economy, what was left within it became a special type of work, housework. We might call this the *work of domesticity* – the tasks that needed to be done to support the home itself and its inhabitants. Although the work of domesticity was unwaged labour, it had an enormous economic impact, and this view is recognized by some (by no means all) economic historians when they talk of the 'marginal product of housework', what it contributes to the family economy by enabling the paid work of others (Mokyr 2000: 3). As Schwartz Cowan notes, the work of domesticity was strongly gendered:

> The allocation of housework to women is . . . a social convention which developed during the nineteenth century because of a specific set of material and cultural conditions. It is a convention so deeply embedded in our individual and collective consciousness that even the profound changes wrought by the twentieth century have not yet shaken it.
> —[1983] 1989: 150

Masculinity also made its contribution to domesticity, in the middle and working classes, and the conventional picture of all Victorian fathers as strict *paterfamilias*, isolated from the day-to-day running of their homes, should be nuanced (Tosh 1999; Strange 2015). Nevertheless, all the evidence examined in this chapter supports the broad generalization that housework was predominantly 'women's work', as Schwartz Cowan indicates.

What was housework? The types of labour that comprise this broad category are reasonably stable from place to place and time to time (Davidoff 1995: 74–75). They include, most prominently, those tasks to do with food (provisioning, storing food, its preparation, serving and clearing away); those tasks dedicated to cleanliness (dusting, sweeping, brushing, polishing, scrubbing); clothing-related tasks (buying, storing, washing, maintaining, mending and sometimes making garments); work to provide heat and light (making and mending fires, cleaning and maintaining lamps); childcare and all its related tasks; and care of invalids and the sick.[1] But if this list of basic categories (producing health, comfort and social status) remains quite stable, the exact nature of the work required varies enormously depending upon the size of the home, the available equipment and technologies, and subjective standards of comfort and respectability. Heating and lighting, for instance, are tasks more or less completely devolved to technology in most modern homes, yet before the twentieth century they would always have demanded considerable labour.

The development of urban infrastructure and the provision of running water, sewerage, gas, electricity and other amenities clearly affected the work done in the home (Daunton 2001a: 19–20, 218–19). This chapter covers the whole of the long nineteenth century, a period of enormous technological change, as well as of marked differences in experience across the social classes. It is thus beyond the scope of the chapter to describe in detail all categories of housework, but a few indicative examples might be useful. Cooking and food, for instance, changed considerably between the early nineteenth and the early twentieth century. Historian John Burnett dates the advent of the kitchen range to the 1820s, and in its many variations it was standard cooking equipment until late in the century when gas cookers appeared (Burnett 1989: 164–65). These were patchily distributed and not always popular, as feeding pennies into the gas meter could be more expensive than using coal to fuel a range, which had the added benefit of producing heat and hot water (Anon. 1862: 105; Daunton 1983: 238–42). Ranges, however, were dirty (coal went in, and soot and ash came out), and nineteenth-century household advice manuals frequently stress the unceasing work involved in keeping a range clean (Browne 1883: 885).

The food that was prepared changed more quickly than the equipment for cooking. The nineteenth century was the period when industrial food production began, with the introduction of new manufacturing and preserving techniques. At the most basic level the production of bread, the staple food, was transformed. From the early nineteenth century onwards, home-baked bread was replaced with that made in commercial bakeries, particularly in the south (home-baking persisted in parts of the north and in rural areas) (Burnett 1989: 5). John Burnett notes that Manchester, described by Asa Briggs as the 'shock city' of British industrialization, and growing rapidly from almost nothing in the 1760s to a great industrial cotton-producing metropolis by the mid-nineteenth century, had no bakeries at all in 1804, yet just eleven years later it was reported that half the population did not bake at home (Briggs [1963] 1993: 56, 88–89; Burnett 1989: 5). The demands placed on women by their increased participation in waged labour outside the home was one factor, as was overcrowding and poor housing (see Engels [1845] 1967). Bread was not the only industrialized foodstuff. Towards the end of the century, a whole range of novel packaged and branded products appeared, and the popular press of the period is full of advertisements for Cadbury's cocoa, Bird's custard powder, Bovril beef extract and many other industrially produced foods. An advice manual written in 1910 lists packets of soup, tins of sardines and gravy granules amongst a list of store cupboard staples (Leverton 1910: 43–44); these were all products that would not have been available a generation or two earlier and which brought a measure of convenience to kitchens across the social classes.

The most onerous single task in domestic work was the laundry. Here running water and the technology to heat it was the key driver of change (for an overview of complex change in domestic amenities, see Daunton 1983, ch. 10). The act of washing itself was the simple, laborious matter of submerging dirty things in hot soapy water, and rubbing, scrubbing and squeezing them to loosen the dirt, before rinsing, wringing and drying. Some tools existed to help: the washboard had a corrugated surface on which to rub the wet laundry, and the dolly, an item like a small wooden stool attached to a long handle, was thumped about in the washtub with the wet soapy washing. Mangles were used to wring out and smooth wet washing. For items that could stand heat (household linen and cotton garments), the copper or set pot was the best solution. This was a large metal vessel installed over a hearth, so that it could be heated to a vigorous boil. Early washing 'machines' appeared in the late nineteenth century, but these were no more than glorified hand tools for the rotation and agitation of washing with soap and water. The first powered washing machines did not appear until the very end of the period, and even in 1938 only 3.5 percent of British households with electricity had a washing machine (Kelley 2010: 80n.).

Laundry was not complete when garments were washed and dried. Ironing cotton, linen and silk garments and household linens such as tablecloths and sheets was a task that changed with technology. The traditional flat iron, heated on the range, was heavy, and meticulous care had to be taken not to pick up soot in heating it up (Anon 1862, vol. 2: 81). Box irons were cleaner, as the heat came from a slug of hot metal heated separately and inserted into the iron, but they were even heavier than flat irons. The first electric irons were introduced at the very end of the nineteenth century, and, as early models did not have thermostats, temperature control was haphazard (as it was with flat irons and box irons) (Kelley 2010: 81–82).

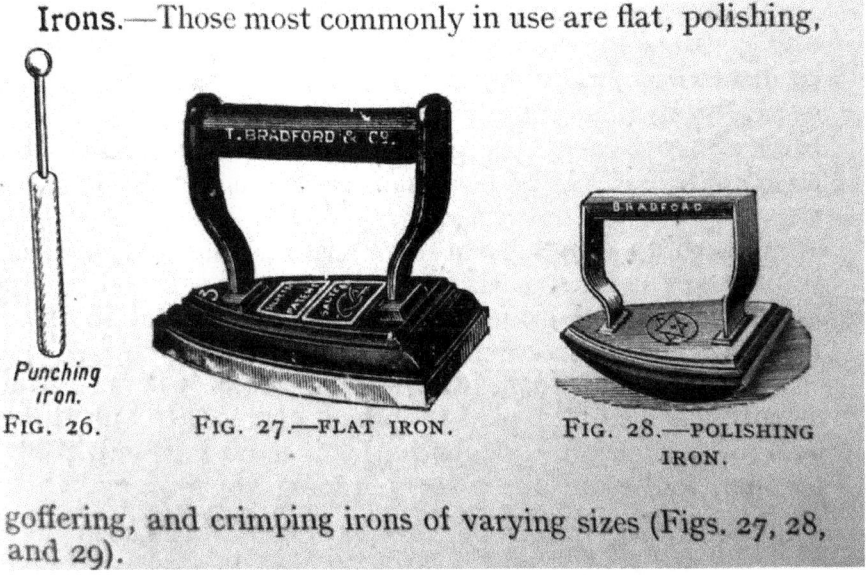

FIGURE 5.1: Domestic irons. The flat iron was standard for simple items like sheets, and the polishing iron was used to give linen its gloss: other sizes and shapes of iron were used to deal with complex frills and ruffles. From E.L. Marsh, *Laundry Work in Theory and Practice* (New York: Longmans, Green, 1914).

The above brief examples mean nothing unless we also consider the material differences in homes that were consequent on poverty and wealth. The slow changes in cooking technology, for instance, had little or no impact on the many poor families who lived in one, two or three rooms in old houses divided into many dwellings, and who might only have a bedroom fireplace to cook on. They might also lack easy access to running water for cooking, cleaning, bathing or laundry. There was an almost unquantifiable gulf between the multi-roomed town or country houses of the middle and upper classes described by Robert Kerr in his 1864 book *The Gentleman's House* ('from the parsonage to the palace') and the fetid cellar dwellings described by Friedrich Engels in Manchester in the 1840s, which lacked ventilation or even drainage, let alone cooking or laundry facilities. As we saw in Chapter 3, by the turn of the century the advent of the 'byelaw' house, the terraced cottage built to minimum standards set by the 1875 Public Health Act, had effected some change (Burnett 1986: 168), but terrible housing conditions persisted for many, especially in crowded areas where houses continued to be divided by subletting. Maud Pember Reeves, describing Lambeth in London in 1913, recorded families faced with the stark choice of a large damp cellar room or a smaller room on a higher floor (Reeves [1913] 1979: 29–33). At the top of the social scale small armies of servants were required to meet the needs of a single family, while at the bottom housekeeping fell away almost completely, as an utter lack of space, furniture and facilities, and of money for food other than the most monotonous, placed the poorest of the poor beyond the reach of domesticity (although aspirations were often retained in the most limiting circumstances). In between these two extremes came the majority of middle- and working-class families.

It is tempting to interpret the development of amenities and household technologies over the nineteenth century as leading slowly but surely to the emergence of the twentieth-century 'labour-saving' house, in other words

FIGURE 5.2: Borax Extract of Soap show-card advertisement, 1900s. Soap was frequently advertised on its capacity to reduce work in the home, or, in this case, to turn labour into 'pleasure'. © Wellcome Library, London.

reducing the hard slog of the work of domesticity. However, Ruth Schwartz Cowan has pointed out (using American evidence) the paradox that as certain domestic tasks (e.g. baking bread) were industrialized and others were lightened by better equipment, the time spent on housework did not in fact decrease. Instead, expected standards improved, so that domesticity was increasingly founded upon the performance of housework, tangled up with complex notions of normative femininity. One driver of increasing expectations was hygiene. As the nineteenth century progressed, scientific knowledge led to growing concern about the links between domestic environment and disease. Edwin Chadwick's 1842 *Report on the Sanitary Conditions of the Labouring Population* linked poor housing and insanitary living conditions to ill health and poverty. The advent of germ theory in the 1870s brought public awareness of the mechanisms of infection (Porter 1997: 431–42), and provoked the writers of household advice literature to urge ever more rigorous action against the 'invisible monsters' that lived in dirt and dust (Stacpoole 1912: 8). From late in the nineteenth century, standards of nutrition were also scrutinized, as for instance when Clementina Black (1915) recorded working women's breast or bottle feeding of their babies as an indicator in infant mortality.

Health was not the only concern affecting standards in housework. Beverly Gordon (1996) sets out the nineteenth-century conflation between women and their domestic setting. Middle- and upper-class women were urged to decorate themselves to suit their homes, and their homes to complement their persons. In *The Art of Beauty* (1883), Eliza Haweis, bestselling author of advice literature on both home and fashion, offers 'a few hints on the decoration of rooms as affecting our personal appearance' (1883: 225), advising that in decorating the home, 'colours about us . . . must always be subservient to the complexion' (1883: 237). It was natural to her to see the home as a woman's expected setting, with similar standards of beauty and taste applied to both. The conflation of woman and home was not just a matter of aesthetics, but also of morality, and the emotional institution of motherhood. In the autobiographies of working-class people, it is arresting how often the mother (always a central character for authors recollecting childhood) is depicted in the kitchen, described through a blend of devotion and domestic tasks, what Ellen Ross (1993) calls 'love and toil'. The account of Elizabeth Flint (born in London around 1905) is interesting here, because she recalls the complicated emotions provoked by her loving mother falling somewhat short of the expected standards of domesticity. Flint was ashamed that her mother's housekeeping compared badly with that of a neighbour who she visited, and who instructed her in the finer points of housework:

'Don't forget the legs of the chairs.'
'No, I'll remember.'

'Only careless housewives forget the legs of things.'
My throat would fill with a lump at this point, but I would say nothing. If I had spoken it would have been to say that Mum never dusted ours, and I must never say that. So I knew for a fact now that Mum had faults. She did not dust chair legs, and she could cuss your ears and shout if she felt in the mood. But Mum was good at lots of things. She was always there to make you feel safe, and she gave you things like stew to eat.

—Flint 1963: 27

Among both the middle and working classes, the work of domesticity was often signalled by spectacular displays of cleanliness and polish, focused on decorative goods to which high status was afforded (Logan 2001: 207). Walter Southgate comments on this in his autobiography depicting a late Victorian working-class childhood in London: 'Every woman prided herself on her parlor mantelpiece . . . heavily draped with cloth pelmets and side curtains. Here were shown off her glass shades and lustres, wax fruits and china vases' (1982: 67). And he recalled how his mother kept her parlour's outside windowsill 'scrupulously cleaned with hearthstone', which was also applied to the front doorstep 'every Sunday morning' (1982: 67).

If the work of domesticity was about display and status within the home, it was also, as suggested by the conflation of women's bodies and their homes, directed towards the material display of status in personal appearance. Advice writer Phillis Browne (1877) describes at length how she trained her three daughters to make their own dresses and underwear, to 'get up' (wash, starch and iron) their cotton 'washing' dresses, to mend and alter garments, and even to grow flowers in the garden with which to trim their outfits and hair. She notes that, 'I consider it a duty we owe to society, and to husbands and fathers, that our appearance and that of our children should be bright and pleasing' (Browne 1877: 186–90), making clear the extent to which this assiduous domestic labour was directed towards the public and fashionable presentation of the self. In working-class families, too, considerable emphasis was placed on maintaining standards of dress and appearance, especially in girls' white pinafores and Sunday best dress for family outings (Loane 1908: 170).

There were thus many ways in which the conspicuous, even spectacular, results produced by domestic work were an important marker of values and status, both within the home and beyond it. The person responsible was the wife and mother, and advice literature in particular, with its prescriptive tone, almost always stressed the centrality of her role in the functioning of the home, busily managing resources and directing labour.[2] Yet if the *results* of work were conspicuous, its *performance* was often not, at least to certain members of the household and to the world beyond. I suggested at the outset that we should consider how work might be conceptualized within a space that was in many respects regarded as the antithesis of the public world of productive labour. One strategy was to play down the extent of the toil involved in housekeeping. The authors of household advice literature were prone to exacting and exhaustive descriptions of domestic regimes. Mrs Haweis, for instance, in her book *The Art of Housekeeping* (1889), describes the duties of a housemaid. Apart from her routine morning tasks of lighting fires and fetching hot water, the maid would be expected to 'turn out' one or two rooms a day, in a never-ending cycle of cleaning:

> Every piece of furniture must be shifted out, the corners must be seriously tackled... All the ornaments have to be removed to another room or packed on a central table and covered with a clean dust-sheet, like the chairs, which should be rubbed and brushed *before* turning out of the room (some ladies prefer these packed in the middle of the room and covered up); then comes the sweeping, after which the housemaid will run down for her 'lunch'... The dust takes half an hour to settle, and during this process a few ornaments can be washed or metal goods polished. Then comes the tidying and the beeswaxing, and last the dusting.
> —Haweis 1889: 84

All this is to be achieved by 1pm, after which the maid changes into a clean uniform to dedicate her afternoons to opening the door to visitors and sewing, polishing the silver plate and cleaning lamps. The labour involved, repeated six days a week, seems to a twenty-first-century reader to be considerable. Yet, as with many other such lists of domestic work to be got through daily, weekly or monthly, Mrs Haweis follows up with an unconvincing disclaimer about the trifling nature of the work just described, counselling her readers to 'keep as few servants as you possibly can' (1889: 82), or run the risk that they will be underemployed and bored. This account is typical: Phillis Browne followed a similar line, but she went one step further, not just de-emphasizing the work involved in housework, but also suggesting strategies to keep it hidden: 'It is impossible to keep the fact of cleaning a secret', she notes (perhaps ruefully) but 'it may be managed so that the worst of the cleaning is got through without the family being inconvenienced' (Browne 1883: 893). And elsewhere she makes it clear who exactly she means by 'the family': 'The cleaning of a large portion of the house may be got over without the gentlemen suspecting that it is going on' (Browne 1877: 41–42). Mrs Waldemar Leverton makes the same point: 'the lord and master will be absolutely oblivious that anything untoward has occurred, and will not have the even tenor of his ways in any way upset, which, after all, is just as it should be – from the masculine point of view' (1910: 104). Housework was a matter for women and for servants. It is difficult to escape the conclusion that there was something about the idea of home that sat uncomfortably with the idea of work, and in consequence those who carried out that work (and this applied in working-class households too) (Kelley 2010: 64–65) were under pressure to organize it discretely, so as not to fracture the atmosphere of the home as a place of leisure, especially for the men who lived there. To this extent, the idea of separate spheres does seem to have some purchase, promoting an ideology of the home as a place that, while utterly dependent upon hard and complex physical toil, should not have its character determined by the conspicuous presence of the work of domesticity. As Deborah Simonton notes, in contrast to 'men's visible work, women's household work became devalued and invisible in a way that their multifarious activities in earlier households had not been' (2002: 91).

HOUSEWORK AS PAID WORK: SERVANTS

Housework was surrounded by rhetoric that played down its scope and diminished its visibility. Sharpening our focus to concentrate on servants reveals this fact in further detail: even when household labour was carried out by people who were paid to do it, it was constrained by pressure to de-emphasize the presence of work within the home.

The period covered by this chapter encompasses a key moment of change in the relationship of home and work, the period of industrialization running from the late eighteenth century into the early decades of the nineteenth. Whatever the debates around the precise nature and scope of this change in its impact upon ideas of public, private, the family and gender roles, there is no doubt that it had enormous implications for the status and work of servants. The pre-industrial household often included many people who were not directly part of the family, but who contributed to the household as a productive unit (apprentices, for instance). The separation of public and private took some of those productive roles out of the home, and left within it servants (predominantly female) whose job was solely to support the home and the family. Although older arrangements of live-in workers and apprentices persisted in some circumstances, many servants came to work (and very often live) in homes that were more private, more intensely focused on the family unit, and more strongly identified than before with leisure and femininity (Simonton 2002: 97). They were caught up in the rhetoric of home as not-work, despite the fact that the home was their workplace.

Deborah Simonton identifies three phases in the development of domestic service in this period: that moment of transition from the eighteenth to the nineteenth century when service became resolutely 'domestic' and increasingly feminized; a mid-century period (*c.* 1830–80) when numbers of servants grew in line with increases in the servant-keeping class; and thereafter a slow decline (2002: 97–98). Lucy Delap notes however that even in 1891 the census showed that 41 percent of women in paid work in England and Wales were in domestic service (the number varying locally in relation to the alternative female occupations available) (2011: 11–12). Throughout the period covered by this chapter, domestic service was a very common experience for women of the working classes, many of whom passed through work as a servant during adolescence and young adulthood, before moving on to marriage and motherhood and continuing to devote themselves to housework in their own homes, on an unpaid basis. These women's entire experience of work, in a lifetime dominated by it, took place within the home. The conditions of service could vary widely, from work in the multi-servant household of a great aristocratic family to toiling as the single servant in a household precariously near the boundary between the servant-keeping and the servant-providing classes. Those in the latter role were often the most exploited, carrying out the bulk of the domestic work required to support an entire family, as Lillian Westall explains in her autobiography:

> I had to be up at six in the morning, and there were so many jobs lined up for me that I worked till eleven o'clock at night . . . I had to clean all the house, starting at the top and working down, sweeping and scrubbing right through. Hearthstoning the steps . . . took me an hour alone.
> —Burnett 1994: 217

Not all servants were badly treated: Lavinia Swainbank, working in a large country house in the 1920s, described her employers as 'people with heart and consideration for all their staff', although she also describes other, less humane masters and mistresses (Burnett 1994: 226).

Although numbers of live-in servants declined from the late nineteenth century, it was not until after the Second World War that domestic service collapsed in Britain (Delap 2011: 14). The First World War saw servants diverted to war work, but levels of domestic service resurged in the 1920s and 1930s (Delap 2011: 11). Yet Delap notes that from around the 1890s there was a persistent culture of crisis, with successive generations bemoaning the 'servant problem', and forecasting the imminent demise of domestic service (a demise identified either pessimistically as the end of an era or optimistically as the advent of modernity) (2011: 2). Delap associates the sense of crisis with the increasing discomfort of both employers and servants, in an era of growing social democracy, with the hierarchical relationships of inequality and obedience that dominated service life (2011: 71).

A further reason may be the uncomfortable pressure on servants to perform work in a home defined as outside the productive sphere. As discussed in the previous section, this pressure affected everyone engaged in housework, but for servants it was reinforced in the very bricks and mortar of standard house plans,

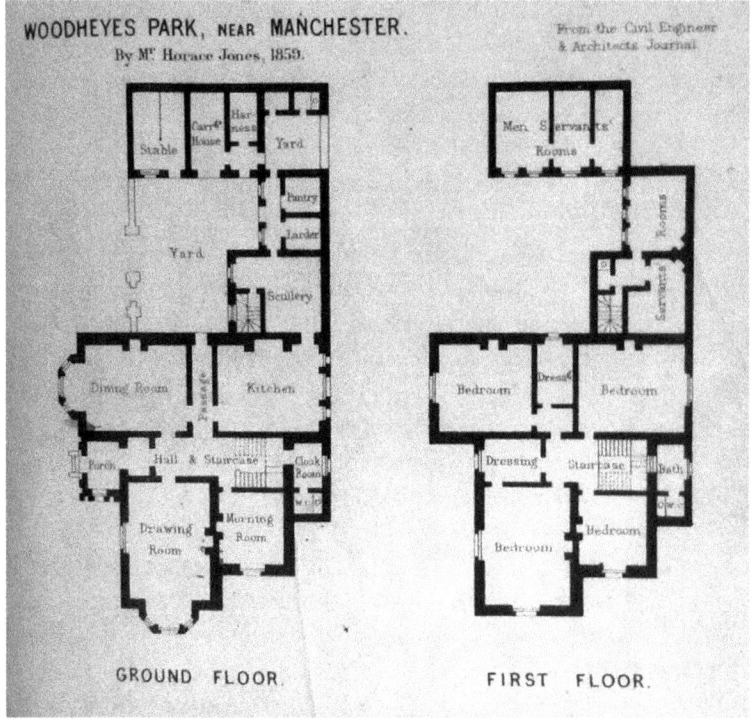

FIGURE 5.3: In this middle-class home, work, and those who do it, are pushed to the margins. Service areas (kitchen, scullery, etc.) are at the rear of the ground floor, and servants' bedrooms are at the rear of the first floor (for women) and above the stables (for men). The house was designed by Horace Jones in 1859. Woodheyes Park, near Manchester. From Robert Kerr, *The Gentleman's House* (London: John Murray, 1864). Reproduced with permission of Guildhall Library, City of London.

in which service areas were segregated from family rooms. The tall, narrow town house used vertical segregation, with kitchen, scullery, pantries and other service rooms in the basement, and servants' bedrooms in the attics. Suburban villas were segregated from front to back, and in the country the separation might be both horizontal and vertical, with separate service wings in larger houses, as well as the positioning of servants' bedrooms in the attics. In smaller homes, the separation of servants and family was more difficult to achieve, but it was nonetheless a well-established idea, as Robert Kerr makes clear:

> The family constitute one community: the servants another. Whatever may be to their mutual regard and confidence as dwellers under the same roof, each class is entitled to shut its door upon the other, and be alone ... On both sides this privacy is highly valued.
>
> —1864: 285

Even in working-class homes where there was unlikely to be any servant, the segregation of work areas and rooms dedicated to leisure and the display of status was strong, with a clear progression from front parlour (often reserved for Sunday use) through the kitchen, which functioned as the family's main living room, to the scullery, where dirty tasks such as laundry were carried out (Kelley 2009a).

Published rules for servants make clear the extent to which their work was marginalized spatially within the home. They were expected to be both silent and unobtrusive:

> Always move quietly about the house, and do not let your voice be heard by the family unless necessary. Never sing or whistle at your work where the family would be likely to hear you . . . When meeting any ladies or gentlemen about the house, stand back or move aside for them to pass . . . Do not walk in the garden unless permitted, unless you know all the family are out; and be careful to walk quietly when there, and on no account to be noisy.
> —Ladies Sanitary Association 1901: 21

We have already seen how wives and mothers were expected to arrange housework so as not to 'inconvenience the gentlemen'. If servants were expected to be discreet in their work, the wife and mother who directed their labour took responsibility for that discretion. Her job was to manage her servants in the performance of the work of domesticity, caught in the classic middle-management fix, pressured to perform (to ensure the attributes of an ordered and well-run house) by her manager and clients (the family) and in order to do so having to direct the labour of servants who might be more or less willing, more or less able, to do the tasks they were allocated. The woman's position was made more difficult, as Lucy Delap has pointed out, by the rather difficult ideological contradictions between her nature as 'woman' and the position of authority that directing the servants demanded. Advice literature struggled to find an appropriate metaphor for this female authority, confusing gender along the way: Delap cites examples where the mistress's management of her home and servants was likened to queenship, or kingship, to the pastoral role of a vicar or priest, or to the captain of a ship (2011: 67).

PAID WORK: CONFUSING THE CATEGORY OF THE HOME

Eleanor Gordon and Gwyneth Nair's 2003 account of women's lives in a Glasgow suburb in the second half of the nineteenth century shows how, in many of the middle-class families they studied, women worked outside the home. Married women might assist their husbands in their business or profession in ways that, while not formally recognized (for instance, in the census) were nonetheless economically significant (2003: 157–58). Single women and widows were often active in very public ways, as, for instance, shopkeepers or hoteliers (2003: 192). Gordon and Nair make an interesting contribution to the debate around women's work by noting that 'the defining concepts of nineteenth-century liberalism' (which they identify as 'individualism, justice, obligation, rights and freedom') could join with Christian duty 'to provide alternative aspirational models for middle-class women which were rooted in self-reliance, independence and self-fulfilment rather than dependence' (2003: 5). The very cultural forces that have been seen as contributing to the sequestering of women in the home might also, in the middle classes, have the opposite effect of encouraging women's public engagement beyond the home. Seth Koven (2002) makes a similar point in his reading of Ruskin's *Sesame and Lilies*, suggesting that it might be interpreted as an encouragement to women to engage with the public world as much as a classic statement of separate spheres ideology.

Yet even those middle-class women who stepped out of the home and into the public world often did so within bounds that still identified them with domesticity, femininity and the family. As Eileen Yeo notes, 'educated women moved into professional employment, where, partly to remain "womanly" (in the eyes of women as well as men), they took supervisory charge of other women workers or dealt with women and children as their primary professional clientele, in medicine or social work, for example' (2002: 85). Such women were involved in what Megan Smitley (2009) calls 'the feminine public sphere'. There was a complex irony in professional middle-class women in this period making a claim on the world of work by reporting on or organizing social interventions for working-class women, who, at least if married, and certainly if they had children, were often themselves condemned for working (Kelley 2009a). The remainder of this section will look at these working-class women. For all that some middle-class women managed to escape or negotiate the constraints of domesticity, for many working-class women paid work was economically essential at the same time as being ideologically uncomfortable, both for outside observers and within their own communities. For brevity, I will concentrate on that large category of paid work that took place within the home, and which could be particularly troubling because it conflated the categories of home and work. Clementina Black's *Married Women's Work* (1915) notes the tendency of many middle-class commentators to associate 'the working for money of married women' with mental pictures of 'rooms unswept, beds unmade and dishes unwashed, of children hungry, ragged, unkempt and running wild' (1915: 1). It was accepted that adolescent girls and young women of the working classes should and did work, and what economic historians call the 'industrious revolution' had partly been based on this (Floud et al. 2014a:

244–47). However, married women, and particularly mothers, had to negotiate complex competing demands in reconciling home and work, demands that in many respects intensified towards the end of the nineteenth century and into the early twentieth.

In the early to mid-nineteenth century, considerable efforts were made to outlaw or marginalize women's work in many industrial settings, with, for instance, legislation ending the work of women and children underground in coal mines (Floud et al. 2014a: 183, 186–89). Intense political debate around women's work resurfaced in the late nineteenth century, and in both these periods the issue of sweated labour (work characterized by particularly low pay and long hours, and which was often casualized through complex systems of subcontracting) was prevalent (Berg 1994: 135; Blackburn 2007: 3–7). Such work was often done by women, and often took place within the home. The extent of women's work in this context can be underestimated as evidence such as the census, so central for historians of male labour, is less reliable for women's work in general and women's home working in particular because census takers could be lax in recording the 'subsidiary' or casual jobs of women in households 'headed' by a working male (Schmiechen 1984: 68). James Schmiechen notes that in industrial centres known for high rates of women's factory working (the Staffordshire Potteries and the Lancashire cotton towns, for instance), as many as 25 percent of married women were employed (it was married women, and particularly those with children, on whom debates around women, work and home were most intensely clustered). Yet in other industrial centres, such as Leicester or London, with considerable home-working industries, the rate of married women working was even higher, and much of this work could take place in the home (Schmiechen 1984: 68–69).

The Royal Commission on Labour (1891–94) thought it necessary to appoint a team of four Lady Assistant Commissioners, led by lawyer and suffragist Eliza Orme, to report specifically on the issue of women's work (outside the home and within it), with their remit to assess 'the effect of women's industrial employment on their health, morality and the home' (Orme et al. 1893: iii). The report contains numerous tables detailing visits to women home workers, and the following example, describing a widowed shirt maker, is typical in its conflation of paid work within the home with poor housekeeping and lax morals. The woman is described as:

> married twice . . . [with] two illegitimate children by two other men. Said that she was in service before marriage. Afterwards, when she had to work, did washing and cleaning; then had a lodger who did shirt-making, and taught her how to do it. Has done shirt-making the last three years . . . Three very dirty children in the room.
>
> —Orme et al. 1893: 79

For a working day that started at six in the morning and ended at eight or nine at night, this woman earned eight to nine shillings per week. From this she had to subtract the cost of her thread and needles (amounting to about 1½ d in the shilling, or 7.5 percent) as was common with this sort of home sewing work (Orme et al. 1893: 79; Schmiechen 1984: 53). This woman worked within the garment industry, where the intense seasonality of production made sweated casual labour, much of it located in workers' homes, particularly prevalent (Godley 1995: 3).

At a similar date to the Royal Commission, Charles Booth carried out his enormous social survey, eventually published as *Life and Labour of the People in London*. For this Clara Collet (who was also one of Eliza Orme's commissioners) undertook a study of women's work in the East End of London, where the issue of home working was particularly acute. London's labour market was notorious for its disorganized nature, with many people, men and women, engaged in casual labour paid at piece rates, or by the day or hour. For men, casual dock work was emblematic, and critics saw women's home working as propping up men's casual labour, enabling the existence of the dock system where men were taken on by the day or even half day, and, in an overpopulated labour market, could rarely get a full week's work (Schmiechen 1984: 50). The fashion trades dominated women's work, with a host of small workshops that employed some labour in-house, but also contracted out work to home workers on piece rates (Schmiechen 1984: 52–59). This was an effective way of keeping down overheads and responding flexibly to the seasonal fluctuations to which the fashion industry was particularly prone. Clara Collet investigated women home workers making 'artificial flowers, ties, trimmings, furs, trousers, vests, and shirts' (1889: 449). We saw earlier how the home was the productive locus of fashionability, as women such as Phillis Browne and her daughters made and maintained their clothes at home. But even when fashionable garments were purchased readymade or bespoke by middle-class consumers, they were often made in someone else's home, under exploitative conditions, so that poor women made goods as home work that were also produced within some households as housework.

As James Schmiechen notes, women home workers became 'the great reservoir of cheap labour ... at starvation wages and under socially objectionable conditions' (1984: 50). Clara Collet found that 'home-workers are to be found in every grade of society among the wage-earning class' from the clerk to the dock labourer, and that the homeworker 'may be working for the barest necessaries of life or to provide for the future, or for luxuries, or it may even be that she works at a trade which is easy to her in order to pay someone else to perform the more distasteful household duties' (the ever-pressing task of the laundry might fall into this category) (1889: 445–46). She analysed in detail the sort of women who might take in work, and ranked her subjects on a sliding scale from agency to

FIGURE 5.4: Blunden was one of many artists who depicted the desperation of women workers sewing for a meagre living, inspired by Thomas Hood's 1843 poem. *For Only One Short Hour (The Song of the Shirt)*, Anna Blunden, 1854. © Yale Center for British Art, Paul Mellon Fund.

desperation, from those who worked because they wanted to, to those who did it because they must. The former had male breadwinners, the latter did not:

> The young wife of the clerk with regular employment but small salary takes sealskin capes home from the warehouse where she worked when a girl, because a good housewife has time to spare when she has only three rooms to keep tidy and only two people to cook for, and is glad to add something to the savings which may be useful some day when the children are being educated or started in life. The wife of the carman with 18s a week may make butterscotch boxes in order that her children and her rooms and her dress may look as well as those of her sister who is married to a mechanic earning 32s a week. The wife of a drunkard in reduced circumstances will do

plain sewing or shirtmaking that she may have a decent dress to wear when she goes to see her friends and may conceal from them the depths to which she has fallen. The wife of the dock labourer out of work will finish trousers to keep herself and her children from the workhouse. The widow . . . will finish shirts at 5d or 4d or 3d a day.

—Collet 1889: 445–46

Whatever their situation and motivation, women's home working was always disadvantaged compared with men's labour, with far lower rates of pay. Very many women took on home working because they had to combine wage earning with the care of young children. Such women were tied to the home and forced to accept work at the lowest wages, which were further undermined by the cost and time-cost of travel to collect and return the goods they worked on. Both Clara Collet in London and a similar study in Manchester reported on women whose slim earnings were decimated by the cost of tram fares (Collet 1889: 448; Black 1915: 169).

James Schmiechen argues, 'while the invasion of work into the home may have been regarded by the middle class as reprehensible, it was a fact of life seldom questioned by the working class' (1984: 52). Yet there is evidence that women's work within the home was seen as a troublesome breach of categories, even by those women and those families for whom it was an inevitable fact of life (Bourke 1994: 64–65). Edith Hogg, investigating fur-pullers in south London in 1897, visited women working long hours in squalid rooms, ripping the coarse hairs from bloody rabbit skins. She describes 'these "homes" in which leisure is unknown . . . In them these mothers with no time to rejoice in their motherhood, to give or to receive love and sympathy and care for those for whom they are responsible'. She named the women as '"home" workers', the scare quotes conveying eloquently how she saw the work undermining the sense of home (Hogg [1897] 2007: 112–13). In one 'stuffy kitchen', its atmosphere clogged with flying fur, she encountered a young woman whose expression was 'a fierce, unavailing protest against the cruelty of fate . . . "Miss, I wish I had your life"' ([1897] 2007: 111–12). The anecdote suggests not just how Hogg saw such work to be incompatible with the notion of home, but how the woman herself might have felt this. Further evidence is provided by Clara Collet when she described how 'over and over again I have met women in comfortable circumstances [working-class women with adequate family incomes] who have told me either that they left off taking in work because it did not pay for the trouble, or that they only worked half the week because they had the washing to do and the clothes to mend' (1889: 450). Many working-class women who had a choice preferred, it seems, not to work within the home, and to prioritize domesticity. Collet also notes how women on the porous border of the upper-working and lower-middle class would take in sewing but disguise the fact that this was paid work, or insist that it was for 'pocket-money' only (1889: 446–47). This sense of shame is revealing, although the fact that this was an attitude prevalent in those on this precarious class boundary may indicate that gendered ideologies around labour had more purchase higher up the social scale, and dropped away as sheer economic necessity became more pressing. For the most desperate women home workers, mothers of young children whose husbands were dead, absent or unable to earn, taking in work was not something they could afford to agonize over. Yet above this level, Eileen Yeo has pointed out, a 'protector/provider masculinity' operated (expressed most strongly in trades unionism with its demand for a 'family wage'), and the corollary of this was a well-established working-class view 'of women as home-based dependents with family and household responsibilities' (2002: 76–77). Women's paid work was seen as less legitimate, and less economically important than men's, an idea that sat alongside the notion that it was home that was women's primary responsibility. Unlike their middle-class sisters, who may by the late nineteenth century have been fighting their way into the world of work, working-class women were more likely to be aspiring to leave it, or at least to clear it out of the home. This was hardly surprising, given the hard and repetitive work for exploitatively low pay that was all that was on offer to women who needed to combine work with domesticity.

CONCLUSION

The Victorian home, despite the powerful, complex ideology of domesticity as separate and different from the world of labour, was nonetheless a site of work. The work that was done in the middle-class home was chiefly (although not exclusively) the work of domesticity, supporting the home itself and its inhabitants, and carried out by servants under the supervision of wives and mothers. This work was constrained by the demand that its performance be as inconspicuous as possible: 'it was to be assumed, I suppose, that the fairies had been at the rooms', recalls housemaid Jean Rennie (Burnett 1994: 241). In working-class homes, the work of domesticity was no less pressing, but for the poorest it was often crowded out by the need to bring paid work into the home, a common practice which was nonetheless troubling to conventional ideas of home, its results, according to social worker Helen Bosanquet, 'dirt, disorder and badly cared for children' (1896: 82–83). What was produced in the home included the comfort and health of its inhabitants, their social status, and public presentation: home was the private site where the public and fashionable self was made and maintained. The home also produced *ideas,* about gender, family and respectability. Above all, perhaps, it produced *contradictions,* as a site of work that could not always be seen or acknowledged as such, and as a productive and wage-earning unit in an age when these activities were normatively regarded as being located outside its boundaries.

CHAPTER SIX

Gender and Home: Domestic Spaces and Families in North America

REBECCA J. FRASER

> In no country has such constant care been taken, as in America, to trace two clearly distinct lines of action for the two sexes, and to make them keep pace one with the other, but in two pathways which are always different. American women never manage the outward concerns of the family, or conduct a business, or take a part in political life; nor are they, on the other hand, ever compelled to perform the rough labor of the fields, or to make any of those laborious exertions, which demand the exertion of physical strength. No families are so poor, as to form an exception to this rule.
>
> —Beecher 1842a: 28

Arguably the American home of the twenty-first century has become increasingly dynamic in terms of the roles that men and women are supposed to play within it, but as Catherine Beecher's quote in the opening vignette to this piece illustrates, in nineteenth-century America the home was inextricably bound to gendered expectations. Such assumptions were grounded in ideals of the public and private whereby the domestic space of the home was explicitly gendered as female. Models of the idealized home in this era were of course class and race bound, whereby the privileges of bourgeois whiteness were held up as aspirations that others were expected – but were unable – to adhere to. This chapter will chart the development of these models of gendered behaviour in relation to the home beginning from the Revolutionary period in the late eighteenth century through the pre-Civil War period of 1861. It will position the middle-class home as the ideal in nineteenth-century America and will explore the subtleties of gender that were central to this conception.

CHANGING IDEOLOGIES IN REVOLUTIONARY AMERICA

The gendered ideals associated with the concept of home in nineteenth-century America had their roots in the late eighteenth-century Revolutionary era, which, coupled with an emerging industrial economy that created distinctions between the home and the workplace, produced a marked transformation in the expectations of men and women within the home and subsequent alterations in the gender order of American society. The colonial structure of the household was hierarchical with the husband's authority over his dependents – wife, children and slaves – as absolute. Although there was no distinction in terms of who laboured – so women, children and slaves worked in addition to the men – there were differences in the types of jobs performed. Women would be mostly charged with domestic duties – cooking, canning, preserving, childcare – although working in the fields was a duty that all, regardless of gender, were required to do. Children were important additions to the household too in the colonial era due to the home-based economies of most families resulting in the need for additional labour. However, exceptionally high infant and child mortality rates in colonial America among European colonists meant that, as C. Dallett Hemphill reminds us, 'most households included no more than three children at a time'. Coupled with high adult mortality rates, particularly in the Chesapeake regions of the southern colonies, this produced complex colonial families with adults remarrying after the death of a spouse and creating new sibling relationships. Indeed, as Hemphill (2011: 16, 28) further points out, 'younger children were . . . more likely to grow up with a variety of stepbrothers and sisters', owing to the death of one or both of their biological parents.

The second half of the eighteenth century marked a gradual shift in such practices, however, and prompted a significant transformation of the structure of the household and the respective duties for men and women within the home. This domestic revolution was part of a much broader ideological movement bound up in an Enlightenment thought which culminated in the Revolutionary War for Independence in 1776 between the original thirteen American colonies and Great Britain. The colonies emerged triumphant and the Peace Treaty of Paris in 1783 ceded massive tracts of land to the newly founded United States as the first modern republic. Anglo-American women loyal to the American colonies and committed to its ambitions of independence were able to demonstrate a domestic radicalism via the Revolution that saw them boycott British made-goods and instead adopt home-spun fabric to clothe themselves and their families and replace produce such as tea, imported to the colonies by the British, with other home-grown goods (see Gunderson 2006; Young 2005; Kerber 1997; Norton 1980). In addition, however, the Revolutionary period heralded much more sweeping changes which saw the emerging new Republic embrace enlightenment ideals of civic virtue, itself a term loaded with gendered connotations that altered in the wake of the Revolutionary era (Bloch [1987] 2003). Leaders of the new nation were to be a virtuous elite, acting not for themselves but for the good of the entire nation. Such righteous objectives, however, were intimately linked to gender, race and class as it was the privilege of a white male elite to form the federal and state governments, lead the newly formed country in terms of their positions as politicians, lawyers, businessmen and professionals, and act out their privileges in the context of the newly formed public sphere and the household. As historian Mark E. Kann has pointed out, 'The American [Revolutionary] founders aspired to create a republic of men, to the exclusion of all others' (1998: 1).

The role that patriot women played during the course of the war and the changing nature of the household and home aligned with ideals of civic virtue for all was embodied in a notion of 'Republican Womanhood', idealizing the two roles which women would play as both wife and mother in the Revolutionary era. According to historian Linda Kerber, 'The model republican woman was competent and confident. She could resist the vagaries of fashion; she was rational, independent, literate, benevolent, and self-reliant' (2004: 119). The idea that the republican women should be literate echoed calls from women of the political class of the era such as Abigail Adams, wife of John Adams, the second President of the United States, for increased education of young women. Abigail argued for better levels of schooling among daughters in the new Republic in order for them to become better wives and mothers. In a letter to her husband, John, who was in attendance at the Continental Congress of 1776 in support of American claims for independence, Abigail wrote that she wished 'that some more liberal plan might be laid and executed for the benefit of the rising generation, and that our new constitution may be distinguished for learning and virtue. If we mean to have heroes, statesmen and philosophers, we should have learned women [too]' (Adams 1875: 213). She was not alone in these thoughts, however, as many reformers of the late eighteenth century and early national period stressed the need for literate women who could educate their children, particularly their sons, into the virtues of the new republic. Educator and reformer, Dr Benjamin Rush, wrote in his *Thoughts Upon Female Education* (1787) that owing to the father's time spent away from families given his professional life, 'a principal share of the instruction of children naturally devolves upon the women. It becomes us therefore to prepare them, by a suitable education, for the discharge of this most important duty of mothers' (1787: 76). Importantly, he added that through a 'peculiar and suitable education . . . ladies should be qualified to a certain degree . . . to concur in instructing their sons in the principles of liberty and government' (1787: 76–77). Rush further argued that the happiness of the country depended on the exclusive expansion of knowledge and virtue to women of the Republic who would not only influence their children, but their husbands: 'Our young men would . . . be restrained from vice by the terror of being banished from their company' (1787: 88).

The sentiments behind Rush's rhetoric were modelled on the idea of republican motherhood, which narrated a version of civic duty in the domestic space of the home which, by the early nineteenth century, had become the exclusive domain of women as wives and mothers. Indeed, in a piece for *Godey's Lady's Book* titled 'FEMELLE AUTORITE' (1847a) concerning modern gallantry, it was suggested that 'It is female influence that nerves the arm of the patriot and causes him to protect the rights of his country', pointing back to the roots of the founding of the Republic as that which was guided by women of the Revolutionary era and the beginnings of their moral guardianship within the family and the nation. In the post-Revolutionary period, the economic structures of American society were developing from cottage-based industries and subsistence farming to an embrace of capitalism with the accompanying industrial and manufacturing changes this incurred. This had a significant impact on the home as a gendered space, especially in the more industrial-developing northeast, given that workplaces were increasingly separate from the home.

Of course, the public/private divisions of the early national period in the United States were grounded in an ideological framework governing the working and domestic lives of the nation's citizens. In reality, however, these strict dividing lines of the domestic or private sphere of the home (supposedly governed solely by women) with the public spaces of the workplace and the developing capitalist market (where men alone apparently operated alongside, and often in competition, with other men) was somewhat illusionary given the household's dependence on the market and vice versa. Yet it served an ideological purpose and it coincided with the growth of an American middle class – entrepreneurs, lawyers, physicians, politicians and the like – who replaced the old elite in the northeast at least and whose insistence on defining themselves as distinct from the labouring classes of white America resulted in a definite bourgeois culture that worked to celebrate these illusionary divisions between the separation of the public and private spaces of American society. Part of this bourgeois cultural world was the development of the concept of romantic love as the only justification for marriage. As a piece for *Godey's Lady's Book* on 'Thoughts on Married Life' (1847b) suggested, 'As husband and wife it is your place, severally, ever to entertain and cherish a high esteem and mutual love for one another, this, indeed, is the proper basis of the strongest and purest amity'. The nineteenth century, then, was an era where middle-class couples of the northeast in particular married increasingly out of choice rather than duty basing their decision of a spouse on mutual attraction and consent and framing this as part of a culture of bourgeois sentimentality and refinement.[1]

THE ADOPTION OF BOURGEOIS CULTURAL IDEALS IN NORTHERN HOMES

Increasingly, the trope of sentimentalization characterized the bourgeois cultural ideal of early-nineteenth-century America and continued to define it through the Civil War of 1861–65 and beyond, albeit in more nuanced and subtle ways (Halttunen 1982). The essence of family life and central to the cultural currency of sentiment for the northern middle classes of the era was bound within the spaces of the home as a means for civilizing and refining the mortal soul. Women alone were charged with this duty as wives, and perhaps, more importantly, as mothers. This was embodied in the ideal of the 'true woman', who had matured from her republican sister in the Revolutionary era to become the moral guardian of the nation through her duties in the domestic spaces of the home. Barbara Welter's ground-breaking essay of 1966 described the prescriptive model of 'true womanhood' in the nineteenth-century United States as a cult, promoted through magazines such as *Godey's Lady's Book*, domestic novels of the period such as Maria Susanna Cummin's *The Lamplighter* (1854) and Louisa May Alcott's *Little Women* (1880), and religious literature like *Pilgrim's Progress* (1678), which although published in the mid-seventeenth century was particularly popular as a gift to young women of the middle class throughout the eighteenth and nineteenth centuries, perhaps increasing in demand as one of the central tenets of the idealized women of the nineteenth century was devout piety. Indeed, Sarah Hicks Williams, who was raised in New Hartford, New York, but had moved south in 1853 following her marriage to physician and slaveholder, Benjamin Williams, was elated with her Christmas present in the winter of 1855, which, as she reported to her parents, was 'a beautiful copy of Pilgrim's Progress'.[2] The true woman, according to the popular literature of the day was, in Welter's words, 'divided into four cardinal virtues – piety, purity, submissiveness and domesticity. Put them all together and they spelled mother, daughter, sister, wife – woman' (1966: 152). These characteristics were held up as the epitome of ideal womanhood and all were judged by such standards, even if the particulars of their circumstances – in terms of their race or class, for example – left them outside of ever being able to achieve this celestial-like version of the feminine archetype.

The true woman of the nineteenth century was typified, then, as the angel of the household; confined to the domestic sphere of the home, it was her role to provide moral guidance and nurturance to her family through her conduct, setting herself up as an example to be followed by her daughters and a model of what a wife and mother should be to her sons and husband. Indeed, the educator and reformer, William A. Alcott (1838), wrote in his publication *From the Young Wife* that 'Woman's true greatness consists, so it seems to me, in rendering others useful, rather than in being directly useful herself. Or, in other words, it is less her office to be seen and known in society, than to make others seen and known, and their influence felt'. Indeed, Catherine Beecher, whose authority on questions of domesticity were rarely if ever questioned in the era, despite never having married and subsequently kept house herself, elevated the status of the American women as wife and mother in the domestic spaces of the home:

> No women on earth have a higher sense of their moral and religious responsibilities, or better understand, not only what is demanded of them, as housekeepers, but all the claims that rest upon them as wives, mothers, and members of a social community. An American woman, who is the mistress of a family, feels her obligations, in reference to her influence over her husband, and a still greater responsibility in rearing and educating her children.
> —Beecher 1842b: 44

The well-known nineteenth-century journalist and poet, Benjamin Park, emphasized further the role of the home in the cultural configurations of gender in the mid-nineteenth century. Writing a piece entitled 'The True Rights of a Women' (1844), Park rhetorically asked himself the following question and detailed his response:

> Where is the proper sphere of woman? . . . My answer is – HOME! – home, which has been eloquently called 'the highest, holiest place in which human agency can act' . . . these are her *true rights*, her true duties, and there should be her supremest [sic] happiness. Sister, mother, wife – dear and hallowed names!
> —1844: 274

Women's prescribed role in the home was part of a wider mission in the young republic which, as Sarah J. Hale reminded readers of *Godey's Lady's Book* (1841/1852) in an editorial, was bound up with the fate of humankind: 'The destiny of the human race is thus dependent on the condition and conduct of women'. This job was to be focussed in the home where women – as wives and mothers – were tasked with 'rais[ing] *humanity* towards the angelic', through their moral guidance.

This elevated role for women was placed in a comparable position to the husband and father of the middle-class family, who was ideally located in the public world of work: professional life including commerce and industry. William

A. Alcott's *Young Man's Guide* (1836) gave several of the early chapters over to aspects of public life such as Chapter One's 'On the Formation of Character', with various sections that spell out exactly how a man should act in the public sphere covering such things as, 'Importance of Aiming High', 'In the Formation of Character', 'On Motives to Action', 'Industry', and 'Economy'. Chapter Two of Alcott's *Guide* is focused 'On the Management of Business', covering aspects such as the importance of integrity in business, methods and application in business, and the art of speculation. Alcott (1836) advises all young men to marry, describing matrimony as a 'duty' and noting, among the 'Female Qualifications for Marriage', such things as 'Moral Excellence', 'Common Sense', 'a Fondness for Children', 'a Love of Domestic Concerns', 'Sobriety', and 'Industry'.

Despite Alcott's stress on the 'public' characteristics required of men during the antebellum era, there was also a domestication of manhood that located them in the home as loving husbands and fathers. As Robert Griswold has argued, this 'cultural redefinition of manhood' (1990: 97) was inextricably linked to the developing middle class and their cultural ideals, which refashioned the requirements of manhood in ways similar to the idealizations of womanhood. As Griswold further comments, the middle-class culture of the antebellum era required men to 'forfeit traditional male prerogatives in exchange for closer emotional and psychological ties with his wife and children . . . the result would be to change the shape of patriarchy, to hone its rough edges, to reconstruct it along lines more appealing to middle-class domestic sentiments' (1990: 97). Evidence of this can be seen in the way that men of the era who were either drawn from or aspiring to be part of the middling classes talked about their home life – particularly their wife and children – in terms of adoration and unrelenting commitment to the family and conceptions of home. James Brown, for example, a store owner from Bloomfield, Ohio, who was active in abolitionist activity in the era, wrote to his father-in-law, Samuel Hicks shortly after James had married his daughter, Mary. In the letter, which James opens with the salutation 'Dear Father', he communicated his desire to be considered part of the Hicks family, as opposed to just an in-law: 'I do not know that I have yet made myself worthy to call you <u>father</u>, yet as with Mary you conferred that privilege, I will use it, and by kindness to her and duty to her own and my new parents, endeavor [*sic*] to deserve to be your son' (Brown 1844, emphasis added). In the same letter, James also wrote of his love for Mary, reflecting on the fact that although the upheaval of departing from the family home in New Hartford, New York, to his home in Ohio had taken a toll on her health, that 'now . . . she is rested, looks better than before she left home. She seems happy and *not only makes me so*, but is a source of joy to all of her Ohio friends as she ever was among her associates in N.H.'. In an evident illustration of how manhood was being refashioned in the era, James can clearly be seen here supplanting the older role of the patriarch in his and Mary's marriage, and replacing this with a closeness and intimacy in the domestic circle. Both women and men of the middle classes, then, were heavily invested in a cultural reconfiguration of gendered ideals of the period, manifesting themselves most explicitly through the domestic spaces of the home.

The homes of the middle classes in mid-nineteenth-century America, then, were examples of refinement and respectability with families that were well-grounded in the cultural codes of gendered conduct. These home spaces were also beautifully ordered with an attempt to pay every last attention to detail, although the realization of this in practice would have proved impossible. Nineteenth-century middle-class homes were not only conversant with the model of true womanhood in terms of domesticity, but also in relation to a middle-class disdain for vulgarity, both in manners and presentation. As Sarah J. Hale wrote in her 'Editors' Table' for *Godey's Lady's Book* in January 1843, 'Purity of heart and correctness of mind, as well as elegance of taste may be shown in the external appearance' (1843: 56). Here Hale was referring to dress and appearance in relation to women, but the same could be said of the *external appearance* of the home. As cultural historian, Richard Bushman (1992: 208, 258), suggests, the home's physical appearance – its exterior, furnishings and wall hangings, for example – most importantly perhaps, was the material evidence that the correct manners and morals were being taught inside it and that only the refined and respectable were invited in. For example, the house of Samuel Hicks at 18 Oxford Road, in the village of New Hartford, Oneida County, New York, was finished in 1826, serving as the family home for himself, his wife, Sarah Parmelee, and their three daughters, Mary, Lucinda and Sarah. It was a two-storey mansion and regarded as 'a splendid example of Georgian architecture', complete with the requisite white exterior and green shutters, which effectively 'rose up and spoke out in brisk white'. It was decorated with an acute attention to detail including the hand-printed English wallpaper, made in eighteen-inch blocks, that decorated the hallway, and which Samuel's granddaughter reported in later years (*Utica Daily Press* 1915) was 'similar to the William Morris design . . . brought at . . . an importer[s] at . . . New York City'. Other notable features of the house included the glass in the fan light and blown glass side panels of the front door. The handrail running down the staircase which was made from mahogany, an expensive and superior wood-type during this period, was complemented by the 'beautiful engraved glass lantern in the hall'. The double parlour at the end of the hallway served the purpose of a dining area and two closets containing blue and gilt china adorned each room. Professional men such as Samuel Hicks devoted considerable energies (and no small amount of the family income) towards fashioning the home to demonstrate the Hicks' achievements and wealth. Alongside this, the manners and morals that Sarah Parmelee Hicks, as his wife, imparted within the confines of the domestic circle to both Samuel and their daughters was vital. Indeed, an inventory provided by the youngest daughter,

FIGURE 6.1: Nineteenth-century home of the middle classes, Hicks' Family Mansion, 18 Oxford Road, New Hartford, Oneida County, New York. © New Hartford Historical Society.

also named Sarah, listing the items she had sent for from New Hartford to Clifton Grove, her new home in Greene County, North Carolina, included a tapestry carpet, a piano and stool, a corner stand, a collection of sofa chairs, two easy chairs, a sofa rocking chair, and a marble-top centre table with a sola lamp and draping. Such high-end items suggested that the Hicks' family were heavily invested in cultivating the 'genteel home', adorning 18 Oxford Road with furnishings that served to further evidence their high moral standing in the neighbourhood and respectability as a family within their domestic space.[3]

SOUTHERN HOMES AND MAINTAINING A RACIAL AND GENDERED HIERARCHY

While this might have been the case within the homes of the northern middle classes during the first half of the nineteenth century, the southern states of North America interpreted models of gender roles and behaviour in the home to better support the system of racial slavery. By the early nineteenth century, slavery in the American South was integral to the southern economy and the cultural world of white southerners. Even though the white southern elite were educated in the same ideals of home and the appropriate gender roles and behaviour accorded to each within it as those in the northeast, the existence of racial slavery and the patriarchal nature inherent in this system saw the reinforcement of conventional models of gender in the home, with deference and submission playing a key part as regards womanhood.

Women, children and slaves were expected to pay deference to their husband, father or enslaver respectively as the master of the household. In return, they were promised protection and for women, as the master's wife, were surely guaranteed esteem in their own domain – the home. The proslavery social theorist, George Fitzhugh, declared in his publication, *Sociology for the South*, that 'as long as [a woman] is nervous, fickle, capricious, delicate, diffident and dependent, man will worship and adore her. Her weakness is her strength, and her true art is to cultivate and improve that weakness' (1854: 214). Fitzhugh charged free society (i.e. those without slavery in the northern states) as having 'robbed women of the softness of their sex' and further declared that 'woman, like children, has but one right, and that is the right to protection. The right to protection involves the obligation to obey. A husband, a lord and master, whom she should love, honor [sic] and obey' (1854: 214). This wifely duty to obey was accompanied by deference and submission to her husband within the domestic spaces of the home. As Caroline Howard Gillman advised all good southern wives of the slaveholding South:

> Her first study must be self-control, almost to hypocrisy. A good wife must smile amid a thousand perplexities, and clear her voice to tones of cheerfulness when her frame is drooping with disease, or else languish alone. Man, on the contrary, when trials beset him, expects to find her ear and heart a ready receptacle, and, when sickness assails him, her soft hand must nurse and sustain him.
>
> —[1838] 1998: 256–57

Although the ideal of the genteel home was part of wider western bourgeois cultural mores by the mid-nineteenth century, it took on a distinct form in the American South given that the home space and the workplace were often one and the same. Compared with the increasing separation of these two sites of labour in the northern states, the rural economies of the Old South meant that this division was largely redundant for many people. Much of the labour that took place on the farms and plantations of the Old South were also where white southern families called home and where enslaved people attempted to create and sustain families of their own. This meant that the households of the white southern elite and yeoman farming families were also often places where white women 'managed' a workforce of enslaved labourers. Depending on the wealth of the family, white southern women could be charged with governing either a few enslaved people as labourers or domestics or, alternatively, a household of housemaids, nurses and nannies, cooks and kitchen hands. The ideals of domesticity, so central to the model of womanhood in the North, were perhaps even more key to definitions of womanhood in the American South during the first half of the nineteenth century. This paradoxically awarded white women of the slaveholding classes a greater degree of power and influence within the home as compared to white women of the urban middle classes in the North. They were permitted to exercise their power over enslaved people within the confines of the domestic spaces in order to demonstrate their racial superiority. Southern

FIGURE 6.2: Sarah Hicks Williams, c. 1850s.

white women as plantation mistresses, however small their enslaved workforce, secured their racial authority while maintaining their subservience to white men as husbands and fathers through their control over the labour of enslaved women within the household. As Thavolia Glymph (2008: 64) points out, 'The call to domestic order highlighted [southern] white women's governance of the home and slave women . . . became projects of the western civilising mission'.

Aware of their power within the context of the home, however, elite southern women wasted little time in complaining about the duties of household management, employing racially derogative stereotypes of their enslaved household labourers in order to accentuate their sense of duty not only to their husband and their children, but also to the southern region of the United States in terms of their civilizing mission involving the African American race. Sarah Hicks Williams, plantation mistress to over forty enslaved labourers at Burnt Fort, Georgia in the late 1850s was conversant with these ideological constructions of racial and gender hierarchy in the home, remarking in the spring of 1859, that 'I lie down at night tired enough to sleep like a rock, & yet cannot tell what I have done but trot after the children, trot after the negroes, trot after the chickens, Egg & hens & turkeys, & trot trot trot all day'.[4] Similarly, Tryphena Fox, a plantation mistress in Louisiana, despaired over the 'wasteful improvident race of the negroes . . . [which] constant attention on my part cannot save' (Fox 1860, cited in King 1993: 104). As Glymph has argued in relation to such perspectives espoused by plantation mistresses of the mid-nineteenth-century South, white women's labours were represented as the central operative mechanism of the plantation household: 'From the hands of white women, not those of black women, came whatever order and cleanliness there was in a world stained by the mere presence of black women' (2008: 64).

While domesticity was central to models of southern womanhood during the era, as it was to women in the urban North, other aspects of ideal femininity that women in the northeast were engaging in outside of the domestic confines of the home, were being performed by plantation mistresses within the home space. Piety, for example, so closely bound to philanthropy and charitable work in the public sphere for middle-class women in the northeast was articulated in the southern plantation context through the private sphere of the home, most especially manifest in the plantation mistresses' duties towards the enslaved population that laboured for her family. Framed by later historians in discourses of maternalism, this was the feminine version of the slaveholding master's ideology of paternalism. As Eugene Genovese defines this concept, it was bound up in ideals of the family and representations of the home as a happy and harmonious space just as in the northeast region of the United States. However, Genovese argues that it was distinctive in the American South during this era in two ways:

> It embraced the laboring class, or the largest section of it, as part of the household, which it identified with the family itself . . . [and fathers] sought ways to maintain a legitimate authority in the household and the polity at a time in which, as they repeatedly noted with alarm, the marketplace ideology was plunging bourgeois though and action in the North and in Europe towards a radical egalitarianism that was slowly eroding the family itself.
> —1991: 72

In idealistic terms, this played itself out in the reciprocal duty and obligations within the context of the family home: enslaved people laboured – in the white slaveholding family's fields and homes – as part of their *duty* to the *family*. In turn, slaveholding masters (who wielded ultimate authority in the slaveholding South) and mistresses held particular responsibilities towards their enslaved labourers as part of *their* family 'white and black' as dependents akin to children who they had responsibility for not only in terms of food, shelter and medical care but also administering discipline if and when required. In reality, this played out in varying measures, with the slaveholding classes justifying the racial order of southern society using the ideology of paternalism to disguise the perniciousness of a system grounded in white power, violent domination and racial privilege.

Slaveholding mistresses performed their maternalistic duties towards the enslaved with varying degrees of compassion. Accounts drawn from slave

FIGURE 6.3: The Old Plantation Home. © Library of Congress Prints and Photographs Division.

narratives and interviews with former slaves and their descendants in the post-slavery era sometimes confirmed the plantation mistresses as far removed from the administering angel of the household, particularly for enslaved women who laboured in the domestic spaces of the home. Ida Adkins (cited in Rawick 1972: 9), who was enslaved in Louisburg, Franklin County, recalled that her mistress, Miss Mary Jane was 'quick as er whip-po'-will. She had black eyes dat snapped an' dey seed everythin'. She could turn her head so quick dat she'd ketch you every time you tried to steal a lump of sugar'. Enslaved domestics were also subject to the capricious whims of their masters and mistresses, as was the case in the household of Dr Flint, the master of Harriet Jacobs. Jacobs recalled in her narrative how Mrs Flint, the slaveholding mistress of the plantation where she laboured in Edenton, North Carolina, had taken Harriet into her own bedroom to sleep at night following her well-grounded suspicious that her husband had sexual designs on the young enslaved girl. Although Jacobs appreciated this intervention on the part of the mistress, she also recognized the assertion of the mistress's power over her demonstrated through such action:

> There I was an object of her especial care, though not of her especial comfort, for she spent many a sleepless night to watch over me. Sometimes I woke up, and found her bending over me. At other times she whispered in my ear, as though it was her husband who was speaking to me, and listened to hear what

I would answer. If she startled me, on such occasions, she would glide stealthily away; and the next morning she would tell me I had been talking in my sleep, and ask who I was talking to. At last, I began to be fearful for my life.

In her narrative, Jacobs recounted several other moments whereby the gendered and racial power dynamics within the southern home were manifest clearly, particularly in relation to the most sacred of gendered spaces in the home: the kitchen. Jacobs explained how the enslaved cook of the Flint household 'never sent a dinner to his table without fear and trembling; for if there happened to be a dish not to his liking, he would either order her to be whipped, or compel her to eat every mouthful of it in his presence. The poor, hungry creature might not have objected to eating it; but she did object to having her master cram it down her throat till she choked' (1861: 54, 22). While the plantation mistress oversaw the work of the enslaved cook and were a visible presence in the kitchens of the southern plantation home – hovering over the preparation of meals – rarely did she cook herself.

The power of the mistress in the southern home, then, lay in their *management* of domestic duties such as cooking, rather than getting their own hands actually dirty. Enslaved cooks held one of the most privileged positions within the homes of the southern slaveholding classes given the ideological links between cooking as a practice and the ideals of domestic womanhood. Usually taught the arts of southern cooking by their own female relatives including mothers and grandmothers, enslaved women who were positioned as cooks in the plantation household often held high rank in the slave quarters and wider communities of enslaved people, using their culinary skills for the benefit of their own and others' families (see Blassingame 1976).

However, slaveholding mistresses employed the talents of their cooks to their own ends, often passing off the meals that came out of a southern kitchen as their own, despite the fact that they had only instructed the enslaved cook and her kitchen helps as regards the menu. When plantation mistress, Sarah Hicks Williams expressed her gratification at having *her* pumpkin pies 'highly complimented' by dinner guests in December 1853, she demonstrated how complete the ownership of her enslaved household was through taking credit for *their* labors.[5]

Certainly in the wake of the Civil War and the subsequent outlawing of slavery on the North American continent via the passing of the Thirteenth Amendment in 1865, many former mistresses bemoaned the difficulties of performing domestic labour for themselves, particularly cooking. Kate Stone, the daughter of a former slaveholding family in Louisiana, wrote of the realities of the daily domestic toil that she was now having to undertake, having seen 150 formally enslaved people that her family had previously held liberated at war's end. Interestingly, however, female members of Kate Stone's family still persisted in their refusal to labour in the kitchen, subsequently hiring a cook,

FIGURE 6.4: North Slave Quarters, East Room, West Wall: Kitchen Fireplace. Hopsewee Plantation, Slave Quarters, U.S. Routes 17 & 701, Santee River, North, Georgetown, Georgetown County, South Carolina. © Library of Congress Prints and Photographs Division.

for as Kate remarked, 'that is new and disagreeable work to us' (Anderson 1995: 373). Similarly, in the final months of the war, Gertrude Clanton Thomas, a slaveholding mistress from Georgia, recounted her efforts at the new chore of baking 'the first cakes I have ever accomplished'. Although she was helped by the family cook, Tamah, she eventually succeeded in producing something edible, while all her children gathered round to applaud her efforts. Gertrude reflected on the experience later that evening, confiding to her journal that 'my back ached when I was through and I have seen things I liked to do better'. Even so, she promised that her intention was to do more cooking for herself, out of necessity if nothing else, although admitted that 'it was about as hard work as I ever did' (Burr 1990: 259).

The order of the kitchen, as an organized domestic space, was held aloft by northern commentators of the antebellum era as symbolic of the heart of the domestic economy and thus central to the ideological conception of the home. Novelists such as Harriet Beecher Stowe, for example, used the physical space of the kitchen in order to illustrate the political differences between a southern system underpinned by racial slavery and a northern one with free labour. In Stowe's 1853 publication of *Uncle Tom's Cabin,* fictional New Englander, Ophelia, remarked on the kitchen of her southern slaveholding cousin, St. Claire. The kitchen, which was run by the enslaved cook, Dinah, looked, Ophelia remarked, 'as if it had been arranged with a hurricane blowing through it' (Stowe 1853: 214). Stowe's delineation of this southern space, with racial slavery at the heart, cleverly linked the chaos of Dinah's kitchen to the impact that slavery had upon both domestic spaces of the home and political disorder in public. Indeed, during the first few months following her removal to the upper-southern slaveholding state of North Carolina in late September of 1853, Sarah Hicks Williams noted the lack of an efficient system in the duties of the southern kitchen compared with the order of her northern home: 'wash, bake, or iron just as the fit takes . . . I think the great fault lies in the want of a system'. In particular, she noted the lack of order in the southern kitchen unless one had control, 'if not I would advise them to keep clear as I have resolved to do'.[6]

Implicit in Sarah's comment above is a critique of the southern order of the home space compared with that of the North. However, other women who had lived in the slaveholding South went much further than simply providing a negative evaluation of the way in which household duties were undertaken. Fanny Kemble is perhaps one of the most acclaimed examples of a slaveholding mistress who challenged the underpinning ideology of slaveholding during the era and the paternalistic images of *my family white and black,* in her account narrating her experience during her time living on her husband's plantations on the sea island coast of Georgia. Kemble, an English actress who had toured the United States

FIGURE 6.5: 'Chloe and Mrs Shelby', Hammat Billings for Chapter 21, *Uncle Tom's Cabin; or, Life Among the Lowly*, by Harriet Beecher Stowe. Illustrated Edition. Original Designs by Billings; Engraved by Baker and Smith (Boston: John P. Jewett, 1853). © Clifton Waller Barret Collection, University of Virginia Library.

during the early 1830s, met Piece Butler when on tour and subsequently married into the slaveholding Butler family in 1834. Fanny's anti-slavery text, *Journal of a Residence on a Georgian Plantation in 1838–39*, published in 1863 following a very public and bitter divorce from Pierce, recounted the horrors of slavery and the plight of enslaved women and children in particular on the plantations her husband owned. Within the *Journal* Fanny portrayed herself as the embodiment of domestic maternalism, in terms of helping those less fortunate than oneself. Ministering to the needs of these people, Fanny requested better medical care of enslaved women during their pregnancies, post-partum, and in cases of miscarriage. She also asked that extra provisions be given to enslaved mothers to ensure they could adequately feed and care for their children. She related the experience of several of the enslaved women in her diary who came to request her assistance. These included enslaved women such as Sophy, who 'came to beg for some old linen. She is suffering fearfully; has had ten children; five of them are dead. The principal favor she asked was a piece of meat, which I gave her'. Another enslaved woman, Charlotte, the wife of Renty, came to Fanny to ask if she might do something for her in the way of relieving her sufferings:

> [she] had had two miscarriages, and was with child again. She was almost crippled with rheumatism, and showed me a pair of poor swollen knees that made my heart ache. I have promised her a pair of flannel trousers, which I must forthwith set about making.
> —[1863] 1984: 230

A third enslaved woman, Fanny, went with a simple request of lightening her load in the field. This woman had borne six children, yet as Kemble ([1863] 1984: 210–11) reported to her journal, 'all [were] dead but one'. Middle-class women of the northeast would have most likely ministered to the poor and suffering populations of their towns and cities as part of their domestic duties extending outside of the home space without the need for formal consent from their husbands to do so. In comparison, Kemble and other wives of the southern slaveholding elite who were concerned to invest the role of mistress with a degree of compassion were obliged to forward enslaved people's petitions to their husband. They often met with little success given enslaved people's legal status as property and the racial stereotypes that many slaveholders held, which gave the lie to any idealization of a southern home including black members as part of the family. As Kemble ([1863] 1984: 229–30) noted:

> I have had a most painful conversation with Mr. [Butler], who has declined receiving any of the people's petitions through me ... their expression silenced by his angry exclamations of: 'why do you listen to such stuff?' or 'why do you believe such trash? Don't you know you know the niggers are

all d---d liars?' . . . He says that bringing their complaints to me, and the sight of my credulous commiseration, only tend to make them discontented and idle, and brings renewed chastisement upon them; and that so, instead of really befriending them, I am only preparing more suffering for them whenever I leave the Place, and they can no more cry to me for help.

SOUTHERN HOMES OF DISREPAIR

While proslavery arguments drew on ideals of domesticity and maternal morality to justify the plantation household of enslaved labourers and different women's role within it, anti-slavery arguments shaped these ideas in different ways to strengthen their own arguments for the abolition of slavery. Abolitionists emphasized that the savagery of the system of southern slavery and its effects on the ideological construction of the home were evident in the rude state of white southerners' domestic dwellings. On his first impressions of the houses of Virginian slaveholders in 1853, for example, northerner Frederick Law Olmsted remarked that:

> A good many substantial old plantation mansions are to be seen; generally standing in a grove of white oaks, upon some hill-top. Most of them are constructed of wood, of two stories, painted white, and have, perhaps, a dozen rude-looking little log-cabins scattered around them, for the slaves. Now and then, there is one of more pretension, with a large porch or gallery in front, like that of Mount Vernon. These are generally in a heavy, compact style; less often, perhaps, than similar establishments at the North, in markedly bad, or vulgar taste; but seldom elegant, or even neat, and almost always in sad need of repairs.
>
> —1856: 17

The political rot at the heart of the economic system in the South was, to Olmstead and other northern commentators, clearly evident in the decay of the physical structures belonging to southern slaveholders. The physical manifestation of the dilapidated southern houses was employed in northern discourse of the era to symbolize the degeneracy of the 'home', ideologically positioned in the North as the scared haven from the heartless world within which ministering angels (read: wives and mothers) would provide moral lessons on conducting oneself in the public sphere for their husbands and sons and teach their daughters how to raise good sons and be dutiful wives. The different models of gender roles and behaviour within the southern slaveholding home in terms of the roles that men and women adopted as the archetype plantation mistress and master, were central to this northern discourse in commentaries such as Olmsted's. They worked to place the corrosion of the

FIGURE 6.6: Southern Planter Home, John B. Williams House, Greene County, North Carolina. © North Carolina State Preservation Office.

FIGURE 6.7: 'Four Oaks' Old Plantation Home, New Orleans, Louisiana. © Library of Congress Prints and Photographs Division.

southern house as 'home', in distinct contrast to the genteel, refined and moral virtues embedded in the middle-class imaginary of what a home should be.

CONCEPTIONS OF THE HOME IN THE AMERICAN WEST

Understandings about the home in both the pre-Civil War North and South were, then, built around discourses of idealized gender roles and behaviour. These were dependent on the socio-economic system that was shaping the cultural worlds of these two regions and accordingly the racial slavery of the South meant for many northern commentators that this region could never achieve parity with the actualities of northerners' experiences of the home. The emerging territory to the northwest, however, most especially Ohio in the context of the period under discussion, was seen as a canvas on which the northern middle classes migrating from the eastern seaboard could plant their cultural ideals of home and gender. Ohio was frontier country previous to the War of 1812 where a violent clash of cultures had been ongoing since Anglo-Americans moved in and the native American populations in the area fought to preserve their claims to land (see Hurt 1998). By the 1830s, Ohio's white population was perceived by many northern commentators and Europeans who visited as being made up of a rough and uncivilized people. Drawn from the migrant classes of Europe who had initially landed on the eastern seaboard in places like New York and Boston and the semi-skilled native born, those bound for Ohio were in search of economic betterment through cultivation of fresh soil. In the popular imagination of political and social commentators, however, the antebellum Ohioan was fiercely independent, thus fulfilling the Jeffersonian ideal of the small independent farmer in the republic of America. And yet because of that autonomy they were removed from the practices of refinement and gentility that supposedly allowed Europeans and middle-class Anglo-Americans in the northeast to instil their homes with the necessary moral guidance to attain a state of civility and respectability. In her caustic review of America and its inhabitants, for example, English novelist Frances Trollope reserved special mention for Ohio and the inhabitants of the region. Although surprisingly complimentary as regards Cincinnati and its people, Trollope (1832) remarked that:

> These people were indeed independent, Robinson Crusoe was hardly more so, and they eat and drink abundantly; but yet it seemed to me that there was something awful and almost unnatural in their loneliness. No village bell ever summoned them to prayer, where they might meet the friendly greeting of their fellow-men. When they die, no spot sacred by ancient reverence will receive their bones—Religion will not breathe her sweet and solemn farewell upon their grave; the husband or the father will dig the pit that is to hold

them, beneath the nearest tree; he will himself deposit them within it, and the wind that whispers through the boughs will be their only requiem. But then they pay neither taxes nor tythes, are never expected to pull off a hat or to make a curtsy, and will live and die without hearing or uttering the dreadful words, 'God save the king'.

However grim the reported picture was of the northwest's lack of civility, there was always hope for improvement. As the area claimed by Anglo-Americans grew in size, some among the middling classes along the northeastern seaboard saw the northwest as a civilizing mission and relocated to the area armed with the idea of bringing civilization to the masses through a process of allowing the inhabitants to learn by example but also through instruction. In the spring of 1833, Catharine Beecher, the author of *A Treatise on Domestic Economy* (1841) and *The American Woman's Home* (1869), which she co-authored with her sister, Harriet Beecher Stowe, announced her plans to establish the Western Female Institute in Cincinnati, a school dedicated not merely to the 'technical acquisition of knowledge', but also to 'mental and moral development'. The central objective of the Institute, as Catharine Beecher (1835, cited in Sklar 1976: 112, 114) explained in her address, *An Essay on the Education of Female Teachers*, was 'to civilize the barbarous immigrants and lower classes of the West'. She would do this through 'the creation of a corps of women teachers' who 'have the highest estimate of the value of moral and religious influence'. She went on to establish more educational institutions across the northwest including Iowa, Illinois and Wisconsin. All of them had moral instruction as one of their primary teaching aims. Catharine envisaged with all her schools that once her pupils were instructed in the moral codes of middle-class behaviour, they would establish their own homes underpinned by the influence of their training in principles of morality, Protestant religious conviction, and domestic duty.

THE AMERICAN CIVIL WAR AND AFTER: BEYOND THE HOME

By April 1861, the American Civil War had begun and four years of war unfolded on a scale that was both wholly unexpected and truly catastrophic. At war's end in April 1865, the death toll of soldiers was at least 750,000 by one recent estimate. The casualties totalled over a million. The physical and cultural landscape had been forever altered. The Union had ultimately failed to overcome the increasing sectional tensions over slavery and state rights that had been threatening to break it apart since its creation and the ratification of the Constitution in 1788. The majority of the former slaveholding states in the South seceded from the Union in the spring and summer of 1861 to claim independent status as the Confederate States of America, determined to maintain their governance over southern institutions including slavery. The remaining ones to the northeast, northwest and on the west coast pledged affinity to the Union.

In moments of conflict, the cultural ideal of the gendered home was used in both Union and Confederate discourses to justify the larger motivations for warfare. The Confederate states to the south particularly employed domestic images of the hearth and home to rationalize the fight. As Aaron Sheehan-Dean has argued in relation to Confederate Virginia, white Virginians 'entered the war with a host of overlapping motivations including a defense of home, a belief in state rights, and a desire to protect slavery' (2007: 1). All across the Confederacy men took up arms to defend their way of life, and thus, in the process, as Drew Gilpin Faust has argued, connected this to their duties and obligations as 'heads of household to protect and provide for their legal dependents – wives, children and slaves' (Faust, 1996: 5). Civil War fiction, published in both the Union and Confederacy, highlighted the domestic sphere as one that was divided. For example, Delphine P. Baker, a Union author, published *Solon; or, The Rebellion of '61: A Domestic and Political Tragedy* (1862), which concerned a courting couple: the young woman a daughter of Lincoln, the President of the Union, and the young man a son of Jefferson Davis, the President of the Confederacy. The courting couple's desire to be married and settle into their own home are prevented from becoming a reality 'while their fathers confront one another in war' (Murrell Taylor 2005: 123).[7]

After the Civil War, cultural conceptions of the home were fundamental to the nation's conception of self as the United States sought to rebuild that which had been lost – both physically and emotionally – during four years of cataclysmic conflict. Discourses of gender remained intimately entwined with such understandings in the post-war era, perhaps even more so as individuals sought a semblance of normality and a need for comfort and nurturance within the sanctity of the family.

During the post-war period in the latter quarter of the nineteenth century, former plantation mistresses and their southern daughters were presented with possibilities for engagement in a public life that they had hitherto been excluded from. The pre-war conventions of white southern femininity that had dictated confinement to the private sphere of the home had rapidly dissolved in the first few months of the Civil War when women assumed a much more public role in the lives of the villages, towns and cities where they lived or had fled to. This shift in the ideological structures relating to the southern gender order persisted in the post-war period, as younger southern women recognized and claimed their right to define their own sense of self while many from the older generations took ideals formed in the antebellum era and both adapted and extended them in the post-war period. As Jane Turner Censer has noted, '[w]hile [southern] genteel white women had never been as thoroughly sequestered in practice as in theory, they greatly increased their paid and voluntary labors after the war'

(2003: 153), extending their activities out into the public arenas of southern life particularly in relation to the Church and memorialization of the Confederate war-dead. Young southern women assumed revised notions of their womanhood too, laying the stress on self-sufficiency and their own efficacy, and 'promulgated an ethic that emphasized "nondependence" in domestic or other roles', increasingly entering positions such as teachers (2003: 7).

Southern gender ideals in the late nineteenth century remained entwined, however, within a familial discourse that still emphasized the home as a particular cultural space with defined gender roles within it. Yet, in the northeast, middle-class women were rapidly moving further from the ideological confines of the domestic ideal bound up in the home to define new ways of being in the public world. They did this through increasing activism on particular moral issues such as temperance and campaigning for a greater role in the public life of America through agitating for women's suffrage. The 'new woman' as a feminist ideal, who was educated, financially independent and sexually autonomous, was gaining increasing popularity in the North if not always grounded in the realities of women's lives during the closing years of the nineteenth century (see, for example, Crocker 2006). Catharine Beecher's claim in 1842, which this chapter opened with, regarding the gendered conceptions of the home, can be clearly traced from the very beginnings of the American republic in the late eighteenth century through to the early 1860s. Degrees of change were evident in the post-war era, particularly in the gradual movement of middle-class women outside of the home into the public arena, whether through paid employment as an economic necessity or engagement in public reform and social activism. However, despite this there remained a central investment in the place of the home and the gendered roles within it during the latter part of the nineteenth century, and which arguably still form a persistent discourse in relation to cultural conceptions of the home in modern America today.

CHAPTER SEVEN

Hospitality and Home: Dining Spaces and Practices in England and North America[1]

JANE HAMLETT AND MARIE DREWS

During the nineteenth century, people in Britain and North America found new occupations, worked in new industries, travelled the globe faster and migrated in large numbers. These changes affected how rituals of hospitality were performed, and how an increasingly geographically and socially mobile population received them. Felicity Heal has convincingly argued that the culture of hospitality in early modern Britain, and in particular the idea of a natural host who welcomed all outsiders to his table, accruing honour through aristocratic benefactions, fell away during the eighteenth century (1990: 389). While there was certainly a shift in aristocratic cultures, a different kind of hospitality remained important to the middle classes in Britain and the middling sort in North America. Indeed, the British middle classes in the early nineteenth century are often thought to have been under particular pressure to socially impress, developing new forms of social etiquette for visiting and entertaining to cope with the heady rush of social transformation (Davidoff 1973). Amongst the middle classes at least, there was an emphasis on entertaining at home, as families sought to develop their local social circle, as well as spending time with kin and celebrating special occasions. In this context, dining spaces and practices

– and their corresponding wares and decorations – were viewed as increasingly important. Cutlery and tableware became more elaborate, and were produced in greater quantities (Davidoff and Hall [1987] 2002: 399), and in the United States the increased availability of and demand for silver resulted in the industry's creation of display-worthy specialty pieces fit for the stand-alone dining room (Williams 1996: 67–68).

Yet older rituals of hospitality were not quite swept away on a tide of silver-plated cutlery. Rather, they were transformed for a new age, and appropriated by larger groups of people who used them to claim new kinds of status for themselves. As this chapter will show, hospitality and dining rituals were reinvented in the nineteenth century. Because these rituals and practices were often based on idealized models of etiquette touted in British and American domestic manuals, women's magazines and print culture (models which themselves were being revised and updated as the century progressed), when enacted by middle-class families, their corresponding performances of hospitality that took shape in dining rooms, kitchens and parlours reflected complex patterns of social stratification. In both Britain and North America, increasingly urban and mobile societies brought about by industrialization produced new, transient domestic spaces, including hotels and lodging houses, residential institutions that housed working men and factory girls, and institutional living facilities like asylums and workhouses. These temporary or community-based housing models reworked older versions of hospitality in modern commercial or correctional contexts.

While the home remained important for sociability, historians of both Britain and America have tended to define it as separate from the public world, as a closed space that created status through exclusivity rather than an open one which welcomed strangers (Davidoff and Hall [1987] 2002; Cott [1977] 1997: 64–74). Leonore Davidoff and Catherine Hall argued that the late eighteenth and early nineteenth centuries saw a consolidation and growth in a new middle-class culture that emphasized the value of gentility (Davidoff and Hall [1987] 2002: 398). This involved the extension of hospitality to business contacts, important neighbours and kin – but this was a select social circle (Davidoff and Hall [1987] 2002: 399; Davidoff, 1973: 80). However, recent work has shown that domestic space must be seen as public and permeable in a variety of ways – through the presence of visitors, men who worked from home, and servants as well as through print culture (Donald 1999; Hamlett 2010: 29–72). In their study of Glaswegian middle-class homes, Eleanor Gordon and Gwyneth Nair challenged the long-standing view of the home as private and concluded that: 'The abundant hospitality offered to family, friends and sometimes strangers gave the Victorian household a sociability and public character which seem far removed from the rather sedate and claustrophobic family-centered life portrayed in some of the literature' (2003: 118). They also pointed out that the majority of socializing in middle-class families took place on a casual, relaxed basis, with little to do with formal visiting rituals (2003: 115–17).

On both sides of the Atlantic it was women who were charged with cultivating and delivering the century's evolving domestic practices. In Britain, there was a new emphasis on the role of the hostess, and domestic sociability became increasingly female-dominated over the century (Davidoff and Hall [1987] 2002: 398; Tosh 1999: 170–94). Women's leadership and expertise drove advances in home management in the United States, and was especially important in the development of domestic science at the turn of the century (Shapiro [1986] 2001: 9). However, scholars' reconsideration of the prevailing 'separate spheres' approach to public and private spaces, which once dominated thinking about American domestic life, has prompted an examination of the public influence of the private, not only in terms of the public and political value of women's work, but, as Monika Elbert suggests, the interdependence and convergence of men's and women's roles within and outside the home (Elbert 2000). Such an approach suggests women's and men's interdependence in the performance of hospitality rituals.

The practice of being hospitable, especially in the context of the shared meal, took different forms in different social groups. As Frank Prochaska has shown, gifts of food and material support remained a crucial part of working-class networks of mutual support in the nineteenth century (1990: 362). And in common lodging houses, small hospitalities such as a share of beer or bacon were an important means of establishing friendship (Hamlett 2015: 133). Class difference became especially important in US writers' approaches to domesticity. Nicole Tonkovich points out that, although initially inspired by their English counterparts, US domestic manual writers cultivated their own brand of advice grounded specifically in American class differences and geographical diversity; attention to class would acknowledge – and simultaneously produce – a distinctly American vision of hospitality and home management (Tonkovich 1997: 92–94). In contrast to Britain, scholars looking at the domestic history of North America tend to interpret the growth of refinement in domestic practices as having a broader social remit and being more inclusive (Bushman 1992; Grier 1988: vi–vii).

To what extent do we see a common narrative of civilization or refinement across the nineteenth-century West? This essay uses the techniques of both social history and literary studies to consider the question. The first two parts explore the representation of hospitality and dining practices in Britain and North America – revealing different understandings of what hospitality should constitute, and where and how sharing a meal should take place. The first section takes a cultural history approach to advice literature on dining and entertaining in middle- and upper-class homes published in England in the second half of the nineteenth century, exploring the representation of the rituals of hospitality and showing how new emphases were placed on decorating the key spaces for entertaining in the home – the drawing room and the dining room – as well as the performance of the role of hostess by the lady of the house. The second section employs literary study and close reading of primary texts to show how a selection of American writers used fictional and non-fiction narratives to respond to hospitality instruction appearing in domestic manuals. Through dramatizing dinner table and kitchen interactions, these writers illustrated the complex web of social expectations and interactions implicit in the performance of hospitality rituals and offered important commentary on the social hierarchies reinforced through these performances, especially as their characters or subjects fall short of carrying out appropriate hospitality practices. Finally, drawing on recent cultural and social histories, the essay offers an overview of the emergence of other types of hospitality beyond the home in Britain and the US in commercial spaces such as hotels, restaurants and lodging houses as well as new residential institutions, including lunatic asylums and workhouses.

ADVICE ON HOSPITALITY AND DINING FOR THE ENGLISH MIDDLE AND UPPER CLASSES

In nineteenth-century England, advice on how homes should be decorated, arranged and managed, and how one should behave in them, proliferated in print culture.[2] This was partly a product of an expanding print market that drew on new technologies, but was also driven by consumer demand from the expanding middle classes (Hamlett 2010: 15). We cannot necessarily assume that advice was followed, indeed it has been argued that the very presence of prescriptive literature is evidence that people did not adhere to it (Vickery 1993). But while we cannot take advice as an indicator of what people actually did, we can use it, as Rachel Rich has recently argued, to uncover shared cultural views on what domesticity should consist of (2011: 30). It is also clear that domestic advice writers did not speak with a single voice. Disagreement among commentators, or different points of view, can reveal the process of the construction of domestic rites and rituals, and it is also a reminder that then, as now, people exercised their own choice and agency to interpret domesticity in their own way. Reading advice on decoration, domestic management and etiquette allows us to see the emergence and evolution of ideas about how spaces should be used for entertaining in English homes, and how certain rituals developed, including the use of calling cards, 'At Homes', dinner parties and the 5 o'clock tea. As we will see, there was an emphasis, from mid-century, on the creation of drawing rooms and dining rooms with certain decorative styles linked to ideas of national identity and gender. The social value of hospitality continued to be stressed, and increasing attention was paid to the role of the hostess.

From the mid-century there was a consensus that middle-class English homes should have a drawing room and a dining room. This allowed the separation of spaces for socializing and eating; the drawing room was the main reception room for visitors, but large-scale entertaining such as luncheons or dinner parties took place in the dining room. Ideas about how these public spaces should be decorated and furnished were quite set, and associated with gender and national identity (Kinchin 1996; Hamlett 2009). According to the architect Robert Kerr, whose seminal book *The Gentleman's House* was first published in the 1860s (discussed at length in Chapter 3), 'The character to be always aimed at in a Drawing-room is especial cheerfulness, refinement of elegance, and what is called lightness as opposed to massiveness ... to be entirely ladylike. The comparison of dining-room and drawing-room, therefore, is in almost every way one of contrast' (1871: 107). It was recommended that drawing rooms were decorated in a light 'feminine' style, perhaps using French furniture, whereas dining rooms were to be given a darker, more solid treatment. English oak was one of the preferred woods for dining room furniture. These stylistic prescriptions were linked to the idea that the rooms were seen as separate terrains of the master and mistress of the house (Hamlett 2009) (Figure 7.1).

By the 1870s, these conventions drew the ire of a new generation of decorative advisers, fed up with what they saw as stultifying practices that prevented the expression of artistic taste (Eastlake 1878: 71–72). Groundbreaking female interior designers Agnes and Rhoda Garrett found dining rooms particularly wanting: '[screens] together with the gloomy appearance of the rest of the room, remind one of the British boast that every Englishman's house is his castle, and that he wishes neither to observe or be observed when he retires in dignified seclusion to this, the most masculine department of the household' (1877: 28). In the final decades of the century, this dense, dark space had begun to be decorated in new ways as an interest in aesthetic or artistic furnishing began to take hold (Gere and Hoskins 2000). In 1902, H.J. Jennings, in his book *The House Beautiful*, reflected on the decoration of the historical and the contemporary English home, offering reworked versions of the drawing and dining room that picked up on new trends in art nouveaux furnishing. Significantly though, while the style of furnishing had changed, the basic gendered associations of the space, and kind of atmosphere it was expected to foster, remained the same. Jennings writes of the drawing room: 'The whole atmosphere of the room is changed with the gracious refinements of woman's subtle spell' (1902: 173).

The major social event that took place in Victorian dining rooms was the dinner party. During the nineteenth century, the timings of meals changed – more men worked outside the home, not returning until the evening, and the arrival of oil and later gas light encouraged meals to become more spread out during the day. By the 1850s, it was normal to have breakfast, lunch, tea and

FIGURE 7.1: The ideal drawing room and dining room, and masculine and feminine behaviours, reversed. From 'The Ladies of Creation', in J. Leech, *Pictures of Life and Character. . . from the Collection of Mr Punch* (London: Bradbury & Evans, 1857), 14.

supper, and amongst the middle classes there was a stronger emphasis on evening dinner parties as social occasions (Rich 2011: 73–74; Davidoff 1973: 47). Rich argues that from the mid-nineteenth century, the hostess began to be expected to take the main responsibility for the dinner party rather than the host (2011: 49). This would have included sending invitations, organizing food and rooms, writing menus, tactfully instructing guests in the drawing room on who they were to lead into dinner and standing up at the end of the meal to signal the ladies' departure for the drawing room (2011: 106–9). This hostess role was emphasized in didactic advice to girls. A 1910 piece in *The Girl's Own Paper*, 'Good Taste as a Hostess', listed lengthy duties including the need to be aware of everyone's rank and to match up male and female pairs who were to be sent into dinner together accordingly (Anon. 1910: 97). Women were also charged with the maintenance of basic etiquette and table manners. As *Hostess and Guest* put it in 1877, careful guidance in this matter would insure against 'misguided individuals who eat peas with their knives, sending shudders through their fair neighbors with each knife load' (Anon. 1877: 2). Men, however, were able to escape from the rigours of dinner-table etiquette when the ladies withdrew to the drawing room after dinner. The behaviour that ensued was satirized by the artist John Leech in a cartoon originally published in *Punch* in the 1850s, showing role reversal in the drawing room and dining room (Figure 7.2).

Discussions of new ways of serving dinner and table decoration also implied a greater female involvement. Dining à la Russe (in the Russian style) – in which courses were served in succession by servants rather than the whole meal being spread out on the table in front of guests and carved by the host – was popular from the 1860s.[3] Serving the meal in sections left more space on the table for decorations and these became increasingly elaborate. Magazines often offered schemes for this, for example *House* magazine offered a monthly design for 'The Table Tasteful' – a series of extremely complex decorative creations that must have been hard to realize in practice.[4] While this emphasis could be read as the use of female labour to demonstrate social status, it is important to remember that dinner parties were also emotional expressions of sentiment and family feeling (Gordon and Nair 2003: 121–23). A wife or daughter who invested time in a table decoration might see this as an emotional investment in family life. Some writers also celebrated the beauty of the laid table, in flowing prose that acknowledged it as an artistic creation in its own right. Mrs Loftie writes of the dining table: 'There is something most attractive, particularly in hot weather, about a table where all the sweet things, the salad, the milk, the cream, the salt, the flowers, and some of the fruit are in bright, transparent flashing glass, and everything looks pure and clean, cool and inviting' (1878: 35).

Women also led the way in the creation of broader practices of domestic sociability including the use of calling cards, visiting and holding 'At Homes'. During the first half of the century, new social rituals for visiting developed amongst elite society in London. A calling system was used to establish social links and there was an expectation that a call would be returned, if the recipient felt that it was appropriate that the caller should enter their social circle (Davidoff 1973: 42). A complex etiquette developed around the practice of leaving cards, which were sometimes used as a means of establishing whether or not a lady of higher social status would receive an acquaintance from lower down the social scale (Davidoff 1973: 43). Cards and calling continued to be discussed in women's magazines, etiquette manuals and domestic advice in the second half of the nineteenth century, but they often remained bewildering. In 1877, the anonymous author of *Hostess and Guest* reported 'considerable uncertainty about card leaving' (Anon. 1877: 120). The domestic advice writer Jane Ellen Panton dismissed the practice completely: 'Formal visiting I never will and can go in for . . . if people are only known casually and in such a manner that to call on them is an effort . . . cherished with the hope, that the person one calls on, card-case in hand, will be out: life is too short for such nonsense' (1873: 112). All the same, a grasp of the intricacies of calling and card leaving continued to be seen as an important part of the education of well-to-do young women. In a piece in *The Girl's Own Paper* in 1900, a wayward young girl who is at first bored by the complexities of the calling card system is taught its social value (Anon. 1900a: 427). Busy women who did not have time to devote to receiving calls throughout the week were also recommended to adopt the practice of having an 'At Home' – a day or afternoon set aside every week or so where they were officially at home to friends. Panton was a keen supporter of this practice, as she believed it freed up more time for women – she dismissed the idea that middle-class women who held 'At Homes' were 'aping their betters', remarking on the practical benefits of being able to prepare tea and refreshments in advance, and to have servants on standby (1873: 112).

The second half of the century saw the growing prominence of the 5 o'clock tea as both a ritual within the family and a social meal extended to guests. The tea was a particularly female event (in some homes men would not return from work in time for it) held in the drawing room and presided over by the lady of the house who would pour out the tea and distribute light foodstuffs. While a basic family tea might consist solely of bread and butter, an 'At Home' tea could be quite extensive. Mrs Beeton's *Cookery Book* included a number of menus specifically for 'At Home' teas, including extensive lists of delicacies, tea, coffee and even alcoholic drinks such as champagne and claret cups (Beeton 1891: 264). The growing popularity of the 5 o'clock tea in England was underpinned by rising consumption of tea imported from colonial India, which as Suzanne Daly has shown, was a colonial product that was reinvented in the nineteenth century as an 'emblem of English middle-class domesticity' (2011: 84). Panton was a strong advocate of the afternoon tea, as a cheaper and more practical

FIGURE 7.2: Illustration showing a number of possible cakes. 'Cakes', from Mrs Beeton, *Mrs Beeton's Cookery Book and Household Guide* (London: Ward, Lock, Bowden, 1891), 151.

FIGURE 7.3: Illustration showing an ideal five o'clock tea. From Mrs Beeton, *Mrs Beeton's Cookery Book and Household Guide* (London: Ward, Lock, Bowden, 1891), 263.

alternative to the dinner party for young women starting out on housekeeping. Her depiction of the tea paraphernalia evokes a cosy sense of domesticity and intimacy. Small and sturdy tea tables were essential, to be laid with 'The best five-o'-clock teacloth ... a fine white damask edged with torchon lace ... A nice copper kettle and a trivet should also be brought in with tea' (Panton 1873: 89–90). The 5 o' clock tea, as an expression of the female domination of home, was, according to John Tosh, one of the factors that drove men out of the domestic sphere in the late nineteenth century, in what he argues was a 'flight from domesticity' (1999: 180). But some men viewed feminine domesticity with a more humorous eye. The art critic and advice writer Charles Locke Eastlake, for example, wrote an amusing commentary on his wife's tea parties – while he made it clear he absented himself from them: 'I am seldom present on these festive occasions' – his bantering tone suggests that he did not feel unseated or threatened (Easel 1895: 59).

DINING SPACES AND PRACTICES IN NORTH AMERICAN NOVELS

In the United States, writers of both fictional and non-fiction narratives dramatized the calls for domesticity that appeared in home manuals, cookbooks and other advice literature; in doing so, their narratives actively prescribed and critiqued hospitality practices that shaped American home life. As these narratives introduced kitchen and dining scenes, their casts of characters often experienced culinary failures, perpetuated domestic misunderstandings, or engaged the dinner table as a site of misconduct. In these moments when the performance of domestic practices and hospitality rituals is not carried out effectively – or is carried out to exclusive ends – authors are able to critique the social expectations and exclusions inherent in the domestic manual tradition.

In *Little Women* (1869), Louisa May Alcott provided a persuasive vision of girls' domestic coming of age during the latter half of the nineteenth century, as Meg, Jo, Beth and Amy March recognize not only the discipline and practice required to be a housekeeper but also the degree to which dining spaces, culinary offerings and table rituals can reflect class stratification. Through illustrating a series of domestic failures, Alcott shows the transformation in behaviour and mindset that must occur in order for the girls to perform the ideal hospitality rituals practised by their mother. The March girls' education is best illustrated when their mother grants their wish to take a 'vacation' from their regular chores and duties (Alcott 1922: 87), the consequences of which are telling as they attempt to prepare their own meals in their cook's absence. Even after Meg's failed breakfast, Jo overestimates the ease of cooking and serves an inedible dinner not only to her sisters but to two guests. The girls end their experiment recognizing that 'housekeeping ain't no joke' and that 'something more than energy and good-will is necessary to make a cook' (Alcott 1922: 89, 92). Given their failure, their mother is able to reinforce a now meaningful lesson that 'plain cooking' should be central to the girls' domestic education and that the girls should balance 'work and play' to ensure a well-run home (Alcott 1922: 94–95).

The March girls' route to being domestically capable calls into question the efficacy of the prevailing culture of domestic manuals and cookbooks. In *Little Women*, when employed, advice books alone cannot ensure a successful cook and hostess; trial and error is what precipitates growth. In a scene that Ann Romines suggests mirrors the 'domestic chaos' described above, albeit with 'graver implications' (1992: 10), newly married Meg attempts to make jelly. Consulting her copy of *Mrs. Cornelius's Receipt Book* (possibly *The Young Housekeeper's Friend* (1858) by Mary Cornelius), Meg 'asked advice of Mrs. Cornelius', yet she is unable to get her jelly to jell, a failure that leaves her sobbing, her kitchen overtaken by 'confusion and despair' (Alcott 1922: 222). Even through calling on the manual, Meg experiences, as the real Cornelius's *Friend* suggests, the 'mortification and discomfort in the parlor, and waste and ill temper in the kitchen' that use of such a text sought to remedy (Cornelius 1858: 7). Meg's culinary inexperience reflects poorly on her duties as a wife and hostess, who had otherwise promised to make her home a hospitable place. Embarrassed by the state of her kitchen, Meg refuses to accept her husband's impromptu dinner guest, which results in the couple's first moment of discord within their marriage.

As is the case in many nineteenth-century novels and short stories, Alcott employs the dinner table as a site where the March girls become aware of their place within the class system. This is the case for Amy when she attempts to impress her higher-class art school friends with a 'proper and elegant' lunch

(Alcott 1922: 208). Despite her effort and expenditures, only one of her peers (of the several she expected) attends. Amy recognizes that she had alienated those close to her and embarrassed herself in attempting to throw 'an artistic *fête*' that was beyond her means (Alcott 1922: 208); as a form of recompense, she takes her lunch leftovers to the impoverished Hummel family. Through showing how Amy learns that welcoming guests should be achieved via measures appropriate to one's class position, Alcott upholds standards of frugality laid out by Lydia Maria Child in *The American Frugal Housewife* (Child [1829] 1830: 5–6), and reflects late-nineteenth-century advice that hospitality was 'not to be confused with ostentation' (Williams 1996: 25). Alcott also prescribes a national message of meal-time belonging: through showing hospitality to those in need, young women might find the unexpected gift of satisfaction in their domestic pursuits. Amy's kindness mirrors a scene early in the novel when the girls pass on their Christmas breakfast to the Hummel family. While limited in their own means, the girls recognize that they can – and, per Catharine Beecher's advisement, should ([1841] 1843: 257) – bestow goodness unto those less fortunate. In appreciation for their generous act, Mr Laurence, the girls' rich neighbour, sets their table with 'ice cream, actually two dishes of it, pink and white, and cake and fruit and distracting French bonbons and, in the middle of the table, four great bouquets of hot house flowers' (Alcott 1922: 17). Thus, Alcott suggests that through self-sacrifice and benevolence the girls might reap rewards beyond those their class position might afford them. Yet, as recipients of 'charity', Yvonne Elizabeth Pelletier points out, the March girls are situated within the class system as a family who, like the Hummels, benefit from the generosity of their higher class neighbour (2009: 195).

Kitchen and dining spaces served as sites of hospitality education and class performance; these spaces also gave American women the opportunity to access the far reaches of the globe without having to step too far away from their dinner tables. Kristin Hoganson argues that whereas prior to the Civil War, homemakers might have suppressed their interest in foreign foodways in the spirit of nationalism, towards the turn of the century, global goods and a global worldview developed 'cachet' (2007: 106). Through hosting luncheons and dinner parties that featured international recipes and decor, middle-class American women created their homes as spaces of 'global encounter' (2007: 110). Given the cultural capital of demonstrating a cosmopolitan sensibility, the home, Hoganson suggests, became a place where white middle-class women were able to demonstrate their worldliness yet also participate – even if tacitly – in acts of empire, re-centring the superiority of their race, class and national positioning as they hosted ethnically themed parties.

The increase in travel abroad marked widening popularity in travel tales; domestic writing and advice columns, too, fed armchair travellers' longing for experience. However, these portrayals often marginalized ethnic groups, reducing ethnic identities to material props, Americanized recipes and costumed performances. In the latter part of the nineteenth century and into the twentieth century, American Orientalism was perpetuated via white middle-class women's engagement with material culture, especially Asian objects and novelties that became available for purchase (Yoshihara 2003: 17–18). The increase in the availability of global foods and global decor made it possible to bring this kind of engagement into one's dining room. Whether it be for Javanese coffee (Coleman 1899: 116), Japanese teas (Anon. 1903: 275) or Chinese luncheons (Bosse 1913a), women's periodicals doled out instructions for how to create meals that would suit the globally minded palate, and perhaps more importantly, suggestions for how to transform the dining room and parlour to create an authentic experience. Such articles often included instructions for appropriate table arrangements, flowers, wall pieces, and costumes, as well as suggestions for where such accoutrements might be purchased. In a January 1913 article on throwing a Chinese luncheon, Sara Bosse instructs readers that with appropriate attention to offering 'Oriental embellishments and decorations . . . one's guests will become imbued with that quaint far-away feeling, as if you had transported them into a new and charming land' (1913a: 135). In addition to offering supposedly authentic recipes, Bosse also suggested in an article to women hoping to throw a Chinese party for their church or club that they might want to 'enlist' the help of Chinese boys as a further authenticating measure (1913b: 113).

While instructions for the ethnic-themed party made global encounter seem possible – 'a cultural, educational, and liberating experience akin to the grand tour' that so many white women were unable to take (Yoshihara 2003: 18) – therein also existed the potential for these parties to result in a domestic failure and embarrassment for the hostess. Edwin L. Sabin's short story 'Tea from Japan' (1911) pokes fun at the artificiality of foreign-themed dinners and the gullibility of the hostesses who were so captivated by them. Mrs Johnson, Sabin's hostess, throws a Japanese tea party with an eye for authenticity: she purchased eggshell cups and saucers and chrysanthemums for the table; borrowed a Russian samovar; and goaded her servant boy to dress 'Japanese' as he served her guests. But, she accidentally steeps the fine tea's packaging rather than the small quantity of tea and serves that to her guests, all while praising its excellence. Sabin's story illustrates the capacity for white hostesses like Mrs Johnson to, as Hoganson notes, assert not only their whiteness as they attempt to authenticate their ethnic entertainments, but also their class status (2007: 148–49). In an attempt to woo her guests and demonstrate her access to cosmopolitan refinement, she reveals her own ignorance.

The American domestic manual tradition encouraged a measured and practised approach to dining and housekeeping rituals; in doing so, these texts set a clear power structure in place concerning the role of the mistress of the house and her servants – whether they be enslaved, indentured or hired. Manuals offered guidance on training servants; in doing so, they also laid out a set of appropriate behaviours for servants but also leadership practices for the mistresses themselves. As writers of colour accessed the literary marketplace and published their own accounts of domestic interaction, real and fictional, they illustrated moments in which servants and slaves rejected the proper etiquette forced upon them as labourers. They also illustrated how, in their abuse and mistreatment, mistresses' failed to engage in the suggested patterns of leadership etiquette. Consequently, both the labourers' resistance and the mistresses' failures impacted hospitality practices within the home as they situated the kitchen and dining room as a site of resistance to expected social codes.

Harriet Jacobs, writing under the pseudonym Linda Brent, told of her harrowing experience of enslavement with the Flint family in her 1861 book *Incidents in the Life of a Slave Girl*. Within her non-fiction account, Jacobs suggests that the plantation kitchen and dining room were places the mistress and master of the house executed their control over their slaves in such a way that reveals what Mary Titus suggests the 'perversity of white domination' and thereby the parameters of hospitality and good manners expected of middle-class whites (Titus 1997: 249). Mrs Flint spat in the dishes her cooks had prepared after the dinner service to keep them from eating extra food. Mr Flint forced one of the slaves to eat food she had prepared for the family's dog (Jacobs 1861: 22–23). The Flints' failures contrasted sharply scenes where Jacobs witnessed true hospitality, namely at her grandmother's house, where she is able to receive food and comfort (1861: 19).

In fiction, too, the kitchen and dining rooms became spaces of resistance where black characters were able to resist the hospitality rituals that diminished their own personhood, but also where the white families in power showed how, in their oppressiveness, they defied appropriate practices for hostesses. In Harriet Wilson's *Our Nig* (1859), Frado, a young black servant in a Northern home, is deliberately disruptive after being forced to eat off her mistress's plate; rather than acquiescing to her mistress's demands, Frado has the dog lick from her plate. The scene, which seems to overturn the ideal table etiquette presented in Catharine Beecher's *Treatise on Domestic Economy* (1841), illustrates the dining space where white power can be temporarily called into question. Here, especially, it is the mistress who resists accepted dining rituals and showcases her own domestic failure as she seats a guest, Frado, at her table with neither a clean place setting nor a napkin (Drews 2009: 100). Such accounts of the domestic failures of slave owners and Northern mistresses confirmed Frederick Douglass's argument that 'the fatal poison of irresponsible power' inherent under slavery could turn an otherwise 'angelic' white mistress into 'a demon' (1845: 33); this 'poison' would continue to impact how Americans would regard the irony of hospitality rituals, where providing a site of welcome and comfort was grounded in the dehumanizing treatment of others.

Writers of colour produced their own domestic manuals, cookbooks and domestic fiction as a way of combating racism that played out in the domestic sphere and giving evidence of their progress and civility as keepers of their own homes and traditions. Booker T. Washington published a short piece in the *Colored American Magazine* in 1902 extolling the order and cleanliness of African American homes in the South: 'There was from kitchen to parlor a measure of delicacy, sweetness and refinement that made one feel that life was worth living' (1902: 379). W.E.B. DuBois celebrated the domestic progress of black families at the turn of the century when he presented his 'American Negro' exhibit at the 1900 Paris World's Fair. Special attention was given in the exhibit to showcasing images of African American homes (Richter 2015: 107). Rafia Zafar points out that long before writers like Lydia Maria Child and Catharine Beecher gained notoriety for their domestic manuals, Robert Roberts, an African American butler, published *The House Servant's Directory; or, A Monitor for Private Families*, in 1827. Written as a manual to help servants best fulfil the expectations of their employers, Roberts' work illustrated the ways in which servants' pathway to 'secur[ing] independent livelihoods' required working within master/servant hierarchies, or, Zafar notes, 'at least pay[ing] lip service to' them (2009: 140–41).

HOSPITALITY AND DINING BEYOND THE HOME IN BRITAIN AND NORTH AMERICA

While the nineteenth century saw a growth in the celebration of the home in both Britain and North America, this was also the period in which more people lived outside it than ever before – in new commercial living spaces as well as residential institutions. These places did not offer hospitality in the sense of an individual host providing for a guest, but they did provide a place to stay or to live, and meals for large numbers of people together, with a company or superintendent acting as a host on a commercial or institutional basis. Within these places, older ideas of hospitality, and dining spaces and the rituals that went with them were transformed. While hotels developed in both Britain and America, US establishments grew faster and were larger. By the 1820s, these 'Palaces of the Public' dotted the East Coast and became more elaborate in the following decades. Notable establishments included Boston's Tremont House (1829), Astor House in New York (1836) and Fifth Avenue Hotel (1859), the first to introduce a passenger elevator (Berger 1998: 41–46). Increasing mobility, migration from Europe and large numbers of people travelling across the continent drove the expansion of hotels in the US. By offering elite hospitality to anyone who could afford to pay, hotels were associated with a specifically

American idea of democracy and sociability (Cocks 2001: 72). There was much commentary on their particular style of hospitality, which revolved around the use of a table d'hôte or host's table – at which all the guests ate together at a set hour, presided over by the hotel manager, from a large number of dishes set before them on the tables. This form of hospitality that was both commercial and communal was thought to convey a national sense of community and public culture (Sandoval-Strausz 2007: 143). For the writer Nathaniel Willis, the shared dining hall in the American hotel was 'a tangible republic', that was much mourned when it was replaced with the European system of ordering from an à la carte menu later in the century (Cocks 2001: 74).

While American establishments led the way, elaborate hotels also began to develop across the Atlantic in Britain from the 1860s and 1870s. Geographical mobility was a key driver, and the railway hotels were often the first and best (Burnett 2004: 70–76). In London, Claridge's, the Savoy and the Ritz emerged in the final decades of the century and were followed by more populist establishments such as the Strand Palace Hotel, opened in 1909 by Lyons and Co., offering something of the glitz of the elite for more limited budgets (Holcombe 2013: 126–29). Although British and US hotels initially operated different systems of hospitality, with the American hosts presiding over shared dining tables, gendered notions of domesticity influenced both. On both sides of the Atlantic there were separate parlours or drawing rooms and sometimes dining rooms for female use. Male protectors and relatives were allowed into the spaces assigned to women, so patriarchal status allowed men to enter both spaces (Berger 1998: 53).

Urbanization, migration and the movement of people also meant that lodging or boarding in commercially run houses were very familiar experiences in the nineteenth century. One estimate suggests that between a third and a half of American urban residents were boarders or took in boarders themselves (Gamber 2007: 3). But there were also large numbers of lodging houses in England, which were rapidly increasing in the second half of the nineteenth century both in smarter boarding houses intended for white-collar workers and the infamous common lodging houses where a bed could be rented on a nightly basis (Kay 2003: 43; Hamlett 2015: 112). Even just looking at the more genteel examples, there was a great deal of cultural commentary on the kinds of hospitality meted out in these places. In England, the social situation of lodgers was often the butt of jokes in publications such as *Punch* (Hamlett 2010: 168). As Wendy Gamber has shown, North American cultural commentators were particularly exercised by the provision of food and dining practices in boarding houses (2007: 77–90). By the end of the century, the term 'boarder's reach' was widely recognized – signifying lapses in men who, accustomed to competing with fellow boarders, grabbed at victuals when they arrived on the table (Gamber 2007: 92). In the British *Girl's Own Paper*, young women living away from home in lodgings for the first time were cautioned not to become lax in laying the table for themselves – the correct cutlery, including butter knives, was always to be used (Hamlett 2010: 164).

The excess of cultural commentary on these issues probably reflected a wider anxiety in society on the effects of people living in commercial spaces outside what was perceived to be the ideal home. Landladies on the make were problematic, as they conflicted with conventional expectations about hospitality and the image of the generous lady hostess. However, personal testimony from boarders on both sides of the Atlantic also suggests that life in lodging houses could be genuinely difficult (Gamber 2007: 87; Hamlett 2010: 166–70). The diaries of George Rose, a clerk at a gas works in Dalston in London, who lodged in Kilburn in the early 1900s reveal the failings of hospitality in boarding houses. He found it particularly difficult to cope with his landlady's failure to serve meals at a regular time, writing in October 1904: 'What a wretched poor existence this is when there is a landlady to combat, when meals are irregular and time is wasted'.[5]

In addition to the growing number of commercial spaces, the second half of the nineteenth century was an era of the growth of residential institutions and spaces for the containment of the poor. Following the introduction of the New Poor Law in 1834, workhouses were built across the England and Wales, in an attempt to reform the older system of poor relief which was predominantly based on outdoor relief and was administered on a local basis. While the care of the poor had not been seen as the direct responsibility of aristocratic households since the sixteenth century (Heal 1990: 402), the new system dramatically reversed the basic idea of hospitality that had been present in older institutions of relief such as hospitals and almshouses that were maintained by parishes and benefactors (Stevenson 2000: 2–3). Designed as a deterrent, living arrangements in the workhouse were made as unpleasant as possible, to discourage the poor from seeking help. Officials spent time calculating the exact amounts of food they believed necessary to keep human beings alive and just about functional (Gurney 2015: 72–76). The degree of privation varied between workhouses but at their worst, as in the Andover Scandal of 1845, where inmates were found gnawing at old bones they had been given to crush, conditions were very bad (Longmate 2003: 129). Meals were doled out into tin receptacles designed not to allow extra portions, under the watchful eye of overseers (Fowler 2007: 62). Later in the century, photographers captured the dehumanizing effect of workhouse dining arrangements, where large numbers of paupers were ranged on benches, facing in the same direction, eating their identical portions (Figure 7.4). Dining room scenes conveyed the inequities of the workhouse and were often evoked by reformers, from Dickens' depiction of Oliver Twist's pleas to George R. Sims' famous poem 'In the Workhouse: Christmas Day' (1877), in which an elderly pauper confounds the workhouse

FIGURE 7.4: 'At Dinner', St. Marylebone Workhouse, *c.* 1901. From George Sims, *Living London*, vol. 2 (London: Cassell, 1902–3), 102.

authorities by refusing Christmas pudding on the grounds that it is a reminder of his wife's death a year before, when she was refused outdoor relief by the same parish officers (Longmate 2003: 223–24). The poem draws attention to the inadequacy of the small hospitalities meted out to inmates at Christmas in the context of a larger framework of social injustice.

Both Britain and the United States were fundamentally opposed to significant state intervention and welfare provision in this era, and instead attempts to assist the poor in society came largely from private individuals and philanthropists. These schemes were often focused on developing new kinds of living spaces for the working classes. Britain was thought to lead the way in housing reform, and American social reformers were strongly influenced by British schemes (Adam 2007: 158). In Britain, particular attention was paid to creating model lodging houses and large-scale institutions for working men (Hamlett 2015: 135–59). While these schemes were designed to help, they were not straightforward exercises in charitable hospitality in the older sense. On the contrary, it was now seen as important that they should be financially sustainable and not undermine the integrity of the men, so a fee was usually charged for board and residence. A notable scheme was the creation of Rowton Houses by a company founded by the Tory peer and philanthropist Lord

Rowton (Hamlett and Preston 2013: 93–108). Six large institutions (billed as 'hotels for working men') were built in London in the late nineteenth and early twentieth centuries and particular attention was paid to the creation of dining spaces within them. While men were given space to do their own cooking if required, there were also large, airy dining rooms. The images chosen for their walls were notable for their popular and inclusive cultural range (Hamlett and Preston 2013: 96). In Britain, less attention was paid to the needs of working women and institutional lodgings were not successfully established for them until the early twentieth century (Gee 2009). In the US, attempts were made to provide special lodgings for female workers much earlier, as the rapid spread of industry in rural areas and villages put pressure on factory owners to create housing for workers, who were often female. The Boston Manufacturing Company, founded by Frances Cabot Lowell, employed young women almost exclusively in its textile mills. Special boarding houses were constructed for the young female employees, where they were watched over by a respectable housemother and ate, slept and attended church at appropriate times (Wright 1981: 66–69). The food was apparently good but some of the ambiguity residents felt about their institutional existence is conveyed in the way that the 'eating room' is described in a resident's own writings as 'demolished in its precincts' yet 'always amply furnished with chairs and tables . . . for, amidst all our deprivations, we have never been deprived of the privilege of sitting at our meals . . .'.[6]

In addition to creating new places for the working classes, the nineteenth century was also an era in which a large number of new institutions for the care of the mentally ill were established. Older hospitals, such as London's Bethlem, established by charitable benefactors in the early modern period, now existed alongside a new range of lunatic asylums, built and administered by state and local authorities in Britain and America. In these modern and increasingly large institutional spaces, the domestic rituals of hospitality and dining came to play an important role. On both sides of the Atlantic, doctors and asylum authorities increasingly emphasized the use of moral treatment in caring for patients (Digby 1985; Dwyer 1987). Moral treatment consisted of keeping patients warm and dry, providing decent meals and clothes, and attempting to get patients to work and live according to 'normal' domestic patterns (Hickman 2009; Yanni 2007; Dwyer 1987: 4, 13; Hamlett 2015). At the New York State Asylum in Utica, patients rose early for a 7 o'clock breakfast, dinner was at half past twelve and tea at six was followed by an early bedtime (Dwyer 1987: 15). Instructions for asylum attendants laid great stress on the need to make sure that meals proceeded in an orderly fashion: tables were to be correctly laid, patients were to be clean and tidy, and to be encouraged to behave as well as possible. According to a manual for staff at Brookwood Hospital, Surrey's second county asylum: 'The Attendants . . . at the table must encourage them [the patients] to use the knives and forks in a proper manner, and not to eat with their fingers as some are inclined to do'.[7] In the English system, institutions set up for middle- and upper-class patients placed an even greater emphasis on dining as a performance of social niceties. Holloway Sanatorium, for example, offered an elite form of hospitality. Deliberately drawing on the conventions of new hotels, dinner was advertised as a table d'hôte and served in an elaborately decorated dining hall, at individual tables (Hamlett 2015: 52) (see Figure 7.5). But such spaces did not always have the desired effect. Alice Rose O., a former governess who was a patient at Holloway in the 1900s, wrote home to a relative: 'I have just come from afternoon tea (more like that of a workhouse tea), one patient is just filthy, there is no other word, it makes one fairly sick. The poor lady is

FIGURE 7.5: Interior of the dining hall at Holloway Sanatorium. From *The Graphic*, 22 October (1881), 425.

irresponsible that is one thing. The table cloths are not as good as our kitchen ones'.[8] For this patient, the asylum's institutional associations overrode its attempt to create an elite form of hospitality.

CONCLUSION

In nineteenth-century England and North America, hospitality remained a fundamental part of home life, but it was also transformed as it was taken up and practised in new contexts by different social groups. Domestic advice published in Britain in the second half of the nineteenth century reveals that entertaining was seen as crucial in middle- and upper-class homes, and there was a strong emphasis on the role of the lady of the house as hostess in achieving it. The celebration of the hostess, and the great emphasis placed on her behaviour and attention to detail was partly a product of a new, Evangelical middle-class ideology that put virtuous womanhood at the centre of the home, but it was also a continuation of an older idea of hospitality as a display of beneficence and virtue, albeit one that was now practised more exclusively within middle-class families and social and business circles.

As writers in North America illustrated scenes where domestic advice was put into practice, readers were able to see the disconnect between the domestic order such advice intended and the failures, misinterpretations and misconduct writers dramatized in their narrative accounts. Ultimately, this disconnect identified the ways in which hospitality rituals and other domestic practices, when performed, could perpetuate divisions among class, nation and racial groups but could also serve as opportunities for subversion. While works like Alcott's *Little Women* suggested domestic education – especially that of cooking and hosting a meal -- was an important part of young women's coming of age, that education was at times only earned through failed attempts. Advice literature that spoke to readers' interest in world travel encouraged the performance of ethnic identities through throwing themed luncheons or dinner parties. Such events might have allowed women access to a form of global encounter, but they perpetuated concerning stereotypes and reaffirmed Western ideals. Black writers, especially those writing in the context of slavery or enforced servitude, illustrated the failures of white families' domestic management, failures that often overturned prescriptions for domestic management, and the ways in which black writers were able to respond to those prescriptions as a form of resistance.

Older ideas of hospitality also informed the wide range of new commercial and residential institutions that were established during our period. Society in Britain and North America was modern, increasingly industrial and above all mobile. This created the conditions for grand hotels and boarding and lodging houses to flourish. However, the critical discussions that some of these places attracted reveal a discomfort with hospitality as a form of commercial exchange, that contrasted with idealized visions of domestic life. The plight of industrial workers produced attempts to provide them with suitable accommodation, often provided on a semi-philanthropic basis, but usually with the intention of raising the moral standards of the working classes through encouraging adherence to middle-class domestic practices. The increased emphasis on the idea that hospitality should not be doled out to the poor for free was realized in its most extreme form in the workhouse in England and Wales. Workhouses offered a kind of reverse hospitality in that it was hoped that terrible conditions would act as a deterrent. Yet despite this use of domestic practices for social exclusion there was also a basic idea that home routines and dining rituals could be shared across social groups, and it was for this reason that moral therapy and the daily rituals of eating, sleeping and dressing were seen as a potential salvation for even pauper asylum patients – here at least the ideal was inclusive.

CHAPTER EIGHT

Religion and the Home: Lived Religion in Working-Class Households

LUCINDA MATTHEWS-JONES

Britain was a religious place in the nineteenth century. The tenets of Christianity, especially, directed people's personal lives and relationships and permeated their novels, poetry and art. Although Protestantism was the official state religion (with authority vested in the Anglican Church of England and Wales, the Presbyterian Church of Scotland and, until 1871, the Anglican/Episcopalian Church of Ireland), Britain was a religiously plural society. Since the English Civil War, there had been growth in dissenting non-conformist religious groups, including the Quakers, Unitarians, Baptists and Congregationalists. These non-Anglican Protestants did not adhere to the Acts of Uniformity (1559, 1662) and thus questioned the hierarchy of the established Church, simultaneously promoting simplicity of worship. The growth of the interdenominational Evangelical movement from the eighteenth century onward led many Protestant groups, including many Anglicans, to advocate personal salvation, the importance of the Bible and social activism. But Britain was also a largely tolerant society. By 1851, the religious census listed Methodists, Congregationalists, Baptists, Roman Catholics, Presbyterians, Unitarians, Mormons, Quakers, Plymouth Brethren, Moravians and Jews worshipping alongside one another. The 1851 census is perhaps more famous for the proof it provided for declining church attendance. While some historians have taken this as evidence of secularization in the nineteenth century, others have pointed to a transformation rather than a decline of religious practices at this time. The home is a site that can help us understand this transformation.

Homes were religious spaces in the nineteenth century. Not only were they infused with a religious ideology of domesticity, they were also spaces where people experienced, articulated and negotiated their religious identity on a day-to-day basis. Leonore Davidoff and Catherine Hall's *Family Fortunes* (1987) examined how the rise of evangelical domesticity in the nineteenth century enabled a new urban middle class to solidify its identity along with its political and social power. They suggest that the sanctity of home was seen by this class as offsetting the profane and immoral workings of the public sphere, adding that these ideas were adopted, for example, across Birmingham's Anglican, Quaker, Congregationalist and Unitarian groups. This argument was picked up by John Tosh (1999), who likewise suggested that domestic evangelism played a role in patriarchal domestic authority in the nineteenth century. Home was thought of in this context as a place for the cultivation of the religious rituals and character of its inhabitants, directed by the head of the household.

However, the majority of the nineteenth-century population lived in very different circumstances to the newly wealthy middling sorts that are often the focus of discussions of religious experience. According to Sarah C. Williams, working-class religious households have not received the same attention because historians have too often elided religious morality with middle-class identity and made problematic assumptions about the secularization of the working classes in the nineteenth century. She argues that historians have been blinded to the ways in which the working classes developed their own distinct religious domesticity (Williams 2010: 11–31). Traditional historians of religion, such as K.S. Inglis (1964) and E.R. Wickham (1964), argued that the working classes were central to Britain's process of secularization in the Victorian era. Their understanding of working-class religious faith was informed by nineteenth-century social commentators and clergymen who believed, like Horace Mann, that the working class were 'unconscious secularists' (Mann quoted in Williams 2010: 12). Such official discourses not only overlooked the ways in which the working-class home was invested with religious and spiritual meaning by occupants themselves, but also the fluidity and malleable nature of class itself (Hewitt 2004: 305–20). Being working class was not tied to a universalized secular experience, nor should it be assumed that stratification within the working classes led certain economic groups to be more religious than others. Religion was (and is) a subjective experience that demands consideration at an individual and at a family level.

The modern period witnessed new religious practices and religious pluralism. While there is a longstanding association between the nineteenth century and the emergence of a secular society, revisionist scholars argue that this was not the result of an urban industrial working class (see Cox 1982; MacLeod 1996;

Morris 1992). Working-class domestic religion was expressed and experienced differently to the ideals advocated by the middle classes. Indeed, the reluctance on the part of the working classes to let the middle-class domestic visitor into their homes was not always indicative of non-belief or secularization, but rather a way for families to maintain control over their home and their religious expression (Hewitt 1999: 121–41; Christie 2003: 162). This chapter focuses on religion in working-class households – which were in fact the places in which most people first came into contact with religious ideas and had their first religious experiences – and are therefore an essential, although a little told part of the story of religion and home in the nineteenth century.

This chapter will explore how domestic religion was articulated within a prism that emphasized specific rituals (such as prayers and hymns), temporalities (holidays and Sundays) and material objects (bibles, other religious texts, and clothes). Scholars are increasingly thinking about new ways to investigate the relationship between religion and society. It draws on the concept of lived religion to reveal how working-class religious households were both personal and familial spaces of religious belief. They are, as Nancy T. Ammerman (2006) has noted, looking to understand the seeming paradox of religion's simultaneous absence and presence in the modern world. According to Ammerman, everyday religion should be understood as happening outside the remit of organized religion and in the realm of 'non-experts;. She writes: 'It may have to do with mundane routines, but it may also have to do with the crises and special events that punctuate those routines . . . the many ways religion may be interwoven with the lives of the people we have been observing' (2006: 4). Ammerman's decision to investigate the individual dimensions of faith has been matched by a growing awareness that an individual lives and experiences their religion in the personal realm. To fully comprehend the role of religion in modern societies, we must consider what Meredith B. McGuire has described as 'religion-as-lived' (2008: 15).

For historians, this means re-orienting our study of religious faith away from religious dogma and theology to the everyday spaces of belief, which includes the home as a key site. If we do, then we will find that religious faith in the nineteenth century was personal, collective and contested. As David D. Hall (1997), the historian of American religion, has contended, the concept of lived religion forces us to examine the dynamic but small aspects of religious people's daily lives. This builds on the work of Callum Brown, who has suggested that historians consider how our modern historical subjects engaged with the parameters of discursive Christianity. At the heart of Brown's discursive Christianity is a commitment to consider how religious subjectivity is expressed by Christians and 'how they in their words reflected Christianity'. For him discursive Christianity defines a 'people's subscription to protocols of personal identity which they derive from Christian experiences, or discourses' (Brown

2009: 12). These protocols are linked to specific rituals, behaviours and dress (2009: 12–13). Discursive Christianity merges both formal and informal expressions of faith. The religious household provides the space in which to understand the way people lived their faith within Britain's vibrant and varied religious landscape.

Drawing on a wide-ranging survey of working-class life writings from across the nineteenth century, this chapter will demonstrate how religion was experienced. It utilizes the experiences of working-class men and women identified as coming from a religious background by the Burnett Archives of Working-Class Autobiographies to illustrate, firstly, how these authors remembered their homes as religious spaces and, secondly, to reveal the significant role fathers, mothers and their families played in the development of a domestic religious selfhood. It will begin by considering the domestic elements of faith by examining the role of the family and how children were encouraged to engage with religion in their homes. Then it will consider the rituals and rhythms of domestic faith by examining Sunday domestic worship through reading, music and hymns. The chapter then moves on to examine the material dimensions of domestic religion. The final part of the chapter considers the unhomely experiences of religion in the religious household.

DOMESTIC FAITH IN WORKING-CLASS FAMILIES

The family was often the focal point for discussion of lived domestic religion. It is well known how this worked in middle-class families (Tosh 1999; Davidoff and Hall 1987), but autobiographies reveal the extent of this in working households as well. Memoirists reveal how important both parents were for the articulation and dissemination of belief within the family. Working-class fathers evidently played a pivotal role in the religious instruction of their children, challenging both Brown's (2009) and Tosh's (1999) assertions that the nineteenth century witnessed the emergence of a dominant female piety. All of Hilda Rose Fowler's siblings, for example, were taught hymns by their builder 'Dad', but, in keeping with the practices of the day, were encouraged to find their own religious meaning in them. This placed great emphasis on the religious development of children. For Fowler, this meant occasionally misunderstanding the meaning of specific words or ideas. For example, she translated words like 'simplicity' into 'stupidity'. It was only with age that 'the meanings grew and developed as we did'.[1] Alice Maud Chase recollected that her carpenter father, Reuben Moody, 'in a quiet way, was deeply religious'. As a Baptist, 'He read his Bible every day and never laid down to sleep at night, or left his room in the morning without kneeling beside his bed to pray'. While he did not discuss his religious faith with his children, he did answer their questions, and directed them towards religion. Chase was encouraged by her father to temper her 'silly ass' by seeking God's help and wisdom.[2] While it was her mother who gave her a bible on her seventh birthday, it was her father who showed her how to use marginal references and to love the 'Holy Word of God'.[3]

A mother's piety was discussed in the autobiographies but not as much as one would expect given Kelly Mays' contention that working-class life writings convey the image of the 'loving mother' to 'paint a picture of the working-class home as a safe haven in a hostile world' (2008: 347). A handful of accounts do discuss their mother's religiosity. Chase's mother instructed Alice and her siblings in biblical stories while her father was at chapel.[4] For the stonemason and missionary Alfred Ireson, his mother's love and piety were bound up with one another. Hannah Ireson believed that her children were given by God and that it was her duty to 'train the infant mind in all good things'. At the end of the day, she would gather her children around her, according to Alfred Ireson, and 'teach them simple truths of the Bible'. She would also sing hymns to her children including Charles Wesley's 'See Israel's Gentle Shepherd Stand'. For Alfred, '[H]er kindly thoughts and tender prayers were Heaven's best gift'. Hannah Ireson not only made her home sacred, but was sacred herself to her son.[5] Her religiosity would be far-reaching as Ireson moved around England and Scotland for work. Letters from her reminded him, even in some of his more unhomely lodgings, that there were Higher, more noble things to consider.[6] When Ireson ran away from his village home in Peterborough to be with his then domestic servant girlfriend, Emma Holly, who worked in Cambridge, his mother was asked to send on his clothes and tools. She also included his Sunday school bible where she enclosed inside a letter 'full of love and kind thoughts'.[7] Alfred did not stay long in Cambridge, resenting the fact that he could not see his love as much as he wanted to and feeling lonely in an unknown city. He quickly left for London, taking his bible and letter with him.

Yet, fathers' religiosity was discussed in more detail than any of these recollections. Religious authority arguably strengthened a man's position in the home. Similarly, the authors of these autobiographical writings might have been responding to the idea that women are naturally pious. Describing their mother's religiosity might have been about revealing the obvious, whereas a father's religious identity needed to be asserted and reaffirmed in a cultural context that aligned working-class men with secularity and religious disengagement. Callum Brown (2009) argues that separate spheres ideology gendered the home feminine in the nineteenth century. Religious masculinity was instead, he argues, made public through muscular Christianity and voluntary and social clubs. Sarah Williams has argued, conversely, that we 'need to inject variety and dynamism into this period' (2010: 27). Gender was a mirror of society's projections, but it was also a lived experience, and the autobiographies under consideration here seem to challenge the assumption that separate spheres ideology was neatly translated into every working-class home. Turning to memoirs reveals that familial belief was centred on the family, but that usually both parents, rather than just the mother, played a role in constructing religious domesticity.

At the same time, the way in which the working classes wrote about their lives also encourages us to think more carefully about how we define the family in this context. Chase's domestic religion was informed by family members other than parents.[8] Grandparents, aunts and cousins played an important role in a child's experience of religion. Children also appear to have taken it upon themselves to instruct their extended family members in religious matters. Many of the writers of the autobiographies went to Sunday school or attended National Schools. It is likely that they were well versed in moral and theological issues, which they could in turn bring home to their parents and other family members. The child Baptist Nora Hampton made it her mission to sing hymns under her breath to her Uncle Tom in order that she might save him from eternal damnation and hell fire because he did not go to chapel with them, preferring instead to drink.[9] She also took it upon herself to teach her grandmother to read from *The Children's Bible*, a task that she found frustrating, but one that did not stop her becoming a teacher in later life.[10] Despite not being able to read, Hampton's grandmother was a devout woman, leaving her money to the local National School.

Not everyone came to religion as a child or through their family. Some of the autobiographies in my sample are spiritual autobiographies: accounts of spiritual transformation in adulthood. These texts offer a glimpse into lifelong journeys into faith. In the early 1840s, the silk weaver John Castle 'was awakened to a deep sense of my state as a sinner'.[11] In similar language, Emmanuel Lovekin recollected how on turning to the light of God as a young man he had rejected 'Sin and folly'. Having spent much of his younger manhood drinking and spending too much money, Lovekin converted to Primitive Methodism in the late 1840s and knew that 'God through Christ can and has forgiven me'. This was evidenced to Lovekin by the fact that God had spared his life twice, once when he was trapped in the pit, and a second time when he nearly drowned. Lovekin's conversion coincided with his marriage and subsequently the birth of his five children. Unsurprisingly, he 'did what I could to teach them the truth'.[12] In contrast, Castle's faith was more personal and not aligned with a specific religious group. In order to give himself hope, he undertook a sustained tour of local chapels and churches. He was nevertheless left confused by the variety of religious messages he heard by local and visiting preachers.[13] The result was greater personal reflection on the word of God, which lead him to a personal, inward experience of religious faith that centred on the home. He prayed, reading the Acts of Apostles (Acts 15:1–31) and, as a confirmed autodidact, taught himself religion, a practice he extended to those around him. He taught his first wife's brother, Isaac, to read the New Testament.

Other spiritual writers of autobiographies note that their path to religiosity was challenged by domestic activities. Terry found himself turning to religion when he was struggling to be a shopkeeper. 'Having got strong religious impressions', he decided to attend the Chapel and teach at two Sunday schools, one for the Wesleyans and the other connected to the New Connexion Methodists. At home, he planned to read and study the Bible. His intentions were rarely fulfilled, however. In order to subvert his inclination to play the violin in the evening rather than undertake bible study, he took the extreme decision to give his instrument and its green cover, from a former sweetheart, to a beggar, who he thought needed it more than he did. It was only through self-denial that he felt he could give his religious study the attention it deserved.[14] Terry's religious conversion coincided with his decision to marry a woman of 'religious character'. From the time of his 'rough uncultivated' boyhood he had admired a family that lived near his grandmother. Mrs Darley, his school mistress, was noted to be a 'guardian angel' and from a 'higher sphere'. Her children were described as 'neat' and 'orderly', as was her home.[15] On joining the New Connexion Methodists, he was reacquainted with the family and pictures of their domestic idyll came back to him. The love that he held for this family meant that he sought one of the elder girls to be his wife. Sarah Ann Darley invited him to call on her one Sunday evening and for several months he courted her at her home, which glowed even brighter with the flushes of his romantic imagination.[16]

Terry's courtship of Sarah Ann placed him at the centre of her mother's religious household. He visited her in the evenings when he would either read to them as they sewed or join in with them singing hymns and on Sundays in family prayers. He chatted and laughed with her mother and eight siblings, all of which was done within 'a decided religious air'. In this home he was a Christian, even if he had not been in his own. Sarah Ann's beloved mother tempered his more robust sailor language. Although this was not his home, it became 'the new home of my heart where my young aspiring mind drank in at the same time the rich nectar of love, and the cheering and consoling influence of religion'. When Sarah Ann broke off her courtship with Terry he wrote to the family that 'if religion in its pure form was to be found anywhere, it was under their roof'. Twelve months later she did consent to become his wife.[17]

The examples in this section reveal the social dimensions of domestic religion. Religious experience in the home was structured by different kinds of relationships between powerful and less powerful family members, and these familial relations were central to the making of the religious home.

THE RHYTHMS OF WORKING-CLASS DOMESTIC RELIGION

According to David Harvey and Edward Soja, any study of space must consider its temporal dimensions (Harvey 1990: 418–34; Soja 1996). Tine Van Osselaer (2014) has argued that nineteenth- and twentieth-century religious domesticity was dependent on the ritualization of time, noting that 'religious rituals not only structured daily life, they also shaped a family's experience of the week and year' (Van Osselaer and Pasture 2014: 20). Easter, Christmas and Saints Days, as well as the regular punctuation of Sunday, were important breaks in the weekly and yearly calendar.[18] Memoirs in my sample reveal that weekly and annual rhythms were structured around temporal shifts from secular to sacred time. This section considers how working-class dwellings were made religious through specific rituals and everyday rhythms by examining Sunday rituals as well as the daily practices of reading and prayer.

Sunday observance was conferred by the Ten Commandments, which asked believers to rest on the seventh day (Exodus 34:21). The separation of Sunday from other days of the week was perceived to be crucial to Britain's religious identity in the nineteenth century. Various religious censuses, most famously the 1851 Religious Census, argued that Sunday was in crisis because church attendance was declining, especially in working-class districts (Mann 1854). But working-class households continued to mark Sunday out from other days in other ways. Autobiographies resound with evidence of Sunday's significance, even if church attendance is absent. For example, Elizabeth Rignall wrote that 'The Victorian Sunday was a day apart from all others'.[19] Sunday was, in the words of Ireson, 'kept very religiously'.[20] Sarah Williams's argument that the working classes 'continued to separate the Sabbath from the rest of the week by a series of rituals and observances which broke from the rhythm of life' seems to hold good (1999: 7). These rituals included sending children to Sunday school or to church club, a refusal to spend money or play games, and more domestic rituals such as hymn singing, prayers and reading the Bible (1999: 145–56). Turning to working-class homes on a Sunday therefore reveals how religion was observed on the Sabbath without the need to look to church attendance as an indicator of working-class religiosity. It also allows for a broader conceptualization of working-class religion, forming a vital counterweight to the view of Victorian social commentators who perceived the working classes to be responsible for secularizing Sunday.

Domestic religion allowed families to engage in Sunday worship beyond the confines of official religious spaces. Hilda Rose Fowler's Baptist family sung their 'childish evening hymns' around the family organ on Sundays when her parents were at church.[21] Several authors also illustrate how domestic religion was not confined exclusively to the immediate parental home, but could extend into other domestic realms. Sundays appear to have involved a collective overlapping of religious spaces at the domestic level. For example, after Sunday evening services, the Goffin children went to their Uncle Will's house where they sang hymns, chants and solos. They were accompanied by their father who played the harmonium, and his uncle and cousin, who played the violin.[22]

Minnie Frisby's memoir reveals how some non-conformists turned their homes into formal religious spaces. Born in 1877, Frisby highlights how cottage religion continued to be used by Methodists in Worms Ash, Bromsgrove. Cottage religion was practised in non-conformist communities that had no chapel. It enabled iterant preachers and locals to preach and worship outside of the parish church. Frisby's family joined their neighbour John Jones at his house for Sunday evening services and prayer. During the summer, they worshiped under the cherry tree in his garden, singing hymns such as Robert Lowry's 'What Can Wash Away My Sin'.[23] Such recollections challenge Deborah Valenze's assertion that this practice had died out by the 1830s and 1840s with the increased institutionalization of Evangelicalism (1985: 31–56). Practices introduced in the early nineteenth century seem to have been sustained into the Victorian period because of the needs of specific communities, and because domestic rituals were continued by families as a matter of habit.

Sunday was a day of both 'restrictions' and 'compensations' to use the words of Rignall.[24] Memoirists were aware of debates over what constituted appropriate leisure and were keen to align what they did on Sundays with a notion of rational leisure. George Gregory remembered that once when he visited his neighbours he found their son Harry playing the piano in the parlour. Harry's mother walked into the room and promptly asked him to stop because she felt that the dance music he was playing was not in keeping with Sunday.[25] Rignall provides the lengthiest description of her Sunday out of all the autobiographies. Over three pages she richly describes her experience of Sunday from attending Sunday school, eating lunch, to afternoon reading habits. Much of her account is given over to reading.[26] Gareth Atkins has demonstrated how the middle classes policed their reading habits to 'safeguard the purity of the household' (2014: 332). This precaution was mainly taken by worried parents concerned about their children's reading habits. These ideas also extended into households that blurred the boundaries of the working class and middle class. For instance, the only book Rignall's parents would allow her to read was their illustrated copy of John Bunyan's *Pilgrim's Progress*, which she found to be horrifying, frightening but strangely mesmerizing. She reminisced about how she would lie on the family sofa with *Pilgrim's Progress* and turn to the colour illustration of 'Apollyon horned, taloned and leathery-winged, with long, darting beams of sinister light flashing from his eyes as he hovered above poor Christian waiting to pounce'.[27] After she had satisfied her fascination with the illustrations, she would then sit in the bay window of their London home and watch the street scene unfolding outside, which she found far more entertaining. Rignall resented her Sunday reading options because she was denied the delight of reading her preferred *Books for the Bairns*, 'thin, pink paper-backed booklets' that were abridged versions or simplifications of *Gulliver's Travels*, *Robinson Crusoe*, *Cinderella* or *Puss in Boots*, stories that she then converted into plays for her and her friends.[28]

Religious reading was not only confined to Sunday. The nineteenth century witnessed the rise of a vibrant publishing industry that printed classic and new

FIGURE 8.1: An example of a nineteenth-century illustrated page of John Bunyan's *Pilgrim's Progress* for children. This shows Christian's conflict with Apollyon discussed by Elizabeth Rignall in her memoir. From the book *The Pilgrim's Progress* by John Bunyan, late-nineteenth-century edition. © Universal Archive / Getty Images.

moral works (Atkins 2014: 331–42). Reading was a prominent feature of daily life and working-class families benefitted from increasing schooling, with the introduction of the 1870 Education Act. Alfred West's memoir gives a detailed account of regular reading of Bunyan's *Pilgrim's Progress*. Unlike Rignall, he appreciated the spiritual qualities of this book. Over five pages he discusses the profound religious and psychological impact the book had on him as a boy, which he eagerly read, even taking it with him to his grandparents' house while convalescing from tuberculosis.[29] He found the book to be 'a story of a great heroic adventure. It is an allegory, and as such, speaks to the soul in the soul's language, which is composed of myth, allegory, legend and analogy'.[30] What gave this book specific religious meaning for West was Bunyan's biblical voice and simple theological messages. For instance, he argued that the pilgrim's journey from the 'City of Destruction' to the 'Celestial City' is one that every man must undertake. A Christian's journey was not physical, but spiritual and moral. It is an allegorical journey. The spiritual journeyman does not physically leave his family or home, but remains there to become a better husband and father. In his memoir, West notes that 'It spoke directly and significantly to my very soul. Life was an adventure, it called for mental and spiritual effort'.[31] West's remembering of this book was reinforced by his continual assertion that post-1945 society needed to rediscover it in order to connect with religion in simple terms (see Brown 2009: 170–93; MacLeod 2007). His decision to explicitly interweave the present with the past confirms Megan Doolittle's argument that autobiographies have a 'double chronology: the time of the events being narrated, and the time of writing them down and constructing their story' (2011: 248).

Religious books, newspapers and pamphlets gave their working-class readers the opportunity to engage with their religious faith in their homes, both on Sundays and throughout the week. Indeed, many of the autobiographies confirm Williams's assertion that there was more often than not a bible in the nineteenth-century working-class household (2010: 25). Many memoirists mention receiving or reading a bible at home. Benjamin Taylor discussed the 'reverence and solemnity' he experienced reading the Bible because it was a 'divine book coming from God'. In a language of atonement, he asserted that its sanctity came from the fact that it 'plainly described good and evil . . . it will telegraph such faithful and undeniable truths to you as will make you blush, fear, and tremble'.[32] Similarly, in Fowler's childhood home a copy of the Bible, together with *Foxe's Book of Martyrs* and several missionary booklets, were to be found on the sitting-room's round table. On rainy Sundays, Fowler turned to *Foxe's Book of Martyrs* and marvelled at the 'gruesome descriptions' and 'awesome illustrations'.[33]

In some households, the dissemination of reading material appears to have been a key part of the father's religious parenting. Taylor's early-nineteenth-century father borrowed religious books such as Daniel Hebert's 1816 *Hymns*

FIGURE 8.2: Front cover of *Foxe's Book of Martyrs* (Newcastle on Tyne: Adam & Co., 1874).

FIGURE 8.3: An example of the 'awesome' images in *Foxe's Book of Martyrs*. 'Last Moments of George Marsh', *Foxe's Book of Martyrs* (Newcastle on Tyne: Adam & Co., 1874), 780.

and *Poems*.³⁴ West's much loved two-shilling copy of *Pilgrim's Progress* was given to him by his father as a birthday present.³⁵ Goffin's father Fred purchased several religious newspapers and publications for his family, including *The Christian World* and later the *Methodist Times* for himself. For his wife he bought the *Christian Globe* and for his children *The Children's Friend*. Like Fowler, Goffin also read *Fox's Book of Martyrs*, together with Locke's *System of Theology*, *Lecture to Young Men* and *Aristotle's Complete Works*. These latter books belonged to his father who 'secreted [them] at the bottom of a chest-of-drawers'.³⁶ By concealing them in his bedroom, Fred Goffin was asserting the intimate and more private expressions of faith. Similarly, it can be assumed that in hiding these books they probably jarred with the religious persona he wanted to convey both at home and in the wider world.

Sundays were for many workers the only day of true relaxation. West recollected that some of his neighbours 'remain[ed] quietly at home' and did not attend church.³⁷ Non-church attendance should not, however, be read as symbolic of a person's lack of religiosity. Rather, West's observation illustrates the tension that emerged between religious intent and the need to rest after a long working week. Increasingly throughout the century there was growing recognition that the modern body needed to rest and that this was just as important as religious observation (see McCrossan 2000). Sunday's sacred times were thus zoned, to allow time for rest. Goffin's parents broke Sunday into sacred and secular time. Goffin's printer father was a self-taught organist at the local Beccles Methodist Chapel. Between morning and evening service he retired to the family's living room and spent the afternoon in his 'substantial Windsor' chair dozing with his legs resting on another chair. This practice of Sunday relaxing extended to his mother, who retired to her bed when the children were at Sunday school.³⁸ Arguably, anybody peering through this family's netted windows would have supposed that his father was an archetypal working-class secular man. As Winnington-Ingram complained, working men, especially on a Sunday, turned their homes into places of relaxation where they read Sunday newspapers, drank beer and lounged around in shirt sleeves, while waiting for their 'missus' to serve them Sunday lunch (1897: 5; See also Brown 2009: 88–98). But, domestic Sunday observance was not all-encompassing. Being a Christian did not necessarily mean turning every minute of Sunday into a day of active worship.

Domestic worship was also not confined to Sunday. Working-class believers interacted with domestic religion through prayer on a daily basis. Anita Hughes's Lancashire family would say grace before meals: they 'dare not speak' except for when they said their prayers because '[c]hildren were seen and not heard in those days'.³⁹ Meanwhile, Gregory was brought up to say his prayers daily at bedtime. These were taught to them by their mother's live-in elderly cousin, Love Green. His family's poverty (his father was a miner) meant they undressed downstairs in front of the fire. On one occasion, the rush to be in the warmth of

FIGURE 8.4: 'A Child's Prayer'. Illustration from *Hymns and Pictures* (London: SPCK, 1870). © Bridgeman Images, LLM456341.

his bed lead him to kneel down and say the Lord's prayer, their 'formal prayer', quickly and before Green had chance to hear him finish. Seeing him climb under the cover she rebuked him and asked him to say his prayers again, which he refused to do, 'the consequence being that the old lady descended downstairs very grieved'.[40] Domestic arrangements could interfere with a family's religious practices. The desire to say night-time prayers with religious fervour and meaning was arguably affected by the temperature of the room they were conducted in.

Prayers were also used in moments of stress. When his gardener father was unemployed, Francis Hughes notes how her mother prayed for her doctor's bill to be paid. A letter then arrived informing her that the doctor was cancelling all monies owed to him because he had been left a legacy.[41] Meanwhile, Thomas Jordan's Durham miner father's domestic religion extended into the workplace when he knelt in the centre of their kitchen to silently pray for himself and the men he oversaw as a deputy overman before he left for work. When he retired in 1926, after thirty years in the job, he reported to his son that no one had ever been killed or injured during these years. Although his father did not attribute his practice of praying to this fact, his son did. What makes Jordan's recollections all the more striking is the way they are separated from the remainder of the memoir history under the heading 'Just a little holy story of my Dad'. This is the only heading that appears in the typescript but it demonstrates the significance that Jordan placed on his father's religiosity.[42]

Praying was also a source of comfort at troubling and difficult times. From his memoir, it would appear that it was the main source of Castle's domestic religiosity. He wrote prayers at home. He also prayed for his second daughter, Esther, on her death bed, and together with a chapter on the death of Christ, he read aloud from Isaac Watts's *Alas! And Did My Saviour Bleed? At the Cross*. Castle's daughter died in his wife's arms.[43] Bereavement was an important part of working-class life writings (Vincent 1980: 223–47; Strange 2005). Castle's faith, however, was not quashed by the death of his daughter. According to his religious outlook, death had restored her to a higher, happier plane.

Similarly, Harry West reported how he prayed for his own recovery. Having been sent to his grandparents in Upper Stanton after the doctor had advised his parents that he needed to be removed from the 'industrial, smoky, dusty and slummy' district where he currently lived in the Mill House of the Avonside Paper Mill in St. Philips, Bristol, where his father worked as a clerk.[44] Not only did he cry, he also prayed that 'God would spare me from death for one thousand years' to be on the safe side.[45] Later, when it looked like he would not recover, it was his Quaker grandmother, according to West, who restored him to health. Unable to take the cod liver oil the doctor had prescribed, his grandmother declared: 'If thou canst not take it down thy throat, I will rub it into thy chest and back, please God it will get somewhere where it is needed'. This example serves to provide an interesting insight into the ways in which 'God' was inserted into an everyday vernacular in the nineteenth-century home. This informal, lived theology was part of the landscape of religious homes. At a practical level, it meant that as a boy West walked around his grandmother's village smelling 'like a whale station'. But, at a spiritual level, the fact that he did not die confirmed to his grandmother that God was 'pleased'.[46] Lived experience of domestic religion was temporal. This religious temporality was expressed not only through rituals, but at key moments when religious practices brought comfort to the believer.

AT HOME WITH WORKING-CLASS MATERIAL RELIGION

Religious objects played an important part in religious domesticity. Artefacts enabled believers to articulate, reaffirm and display their religious identity (Jones and Matthews-Jones 2015: 1–16). There is a growing literature on the role that objects play in the home (Hamlett 2010; Davidoff and Hall 1997: 149–92). Although much of this scholarship has been concerned with middle-class dwellings, its approach can be extended to consider how things were used to create meaning in working-class homes. We can draw on the work of Deborah Cohen, in particular, who has revealed the growth in the nineteenth century of a discourse which placed religious meaning on specific objects. Framing goods within such narratives enabled Victorians to reconcile themselves with the competing demands of 'religious restraint and the lure of newfound wealth' (Cohen 2006: x). Not everyone became wealthy in the nineteenth century, of course: the working classes, in particular, often struggled and fought hard to survive poverty. But we should not assume that their homes were empty spaces (see Johnson 1988: 27–42). Religious faith brought objects into the domestic sphere (Van Osselaer and Pasture 2014: 21–22). Sarah Williams (1999) maintains that even the poorest Southwark families' religiosity was materially manifested though bibles, amulets and tokens. By taking account of religious possessions in the working-class home, we might fully understand the varied and malleable nature of working-class belief (Williams 2010: 24–25).

Both Doolittle and Strange have discussed how objects were used by working-class families to anchor life narratives (Doolittle 2011; Strange 2015). Their emphasis has largely been on children and their fathers. As I have already shown, books and religious reading materials affirmed fathers' domestic religiosity. Men's engagement with the material aspects of domestic faith were not only confined to books, but nor were they tied only to the family. Goffin, Lanigan and Frisby offer additional glimpses of their fathers' personal and material interaction with faith. Goffin's father's made a scrapbook of Methodist ministers' photographs where he also added 'topical notes' on what they were doing and where they were stationed.[47] Making a scrapbook was a highly subjective experience that bound individuals to larger communities in the Victorian period (Hunt 2006). For men like Goffin, scrapbooking enabled them to take an imaginative flight into Britain's Empire (Francis 2002: 643). Lanigan's alcoholic father engraved the Lord's Prayer on one side of a sixpence that he would carry around with him.[48] Religious objects were not only personifications of faith. Frisby's father, like many of the local men in her community, blurred the boundaries between domestic and religious space by sending their best food produce to the Non-Conformist Chapel's Harvest Festival. Her water-cress farmer father, in particular, always sent a sheaf of wheat, which he prepared and assembled in their barn.[49]

In contrast, mothers' engagement with material religion was written into autobiographical narratives mainly through reference to sewing skills. Henderson, for instance, reported that her mother made new dresses for her and her sister Louie to wear for the Sunday School Anniversary. This yearly treat made them feel like 'duchesses'.[50] Rignall's mother's dressmaking skills made her and her brother the best-dressed children in their parish.[51] In the 'Hungry Sixties', the Sunday best that children wore in Warmington was, according to Ireson, down to women like his mother, who turned their 'tiny needles' into 'instruments of industry in the homes.⁵² The prominence placed on what people wore, when and how, reveals that clothes were necessary for conveying a particular religious selfhood, status and respectability (see Wildman 2011: 118–19).

On first sight, it might be argued that clothes were largely secular concerns: more about conveying a specific image than to do with expressing faith. Yet sewing in this period was understood to be a religious activity (Parker [1984] 2010: 21). Working-class women sewed outfits for their children and to engage with the religious public sphere. This insight invites scholars to think more about why we should turn to objects in order to understand women's involvement with institutional religion. As Timothy W. Jones and I have argued elsewhere, an investigation into material religion shows that belief was not always tied to the written word (Jones and Matthews-Jones 2015: 5). Rather, articulations of faith were conveyed through other means. This has important implications for the history of religion because it prompts us to consider the more varied ways in which women engaged with religion. Maureen Daly Goggin, for instance, contends that the needle should be understood as women's equivalent to the pen, and the stitch the rhetorical device left by women who have been obscured in the historical record (2002: 309–38). Although Daly Goggin's argument is made with reference to samplers, this point can be extended to the clothing made by working women for their children.

Formal religion also intersected with domestic religion through the transfer of goods between church/chapel and home. Books were awarded to Sunday school

FIGURE 8.5: Postcard showing a church parade in Preston in the early twentieth century.

pupils to mark their attendance and conduct during the year. Amy Langley recollected 'the very nicely bound, red-covered book called "The Puzzling Pair"', she was awarded as her first Sunday School Prize. This story remained vivid in her memory, when almost seventy-five years later, she wrote her memoir. She was also given a Moroccan calf-bound copy of Charles Dickens's *A Tale of Two Cities* after her confirmation.[53] Emotional attachment to religious and spiritual objects was not only confined to commercial books. West's aunt Jemima Membrey 'treasured' two pots that had been made out of a domestic pulpit that John Wesley had once preached from. The significance of these objects was heightened by the family connection Membrey had with them, because the pulpit had been for a time in the kitchen of one of her family members.[54]

The nineteenth century was also as a period of conspicuous religious consumption. Religious and moral objects were staples in instructing children about how they should behave. Sunday schools were known to hand out mugs and plates inscribed with religious messages (Riley 1991: 226). Recent archaeological digs have confirmed that religious and moral crockery was also an important part of working-class culture (Crewe and Hadley 2013: 89–105). Despite this, none of the autobiographies discuss this form of material exchange between church/chapel and home. This implies that books were more prominent in their distribution or that they functioned differently in the authors' memories. Objects like cups and plates are less likely to involve active religious embodiment because they were either being stored or used beyond the religious purpose. Fowler, nonetheless, remembered how one Christmas she received a knife, fork and spoon set from Father Christmas with the words, 'For a Good Child', a set that she used whenever she felt that she had been good. This provoked comments and remarks from her elder siblings, reinforcing her behaviour.[55]

Material religion also had temporal dynamics. Sunday was materially marked out for many of the authors not only by what they wore but also by what they ate. Sunday was also marked by the rhythm of luxuries. The notion of what consisted of a luxury depended on family circumstance. For Thomas McLauchlan's South Hetton family, Sunday was a day for butter rather than their staple of dripping.[56] Chase's mother, Priscilla, made the same dinner every Sunday of roast pork, potatoes and apple dumplings. Prepared on a Saturday and cooked at the local bakehouse, this was considered by Alice to be 'SOME dish'.[57] Meanwhile, Anita Hughes's family always had fish for their breakfast on Sundays because it was sold cheaply at Preston's fish-market on a Saturday.[58] Together with her brother, Jack, Rignall would wake up to find on their mantelpiece sweets from their mother and aunt. These might include small chocolate macaroons or Cailler chocolate. After breakfast she went to Sunday school returning home for Sunday dinner. This she notes was cooked for the family by her Salvation Army father, who would 'don an apron' in order that his wife and her sister could attend morning service at their local Anglican church.[59]

FIGURE 8.6: Image showing a fragment of temperance crockery. From www.whatthevictoriansthrewaway.com (designed, Ben Ross). © Tom Licence.

Few of the writers of the autobiographies go into detail about the material objects in their homes. When objects were discussed they were done so in a fleeting manner with little description. Nora Hampton's grandmother, who she frequently visited at her house on Dudley's Round Street, had some 'quite good pictures', which included '2 pictures one of St. John and Mark and St. Peter and James'. Yet, as this section has shown, the working classes did partake in material religion. Objects were not only exchanged between institutional spaces of religion but also as part of the practices of religious domesticity. This was especially the case with the made object – dresses, sheafs and coins – which showed how the working classes extended their belief practices into the public sphere.

UNHOMELY RELIGIOUS HOUSEHOLDS

Religious households were also unsettling places, especially if residents did not adhere to the religious principles set out by their families. Alison Blunt and Ann Varley have argued that domestic inclusion and exclusion depends on 'class, age, sexuality and "race"' (2004: 3). This section will demonstrate that religion can be added to that list. A small but significant number of male memoirists confirm

John Tosh's argument that middle-class men, like Samuel Butler and Edward Carpenter, rejected their familial homes when they clashed with the 'character traits' of the patriarch (Tosh 1999: 183). Such a reading can be extended to working-class homes, where religion was also at the heart of nineteenth-century ideas of patriarchal domesticity (Christie 2002: 3–36). Arthur Frederick Goffin's and Benjamin Taylor's autobiographical writings reveal that their family's religious domesticity was rejected by men not necessarily because they themselves were averse to religion, but because they clashed with their father's religious-patriarchal status in the home. Goffin especially found his strict religious upbringing 'irksome ... resent[ing] the "repression on all sides"'. Goffin's account of his childhood and teenage years reveals that his father used religion as a justification for punishment.[60] He and his father also clashed with one another over religious principles. While Goffin noted that it was his mother who directed his everyday religious practice, it was his father, the more religious of his parents, who was the disciplinarian, which was structured by religious phrases and reference to the Bible. Indeed, on one occasion when he was telling his son off, Goffin's father called him 'Little Herod' after King Herod who ordered the mass killing of new-born children in Bethlehem (Matthew 2:16). Goffin does not explain why his father used this example, or what incident had occurred for him to be described in this way, but it clearly left a lasting impression on him, because he remembers his father biting his tongue, and bleeding from his mouth, in order to avoid physically striking his son.[61]

Home was therefore neither sacred nor sweet for Goffin, but rather a site of conflict to be endured. As Amanda Vickery reminds us, 'the history of the home is as much a saga of power, labor, inequality and struggle' (2009: 2). Goffin's memoir is unusual in the detail used to describe the everyday unease experienced around religion. This was not tied only to his father. His mother was also included, suggesting that religious conflict was not only connected to patriarchy, but also generational. He was 'miserable' living with his parents because of the constant 'quarrels and nerve-racking upheavals'.[62] Similarly, he found his parent's Christian respectability – no swearing, gambling or drinking – hypocritical. His mother was too domineering, his father too placid and unloving. His Methodist home stifled him. Goffin instead found a religious home elsewhere, in the bible classes he attended. By moving his religious dwelling outside of the domestic sphere, he revealed how for some young working-class men, homeliness was not only to be found in the familial home. Even then, his attendance at this class became a site of domestic strife because his father objected to his fellow class members and because, on one occasion, he was late home from class. Faced with such opposition, Goffin reports that a 'chilly atmosphere' pervaded his parental home. He came to see it as somewhere to only eat and sleep.[63]

There were certainly times when a Christian home could be *too Christian*. Benjamin Taylor's spiritual autobiography expands on many of the themes discussed above. He used his spiritual autobiography to chart the religious discomposure he felt both in his familial home and later in the home of his master. His early-nineteenth-century memoir was infused with the language of atonement (see Hilton 1988). Words like 'sin', 'sinner', 'wicked', 'distressed' and 'Satan' fill his fourteen-page account. Taylors's mind was so plagued with concerns over his spiritual worthiness that he once contemplated committing suicide. Throughout his account, the reader is invited to experience his religious torments and to share his parents' concerns that he would not find salvation in Christ. While living with his parents, he described the emotional and spiritual torments he experienced.[64] He recounts three nightmares that centred on the Devil and his fear that he would go to hell. Taylor was not the only memoirist to suffer from religiously infused nightmares. On one occasion, for instance, he dreamt that the Devil had come to fetch his soul. In horror he woke up screaming. His father came to him, but rather than reassure him, he confirmed his son's dream and said that if his son did not change his ways he would be taken by the Devil. The lack of emotional support for the young Taylor had a scarring impact on him. His memoir is written in such a way as to suggest that he was in religious conflict with his parents over his supposed lack of religiosity for most of his childhood.

Not all unhomely moments were a permanent feature in Christian households. George Gregory recollected that it was his mother who was the disciplinarian at home and that when he had misbehaved his 'pious' mother tied him to the bedstead and make him learn the verse of the scripture by heart, which he would then recite.[65] Even though Gregory described his mother as 'illiterate', her commitment to this type of punishment was indicative of her commitment to the Bible and the word of God.[66] Yet, his memoir suggests an intimacy that contrasts sharply with Goffin's above and a determination despite their poverty to see their children prosper.

CONCLUSION

This chapter has demonstrated a rich history of lived religion in the working-class domestic sphere. It has argued that scholars of nineteenth-century religion should turn to the home in order to understand religious belief at a personal and collective level. Peering through the windows of religious households reveals that the religious practices in the home structured the lives of working-class believers in the nineteenth century. The examples in this chapter complicate the binary of secular and sacred, suggesting that historians of religion have been short-sighted in their focus on church attendance as a measure of working-class religiosity. The everyday lived aspects of religious faith evidenced by the autobiographies discussed in this chapter offer a different view of working-class religion and of the secularization process which historians have perceived to be at work in this period. Life writings in the Burnett collection illustrate how working-class men and women understood their religious faith in the nineteenth century. I have shown that working-class religion needs to be understood on its own terms and that by privileging the voices of the working-class people themselves we can see how domestic religion was an integral part of working-class religiosity. Similarly, the autobiographies used for this chapter reveal that religious identity was not exclusively tied to the formal sphere but also bound up with the everyday practices of home. Expressions of domestic faith demonstrate how home was made a sacred place and how religious authenticity was sought in the domestic sphere. As Timothy Jones and I have argued, 'One is not born, but rather becomes religious' (Jones and Matthews-Jones 2015: 3). Being religious is not an immediate or straightforward state of being: rather, domestic rituals and behaviours remind a person of their faith. They also serve to let the believer perform, articulate and personify what they believe beyond the confines of religious institutions.

NOTES

Introduction

1. I have adopted an expansive definition of this, drawing on the secondary literature to discuss Britain, France and what was to become Germany as well as Scandinavia, Italy and Spain.
2. A secluded part of the house for women in high caste families in India and Iran.

Chapter 1

1. See, for example, *The Sydney Morning Herald*, 5 February 1847. Available online: http://nla.gov.au/nla.news-page1516626
2. Bournville Village Trust, Bournville Almshouse Trust Ladies Visiting Committee, Minutes and Reports, 1903–4.

Chapter 2

1. This chapter is based on research undertaken for my PhD thesis (2005), which was funded by the Arts and Humanities Research Board Competition B: 'The Master–Servant Relationship in 19th Century England and India', PhD thesis, University College London, University of London.
2. It is important to note the British population of India constituted a minority of the whole: see W.C. Plowden, *Report on the Census of British India taken on the 17th February 1881*, vol. 1 (London: HMSO, 1883). The majority of domestic servants in India would have been employed in Indian households. For an analysis of the servant–employer relationship in Bengali households, see Swapna M. Banerjee, *Men, Women, and Domestics: Articulating Middle-class Identity in Colonial Bengal* (New Delhi: Oxford University Press, 2004).

3. Estate of Elizabeth Tilyard, Inventories of Deceased Estates, British Library, Oriental and India Office Collections, L/AG/34/27/163.

Chapter 3

1. The National Archives, IR 19/124/105.
2. *Liverpool Mercury*, 16 August 1853, 4.
3. *Liverpool Mail*, 8 June 1837, 3.
4. The inventory is part of the Legacy Duty papers for Thomas Ward, which valued his personal estate at £211,457, The National Archives, IR 19/124/105. In 1858, only 14.6 percent of the population left enough personal property to warrant probate; of this 14.6 percent, only 0.08 percent left personal property valued at more than £200,000, *Twenty-Second Annual Report of the Registrar-General* (1859) PP 1861 XVIII (2897), xlvi, 181. Biographical information is built up from electoral rolls, newspaper reports, parish registers, census returns and contemporary maps.
5. *London Evening Standard*, 25 September 1829, 3.
6. Family and building history is compiled from census returns and maps as well as the memoirs referenced.

Chapter 4

1. See www.beyondthebungalow.com
2. Correspondence with Stuart West, 19 June 2013; Interview with Ian Cooper, Cambridge, 12 March 2014; correspondence with David Potter, 11 October 2014.
3. V&A Collections, Museum Number IS.2376-1883. Available online: http://collections.vam.ac.uk/item/O77358/table-unknown
4. Bodleian Library, Oxford, Special Collections, MSS. Afr. s. 2305/2/28, 69, William McGregor and Isabel Ross Papers.
5. Bodleian Library, Oxford, Special Collections, MSS. Afr. s. 2058 (2): 'Pioneers in Africa', Letters and Memoirs of Edward and Dorothy Powys Cobb.
6. Ibid., 42–43.
7. Cambridge University Library Special Collections, RCMS 169, Langridge Papers 1909–15, *The Leader of British East Africa*, Saturday 7 October 1911.
8. Bodleian Library, Oxford, Special Collections, MSS. Afr. s. 1876/18/34/30: 'Mrs Millington's banda at English Point (interior). Apr 25, 1918', William McGregor and Isabel Ross Papers'.

Chapter 5

1. I have synthesized these categories from a range of household advice books, many of which are cited in this chapter.
2. Advice literature does not always *represent* reality, but it may influence it, and how people think about it. See Grace Lees-Maffei, 'Studying Advice: Historiography, Methodology, Commentary, Bibliography', *Journal of Design History*, 16:1 (2003), 3–5.

Chapter 6

1. For a discussion of romantic love in nineteenth-century America, see Karen Lystra, *Searching the Heart: Women, Men, and Romantic Love in Nineteenth-Century America* (New York: Oxford University Press, 1989); Ellen K. Rothman, *Hands and Hearts: A History of Courtship in America* (New York: Basic Books, 1984). For a discussion of the ideals germane to the American Revolutionary period that established new ideals of family life, see Jan Lewis, *The Pursuit of Happiness: Family and Values in Jefferson's Virginia* (Cambridge: Cambridge University Press, 1983); Jay Fliegelman, *Prodigals and Pilgrims: The American Revolution Against Patriarchal Authority, 1750–1800* (Cambridge: Cambridge University Press, 1982).
2. Hicks Williams, Sarah (1836–68), Sarah Frances Hicks Williams Collection 1836–1868, folders 1–6, Southern Historical Collection, Wilson Library, The University of North Carolina at Chapel Hill, folder 5: 1854–55, 2 January 1855.
3. Hicks Williams, folder 4: 1852–53, 10 December 1853.
4. Hicks Williams, folder 6: 1856–68, 12 April 1859.
5. Hicks Williams, folder 4: 1852–53, 10 December 1853.
6. Hicks Williams, folder 4: 1853–54, 22 October 1853.
7. For further reading around the fictional images of home and the domestic sphere published during the Civil War, see Chapter 5, 'Border Dramas and the Divided Family in the Popular Imagination', in Murrell Taylor, *The Divided Family in Civil War America* (Chapel Hill, NC: University of North Carolina Press, 2005), 123–52.

Chapter 7

1. This chapter was developed from an original idea by Monika Elbert. Special thanks to Rebecca Preston and Lesley Hoskins for their thoughtful comments on an earlier draft.
2. Readers could now avail themselves of many different kinds of advice literature – including compendiums of specific practical advice such as *Enquire Within* and *Cassell's Household Guide*, books on home arrangement and decoration by architects and artistic experts as well as domestic advice manuals aimed at housekeepers and usually written by women. While some of the books were quite expensive, this market aimed at a range of social groups, including the lower middle classes and respectable working class, who were catered for by writers like Mrs. Warren and John Kirton. There were also an increasing number of women's magazines, aimed at different social strata, that frequently dealt with home affairs.
3. Rich suggests that it is not possible to say how complete the adoption was – the French style of laying everything out together may still have been seen as appropriate on special occasions; Rachel Rich, *Bourgeois Consumption: Food, Space and Identity in London and Paris, 1850–1914* (Manchester: Manchester University Press, 2011), 102.
4. 'The Table Tasteful' was a recurring feature in *The House* magazine between 1898 and 1900. *The House: an artistic monthly for those who manage and beautify the home*, January 1889–December 1900, vols. 2-8, no. 11-46.

5. Essex Record Office, D/DU 418, Diaries of George H. Rose, 6 October 1904.
6. 'Home in a Boarding-House', Lowell Offering 3 (1842), 69–70; reproduced in Amy G. Richter, *At Home in Nineteenth-Century America: A Documentary History* (New York: New York University Press, 2015).
7. Surrey History Centre, SHC 3043/1/3/1/2, 'Rules for the Guidance of the Attendants, Servants and all Persons engaged in the Service of the Surrey County Asylum at Brookwood, near Woking Station, 1871'.
8. Surrey History Centre, Letter from Alice Rose O., 1902.

Chapter 8

1. Hilda Rose Fowler, Unfinished autobiography, provisionally entitled 'Look after the Little Ones', Brunel University Library.
2. Alice Maud Chase, 'The Memoirs of Alice Maud Chase', Burnett Archive of Working-Class Autobiography, Brunel University Library, 8.
3. Chase, 'The Memoirs of Alice Maud Chase', 8
4. Chase, 'The Memoirs of Alice Maud Chase', 14.
5. Alfred Ireson, 'Reminiscences', Burnett Archive of Working-Class Autobiography, Brunel University Library, 8.
6. Ireson, 'Reminiscences', 81.
7. Ireson, 'Reminiscences', 50.
8. Chase, 'The Memoirs of Alice Maud Chase', 20.
9. Nora Hampton, 'Memories of Baptist End, Netherton, Dudley in the period 1895–1918', Burnett Archive of Working-Class Autobiography, Brunel University Library, 9.
10. Hampton, 'Memories of Baptist End', 20.
11. John Castle, 'The Diary of John Castle', Burnett Archive of Working-Class Autobiography, Brunel University Library, n.p.
12. Emanuel Lovekin, 'Some Notes of My Life', Burnett Archive of Working-Class Autobiography, Brunel University Library, 32.
13. Castle, 'The Diary of John Castle', n.p.
14. Joseph Terry, 'Recollections of My Life', Burnett Archive of Working-Class Autobiography, Brunel University Library, 36.
15. Terry, 'Recollections of My Life', 39.
16. Terry, 'Recollections of My Life', 41.
17. Terry, 'Recollections of My Life', 44.
18. For the purpose of this chapter, I will look at Sunday. None of the autobiographies mention Easter despite its prominence in the Christian calendar. Whilst Christmas figures predominate in their accounts of childhood, this was framed more around what John Gillis (1996) has described as 'family time'. For a discussion of this, see Julie-Marie Strange, *Fatherhood and the British Working Class, 1865–1914* (Cambridge: Cambridge University Press, 2015).
19. Elizabeth Rignall, 'All So Long Ago', Burnett Archive of Working-Class Autobiography, Brunel University Library, 19.
20. Ireson, 'Reminiscences', 18.

21. Fowler, Unfinished autobiography.
22. Arthur Frederick Goffin, 'A Grey Life', Burnett Archive of Working-Class Autobiography, Brunel University Library, n.p.
23. Minnie Frisby, 'Memories', Burnett Archive of Working-Class Autobiography, Brunel University Library, 10.
24. Rignall, 'All So Long Ago', 19.
25. George Gregory, Untitled, Burnett Archive of Working-Class Autobiography, Brunel University Library, 7.
26. Rignall, 'All So Long Ago', 19–21.
27. Rignall, 'All So Long Ago', 19.
28. Rignall, 'All So Long Ago', 19.
29. Harry Alfred West, 'The Autobiography of Harry Alfred West: Facts and Comments', Burnett Archive of Working-Class Autobiography, Brunel University Library, 12.
30. West, 'The Autobiography of Harry Alfred West', 11.
31. West, 'The Autobiography of Harry Alfred West', 12.
32. Benjamin Taylor, 'A Sketch of the Author's Experience', Burnett Archive of Working-Class Autobiography, Brunel University Library, 1.
33. Fowler, Unfinished autobiography.
34. Taylor, 'A Sketch of the Author's Experience', 9.
35. West, 'The Autobiography of Harry Alfred West', 11.
36. Goffin, "A Grey Life," n.p.
37. West, "The Autobiography of Harry Alfred West," 14.
38. Goffin, 'A Grey Life', n.p.
39. Anita Elizabeth Hughes, Untitled, Burnett Archive of Working-Class Autobiography, Brunel University Library, 12.
40. Gregory, Untitled, 7.
41. Francis Hughes, 'I Remember', Burnett Archive of Working-Class Autobiography, Brunel University Library, 1.
42. Thomas Jordan, Untitled, Burnett Archive of Working-Class Autobiography, Brunel University Library, 19.
43. Castle, 'The Diary of John Castle', n.p.
44. West, 'The Autobiography of Harry Alfred West', 8.
45. West, 'The Autobiography of Harry Alfred West', 37.
46. West, 'The Autobiography of Harry Alfred West', 37.
47. Goffin, 'A Grey Life', n.p.
48. Jack Lanigan, 'Thy Kingdom Did Come', Burnett Archive of Working-Class Autobiography, Brunel University Library, 92.
49. Frisby, 'Memories', 17.
50. Katherine Henderson [pseud. of Katherine Dudley], 'Had I But Known', Burnett Archive of Working-Class Autobiography, Brunel University Library, 1–3.
51. Rignall, 'All So Long Ago', 130.
52. Ireson, 'Reminiscences', 10.
53. Amy Langley, Untitled, Burnett Archive of Working-Class Autobiography, Brunel University Library, n.p.
54. West, 'The Autobiography of Harry Alfred West', 15.

55. Fowler, Unfinished autobiography.
56. Thomas McLauchlan, 'The Life of an Ordinary Man', Burnett Archive of Working-Class Autobiography, Brunel University Library, 1.
57. Chase, 'The Memoirs of Alice Maud Chase', 10.
58. Anita Elizabeth Hughes, Untitled, 10.
59. Rignall, 'All So Long Ago', 130.
60. Goffin, 'A Grey Life', n.p.
61. Goffin, 'A Grey Life', n.p.
62. Goffin, 'A Grey Life', n.p.
63. Goffin, 'A Grey Life', n.p.
64. Taylor, 'A Sketch of the Author's Experience', 4.
65. Gregory, 'Untitled', 2, 7.
66. Gregory, 'Untitled', 7.

BIBLIOGRAPHY

Primary sources

A Lady Resident (1864), *The Englishwoman in India*, London: Smith, Elder.
A Medical Practitioner (1848), *A Domestic Guide to Mothers in India*, 5th edition, Bombay: American Mission Press.
Adams, Charles Francis, ed. (1875), *Familiar Letters of John Adams and His Wife Abigail Adams, During the Revolution*, Cambridge, MA: Houghton. Sourced from Project Gutenberg. Available online: http://www.gutenberg.org/files/34123/34123-h/34123-h.htm (accessed 24 June 2015).
Aitken, E.H. (1897), *Behind the Bungalow*, London: Thacker.
Alcott, Louisa May (1922), *Little Women: or, Meg, Jo, Beth, and Amy*, Boston, MA: Little, Brown.
Alcott, William A. (1838), *From the Young Wife*, Boston, MA: George W. Light. Sourced from Uncle Tom's Cabin: A Multi-Media Archive directed by Stephen Railton. Available online: http://utc.iath.virginia.edu/sentimnt/sneswaaat.html (accessed 30 June 2015).
Alcott, William, A. (1836), *The Young Man's Guide*, 10th edition, Boston, MA: Perkins & Marvin. Sourced from Online Books. Available online: http://www.nimbus.org/ElectronicTexts/YgMnsGde.1836.html (accessed 30 June 2015).
Alden, Percy and Edward E. Hayward (1907), *Housing*, London: Headley Brothers.
'Alexander Mackay', *Church Missionary Gleaner*, (1890), 17 (6): 83–84.
'An African Arts and Crafts Exhibition', (1912), *Church Missionary Gleaner*, 39 (12): 202–3.
'An Almshouse in Shropshire', (1856), *Chambers Journal*, 23 September: 103–5.
An Anglo-Indian (1882), *Indian Outfits and Establishments: A Practical Guide for Persons about to Reside in India*, London: L. Upcott Gill.
An Anglo-Indian (1883), *Indian Cookery*, Bombay: Imperial Press.
Anderson, John Q., ed. (1995), *Brokenburn: The Journal of Kate Stone, 1861–1868*, Baton Rouge, LA: Louisiana State University Press, 22 September 1867.
Beecher, Catharine E. (1835), *An Essay on the Education of Female Teachers for the United States*, New York: Van Nostrand & Dwight.

Beecher, Catharine E. ([1841] 1843), *A Treatise on Domestic Economy: For the Use of Young Ladies at Home, and at School*, Boston, MA: T.H. Webb.

Beecher, Catharine E. (1842a), *Treatise on Domestic Economy*, Boston, MA: T.H. Webb. Sourced from Uncle Tom's Cabin: A Multi-Media Archive directed by Stephen Railton. Available online: http://utc.iath.virginia.edu/sentimnt/snesceba1t.html (accessed 20 June 2015).

Beecher, Catharine E. (1842b), *A Treatise on Domestic Economy for the Use of Young Ladies at Home, and at School*, New York: Harper & Brothers. Sourced from Project Gutenberg. Available online: http://www.gutenberg.org/files/21829/21829-h/21829-h.htm (accessed 14 July 2015).

Beecher, Catharine E. and Harriet Beecher Stowe (1869), *The American Woman's Home*, Boston, MA: A.H. Brown.

Beeton, Mrs. (1891), *Cookery Book and Household Guide*, London: Ward, Lock, Bowden.

Black, Clementina (1915), *Married Women's Work*, London: G. Bell.

Board of Trade (1908), *Cost of Living of the Working Classes: Report of an Enquiry by the Board of Trade into Working Class Rents, Housing and Retail Prices*, London: HMSO.

Bodleian Library, Oxford, Special Collections, MSS. Afr. s. 1876 and 2305: William McGregor and Isabel Ross Papers; MSS. Afr. s. 2058: Letters and Memoirs of Edward and Dorothy Powys Cobb.

Booth, Charles, ed. (1891), *Labour and Life of the People, vol. 2: London Continued*, London: Williams & Norgate.

Borup, K. (1902), 'Industrial Work at Mengo', *Church Missionary Gleaner*, 29 (9): 138.

Bosanquet, Helen (Mrs. Bernard) (1896), *Rich and Poor*, London: Macmillan.

Bosse, Sara (1913a), 'Giving a Chinese Luncheon Party: How to Do It in Your Own Home', *Harper's Bazaar*, January: 135, 146.

Bosse, Sara (1913b), 'A New Dinner for Churches and Clubs', *Ladies Home Journal*, 30 (March): 113.

Bournville Village Trust, Bournville Almshouse Trust Ladies Visiting Committee, Minutes and Reports, 1903–4.

Braddon, Edward (1872), *Life in India*, London: Longmans, Green.

Bradley, Emily (1950), *Dearest Priscilla: Letters to the Wife of a Colonial Civil Servant*, London: Max Parish.

Brandeis, Antonie (1907), *Kochbuch für die Tropen*, Berlin: Dietrich Reimer/Ernst Vohsen.

British Foreign and Commonwealth Office (1901–31), *East Africa Protectorate Blue Book*.

British Parliamentary Papers, *Twenty-Second Annual Report of the Registrar-General* (1859) PP 1861 XVIII (2897).

Brooks, S.H. (1839), *Designs for Cottage and Villa Architecture*, London: Thomas Kelly.

Brown, James (1844), James Brown to Samuel Hicks, 9 June 1844, Williams Family Archive, courtesy of Kathy Wright Fowler.

Browne, Phillis (1877), *Common-Sense Housekeeping*, London: Cassell, Petter & Galpin.

Browne, Phillis (1883), 'House-cleaning', in Shirley Foster Murphy (ed.), *Our Homes and How to Make Them Healthy*, 869–894, London: Cassell.

Burnett Archive of Working-Class Autobiography, Brunel University Library.

Burton, Harry McGuire (1958), *There Was A Young Man*, London: Geoffrey Bles.

Buxton, Mary Aline (1927), *Kenya Days*, London: Edward Arnold.

Cambridge University Library Special Collections, RCMS 169: Langridge Papers 1909–15.
Cassell's Household Guide (1870), vol. 1, London: Cassell, Petter & Galpin.
'Central Africa: Uganda: Industrial Work', (1911), *Church Missionary Gleaner*, 38 (8): 122.
Chadwick, Edwin (1842), *Report on the Sanitary Conditions of the Labouring Population of Great Britain*, London: Her Majesty's Stationery Office.
Child, Lydia Maria Francis ([1829] 1830), *The American Frugal Housewife, Dedicated to Those Who Are Not Afraid of Economy*, Boston, MA: Carter & Hendee.
Church, Richard (1955), *Over the Bridge: An Essay in Autobiography*, London: William Heinemann.
Cocks, Catherine (2001), *Doing the Town: The Rise of Urban Tourism in the United States, 1850–1915*, Los Angeles, CA: University of California Press.
Coleman, Nellie G. (1899), 'A Javanese Coffee', *Good Housekeeping*, 28 (3): 116.
Collet, Clara (1889), 'Women's Work', in Charles Booth (ed.), *Labour and Life of the People, vol. 1: East London*, 406–77, London: Williams & Norgate.
Colonial Office (1914), *Notes for Officers Appointed to East Africa and Uganda*, London: Waterlow & Sons.
Cornelius, Mary Hooker (1858), *The Young Housekeeper's Friend*, Boston, MA: Taggard & Thompson.
Delphine [Baker, Delphine P.] (1862), *Solon; or, The Rebellion of '61: A Domestic and Political Tragedy*, Chicago, IL: S.P. Rounds.
Dickens, Charles ([1853] 2003), *Bleak House*, London: Penguin.
Dixon, Edith, British Library, Asia, Pacific and African Collections, MSS Eur/T26.
Douglass, Frederick (1845), *Narrative of the Life of Frederick Douglass, An American Slave. Written by Himself*. Boston, MA: Antislavery Office.
Dundas, Anne (1924), *Beneath African Glaciers: The Humors, Tragedies and Demands of an East African Government Station as Experienced by an Official's Wife: With Some Personal Views on Native Life and Customs*, London: Witherby.
Easel, Jack (1895), *Our Square & Circle; or, the Annals of a Little London House*, London: Smith, Elder.
Eastlake, Charles L. (1878), *Hints on Household Taste in Furniture, Upholstery and Other Details*, London: Longmans Green.
Eaton, Mary (1823), *The Cook and Housekeeper's Complete & Universal Dictionary*, Bungay: L. & R. Childs.
Editorial, (1876), *The Pioneer*, 19 July.
Engels, Friedrich ([1845] 1967), 'The Condition of the Working Classes in England in 1844', in W.O. Henderson (ed.), *Engels: Selected Writings*, London: Penguin.
'Entertainments a la Japonaise', (1903), *The Boston Cooking School Magazine*, 7 (6): 275.
Essex Record Office, D/DU 418, Diaries of George H. Rose, 6 October 1904.
Estate of Elizabeth Tilyard, Inventories of Deceased Estates, British Library, Oriental and India Office Collections, L/AG/34/27/163.
Fay, Eliza (1925), *Original Letters from India 1779–1815*, London: Hogarth Press.
Fitzhugh, George (1854), *Sociology for the South, or the Failure of Free Society*, Richmond, VA: A. Morris. Sourced from Documenting the American South, 1998. University Library, The University of North Carolina at Chapel Hill. Available online: https://docsouth.unc.edu/southlit/fitzhughsoc/fitzhugh.html (accessed 26 August 2015).

Furley, E.M. (1895), 'On the Way to Uganda', *Church Missionary Gleaner*, 22 (12): 186–88.
Garrett, E.A. (1887), *Morning Hours in India. Practical Hints on Household Management, the Care ... of Children, &c*, London: Trubner.
Garrett, Rhoda and Agnes Garrett (1877) *Suggestions For House Decoration in Painting, Woodwork, and Furniture*, London: Macmillan.
Gilchrist Gibb, Alexander (1936), *Tanganyika Memories: A Judge in the Red Kanzu*, London: Blackie.
Gillman, Caroline Howard ([1838] 1998), *Recollections of a Southern Matron*, New York: Harper & Brothers. Documenting the American South, 1998. University Library. The University of North Carolina at Chapel Hill. Available online: http://docsouth.unc.edu/fpn/gilman/gilman.html (accessed 26 August 2015).
Godden, Rumer (2013), *Breakfast with Nikolides*, London: Virago.
Godey's Lady's Book (1841/1852), 'Editors' Table' (Philadelphia, Penn), August 1841 and January 1852. Sourced from Accessible Archives. Available online: www.accessible.com (accessed 12 April 2010).
Godey's Lady's Book (1843), 'Editors' Table' (Philadelphia, Penn), January 1843. Sourced from Accessible Archives. Available online: www.accessible.com (accessed 9 April 2010).
Godey's Lady's Book (1847a), 'FEMELLE AUTORITE' (Philadelphia, Penn), November 1847. Sourced from Accessible Archives. Available online: www.accessible.com (accessed 9 April 2010).
Godey's Lady's Book (1847b), 'Thoughts on Married Life' (Philadelphia, Penn), January 1847. Sourced from Accessible Archives. Available online: www.accessible.com (accessed 9 April 2010).
'Good Taste as a Hostess', (1910), *The Girl's Own Paper and Woman's Magazine*, XXXI: 97.
Gurdon, Vera, Lady Cranworth (1919), 'Hints for a Woman in British East Africa', in Bertram Francis Gurdon, Lord Cranworth, *Profit and Sport in British East Africa*, London: Macmillan.
Halttunen, Karen (1982), *Confidence Men and Painted Women: A Study of Middle-Class Culture in America, 1830–1870*, New Haven, CT: Yale University Press.
Hattersley, Charles W. (1908), *The Baganda at Home*, London: Religious Tract Society.
Havart, Harry (1912), *The Back Garden Beautiful*, London: Amalgamated Press.
Haweis, Mrs. H.R. [Eliza] (1883), *The Art of Beauty*, London: Chatto & Windus.
Haweis, Mrs. H.R. [Eliza] (1889), *The Art of Housekeeping*, London: Sampson, Lowe, Marston, Searle & Rivington.
Hicks Williams, Sarah (1836–68), Sarah Frances Hicks Williams Collection 1836–1868, folders 1–6, Southern Historical Collection, Wilson Library, The University of North Carolina at Chapel Hill.
Hogg, Edith ([1897] 2007), in Ellen Ross (ed.), *Slum Travelers: Ladies and London Poverty*, Oakland, CA: University of California Press.
Hostess and Guest: A Guide to the Etiquette of Dinners, Suppers, Luncheons, the Precedence of Guests, Etc, Etc, (1877), London, Ward, Lock.
Huxley, Elspeth (1985), *Out in the Midday Sun*, London: Chatto & Windus.
'Industrial Mission in Mengo', (1900b), *Church Missionary Gleaner*, 27 (7): 107.
'Industrial Work', (1920), *Church Missionary Gleaner*, 47 (3): 60.
Jacobs, Harriet A. (1861), *Incidents in the Life of a Slave Girl. Written by Herself*, ed. L. Maria Child, Boston: Published for the Author. Sourced from Documenting the

American South, 2003. University Library, The University of North Carolina at Chapel Hill. Available online: http://docsouth.unc.edu/fpn/jacobs/jacobs.html (accessed 12 February 2016)

James, A.G.F.E.M. (1879), *A Guide to Indian Household Management, etc.*, London: Ward, Lock.

James, Henry (1879), *The Europeans*, London: Macmillan.

Jennings, H.J. (1902), *Our Homes and How to Beautify Them*, 2nd edition, London: Harrison.

Johnston, Sir Harry (1902), *The Uganda Protectorate*, London: Hutchinson.

Kerr, Robert (1864), *The Gentleman's House; or, How to Plan English Residences, From the Parsonage to the Palace*, London: John Murray.

Kerr, Robert (1871), *The Gentleman's House; or, How to Plan English Residences, From the Parsonage to the Palace*, 2nd edition, London: John Murray.

King, Wilma, ed. (1993), *A Northern Woman in the Plantation South: Letters of Tryphena Blanche Holder Fox, 1856–1876*, Columbia, SC: University of South Carolina Press.

Ladies Sanitary Association (1901), *A Few Rules for the Manners of Servants in Good Families*, London: Ladies Sanitary Association, cited in John Raymond Pink (1998), *Country Girls Preferred: Victorian Domestic Servants in the Suburbs*, Surbiton: JRP.

Leigh, Linda (1901), *Zanzibar of To-day: A Practical Guide to Zanzibar and its Environs*, Zanzibar: Zanzibar Gazette Office.

Lethbridge, Katherine, ed. (1990), *Letters from East and West*, Braunton: Merlin.

Letter, (1883a), *The Englishman*, 21 April.

Letter, (1883b), *The* Englishman, 23 April.

Leverton, Mrs. Waldemar (1910), *Housekeeping Made Easy: A Handbook of Household Management Appealing Chiefly to the Middle-Class Housekeeper*, London: George Newnes.

Loane, M.E. (1908), *From Their Point of View*, London: Edward Arnold.

Loftie, Mrs. (1878), *The Dining Room*, London: Macmillan.

Loudon, J.C. (1833), *An Encyclopaedia of Cottage, Farm, and Villa Architecture and Furniture*, London: Longman Rees.

Loudon, J.C. (1838), *The Suburban Gardener, and Villa Companion*, London: Longman.

Loudon, J.C. (1842), *An Encyclopaedia of Cottage, Farm, and Villa Architecture and Furniture*, London: Longman, Brown, Green & Longmans.

Maddocks, Sydney (1932), 'Commercial Road', *The Copartnership Herald*, II (21), November. Available online: http://www.mernick.org.uk/thhol/commroad.html (accessed 15 May 2016).

Maitland, Fowler (1910), *Building Estates: A Rudimentary Treatise*, 5th edition, London: Crosby, Lockwood.

Maitland, Julia (1846), *Letters from Madras during the Years 1836 to 1839*, London: John Murray.

Mann, Horace (1854), *Census of Great Britain, 1851: Religious Workshop in England and Wales*, London: George Routledge. Available online: https://archive.org/details/dli.bengal.10689.16672/mode/2up.

Mann, Thomas (1927), *The Magic Mountain*, London: Martin Secker.

Marryat, Florence (1868), 'Gup'. Sketches of Anglo-Indian Life and Character, London: R. Bentley.

McCullock and Others (1858), *India: Geographical, Statistical, and Historical, Compiled from the London Times Correspondence*, London: G. Watts.

McIntosh, Charles (1828), *The Practical Gardener and Modern Horticulturist*, vol. 2, London: Thomas Kelly.

Mill, J. (1820), *History of British India*, vol. VI, London: Baldwin, Cradock & Joy.

Moffusilite (1876), Letter, *The Englishman*, 26 July.

Murphy, Shirley Forster, ed. (1883), *Our Homes and How to Make Them Healthy*, London: Cassell.

Murray Mitchell, J. (1876), *In India. Sketches of Indian Life and Travel from Letters and Journals*, London: T. Nelson.

Muthesius, Hermann ([1904–5] 1979, 1987), *The English House*, trans. Janet Seligman, Oxford: BSP Professional Books.

Nicol, Walter (1809), *The Villa Garden Directory*, Edinburgh: Constable.

Olmsted, Frederick Law (1856), *A Journey in the Seaboard Slave States: with Remarks on their Economy*, New York: Dix & Edwards. Sourced from Documenting the American South, 2001. University Library, The University of North Carolina at Chapel Hill. Available online: http://docsouth.unc.edu/nc/olmsted/olmsted.html (accessed 12 February 2016).

Orme, Eliza et al. (1893), *The Employment of Women*, special report of the Royal Commission on Labor (1891–4). Accessed via: http://parlipapers.chadwyck.co.uk/home.do (April 2016).

Orrinsmith, Lucy (1877), *The Drawing Room, its Decorations and Furniture*, London: Macmillan.

Panton, Jane Ellen (1873), *From Kitchen to Garret: Hints to Young Householders*, London: Ward & Downey.

Park, Benjamin (1844), 'The True Rights of a Woman', in *Godey's Lady's Book*, June (Philadelphia, Penn). Sourced from Accessible Archives. Available online: www.accessible.com (accessed 12 April 2010).

Parkes, Mrs. William (1828), *Domestic Duties*, London.

Patmore, Coventry (1860), *The Angel in the House*, London: Macmillan.

Perrin, Alice (1912), *The Anglo-Indians*, London: Methuen.

'Pictures from Uganda', (1894), *Church Missionary Gleaner*, 21 (6): 90.

Plowden, W.C. (1883), *Report on the Census of British India taken on the 17th February 1881*, vol. 1, London: Eyre & Spottiswoode.

Pultuney, P. and J.W.S. Kaye (1844), *Peregrine Pultuney; or, Life in India*, London: Henry Colburn.

Rawick, George (1972), *The American Slave: A Composite Autobiography*, vol. 14, Westport, CT: Greenwood Press.

Reeves, Maud Pember ([1913] 1979), *Round About a Pound a Week*, London: Virago.

Riddell, R. (1871) *Indian Domestic Economy and Receipt Book . . . By the Author of Manual of Gardening for Western India*, 7th edition, London: Thacker & Spink.

Roberts, Emma (1835), *Scenes and Characteristics of Hindostan, with Sketches of Anglo-Indian Society*, London: W.H. Allen.

Roberts, Robert (1827), *The House Servant's Directory; or, a Monitor for Private Families*, Boston, MA: Munroe & Francis.

Rolph, C.H. (1982), *London Particulars: Memories of an Edwardian Boyhood*, 2nd edition, Oxford: Oxford University Press.

Rush, Benjamin (1787), 'Thoughts Upon Female Education' (Boston, 1787). Sourced from *Google Books*. Available online: https://books.google.co.uk/books?id=xtUKA

AAAIAAJ&pg=PA75&lpg=PA75&dq=Thoughts+upon+female+education&source=bl&ots=aK3AS0mXdT&sig=WTlJr377ytBDL2WAjrs8aREGOtQ&hl=en&sa=X&ved=0CEQQ6AEwATgKahUKEwicqNfIvpTHAhWkCNsKHRrNCUU#v=onepage&q=Thoughts%20upon%20female%20education&f=false (accessed 10 July 2015).

Sabin, Edwin L. (1911), 'Tea from Japan', *Lippincott's Monthly*, 88: 231–36.

Said Ruete, Emily ([1888] 1907), *Memoirs of an Arabian Princess*, trans. Lionel Strachey, New York: Doubleday, Page.

Schuyler Matthews, F. (1894), 'An Oriental Den in the Indian Style', *The Decorator and Furnisher*, 24 (1): 11–12.

Seebohm-Rowntree, B. (1903), *Poverty: A Study of Town Life*, London: Macmillan.

Shore, Frederick John (1883), British Library, Asia, Pacific and African Collections, MSS Eur/E307/5 MSS Eur/E307/5, 23 December, Frederick John Shore Collection.

'Some Account of the Ancient and Present State of Shrewsbury', (1808), Shrewsbury: P. Sandford.

Soyer, Alexis (1849), *The Modern Housewife or Ménagére*, London: Simpkin, Marshall.

Stacpoole, Florence (1912), *The Mother's Book: On the Rearing of Healthy Children*, London: Wells Gardner, Darton.

Steel, F.A. and G. Gardiner ([1890] 2010), *The Complete Indian Housekeeper and Cook*, ed. Ralph Crane and Anna Johnston, Oxford: Oxford University Press.

Steel, F.A. and G. Gardiner (1898), *The Complete Indian Housekeeper and Cook*, 4th edition, London: Wm. Heinemann.

Steel, F.A. and G. Gardiner (1904), *The Complete Indian Housekeeper and Cook*, new and revised edition, London: Wm. Heinemann.

Stocqueler, J.H. (1844), *The Hand-book of India: A Guide to the Stranger and the Traveller, and a Companion to the Resident*, 3rd edition, London: W.H. Allen.

Stowe, Harriet Stowe (1853), *Uncle Tom's Cabin; or, Life among the Lowly*, London: Nathaniel Cooke.

Surrey History Centre, SHC 3043/1/3/1/2, 'Rules for the Guidance of the Attendants, Servants and all Persons engaged in the Service of the Surrey County Asylum at Brookwood, near Woking Station, 1871'.

The Book of the Household, (1862), 2 vols., London: Ward, Lock.

'The Law of Order and How Beryl Came to Observe It', (1900a), *The Girl's Own Paper*, no. 1058, 7 April, p. 427.

The Sydney Morning Herald (1847), 5 February. Available online: http://nla.gov.au/nla.news-page1516626.

The Sydney Morning Herald (1866), 9 June. Available online: http://nla.gov.au/nla.news-page1473635.

The Workwoman's Guide, (1838),London: Simpkin, Marshall.

Trollope, Fanny (1832), 'Cincinnati—Forest Farm—Mr. Bullock', in *The Domestic Manners of the Americans*, 1832. Sourced from Project Gutenberg, 2003. Available online: http://www.gutenberg.org/cache/epub/10345/pg10345-images.html (accessed 12 February 2016).

'Two Portraits from Toro', (1901), *Church Missionary Gleaner*, 28 (5): 77.

Unwin, Raymond (1912), *Nothing Gained by Overcrowding: How the Garden City Type of Development May Benefit Both Owner and Occupier*, London: P.S. King.

V&A Collections, Museum Number IS.2376-1883. Available online: http://collections.vam.ac.uk/item/O77358/table-unknown.

Walker, Rev. R.H. (1893), 'Mika Sematimba, Chief in Uganda', *Church Missionary Gleaner*, 20 (3): 37–39.
Walter, Emma (1839), Indian Journal of Emma Walter, British Library, Oriental and India Office Collections, MSS Eur/B265/1, 28 November.
Ward, H.F. and J.W. Milligan (1912), *Handbook of British East Africa*, London/Nairobi: Sifton Praed/Caxton (B.E.A.).
Waring, Edward J. (1866), *The Tropical Resident at Home: Letters Addressed to Europeans Returning from India and the Colonies on Subjects Connected with their Health and General Welfare*, London: John Churchill.
Washington, Booker T. (1902), 'Negro Homes', *Colored American Magazine*, 5: 378–79.
White, F.H. (1920), 'Kavirondo Boys Make Good', *Church Missionary Gleaner*, 47 (3): 55.
Wilson, Anne Campbell (1904), *Hints for the First Years of Residence in India*, Oxford: Clarendon Press.
Wilson, Anne Campbell (1911), *Letters from India*, Edinburgh: William Blackwood.
Wilson, Harriet E. ([1859] 1983), *Our Nig; or, Sketches in the Life of a Free Black, in a Two Story White House, North. Showing that Slavery's Shadows Fall Even There*, New York: Vintage.
Winnington-Ingram, Arthur (1897), *Work in Great Cities: Six Lectures on Pastoral Theology Delivered in the Divinity School, Cambridge Easter Term, 1895*, 3rd edition, London: Gardener, Darton.
Wood, Maria Lydia (1857a), Letters of Maria Lydia Wood, Asia Pacific and African Collections, British Library, Letter of 10 March 1857.
Wood, Maria Lydia (1857b), Letters of Maria Lydia Wood, Asia Pacific and African Collections, British Library, Letter of 27 March 1857.
Wood, Maria Lydia (1857c), Letters of Maria Lydia Wood, Asia Pacific and African Collections, British Library, Letter of 29 March 1857.
Wood, Maria Lydia (1857d), Letters of Maria Lydia Wood, Asia Pacific and African Collections, British Library, Letter of 22 July 1857.
Wright, Thomas (1868), *Some Habits and Customs of the Working Classes by a Journeyman Engineer*, London: Tinsley.
Younghusband, Ethel (1910), *Glimpses of East Africa and Zanzibar*, London: John Long.

Secondary sources

Abey-Koch, Madelaine (2006), 'History of Housekeeping', in *The National Trust Manual of Housekeeping: The Care of Collections in Historic Houses Open to the Public*, 20–33, Oxford: Elsevier, Butterworth-Heinemann.
Adam, Thomas (2007), 'Housing Charities and the Provision of Social Housing in Germany and the United States of America, Great Britain and Canada in the Nineteenth Century', in Bernard Harris and Paul Bridgen (eds.), *Charity and Mutual Aid in Europe and North America since 1800*, 158–88, London: Routledge.
Adams, Annmarie (1996), *Architecture in the Family Way: Doctors, Houses, and Women, 1870–1900*, London: McGill-Queen's University Press.
Adie, J.J. (1949), 'Zanzibar "Arab" Chests', in *A Guide to Zanzibar*, 104–7, Zanzibar: Government Printer.
Algotsson, Sharne (2000), *African Style: Down to the Details*, New York: Clarkson Potter.

Ammerman, Nancy T., ed. (2006), *Everyday Religion: Observing Modern Religious Lives*, Oxford: Oxford University Press.
Anderson, Michael (1990), 'The Social Implications of Demographic Change', in F.M.L. Thompson (ed.), *The Cambridge Social History of Britain 1750–1950, vol. 2: People and Their Environment*, 1–70, Cambridge: Cambridge University Press.
Ansari, Sarah (2004), 'Book Review', *History in Focus*, 8. Available online: http://www.history.ac.uk/ihr/Focus/Gender/ansari.html.
Appadurai, Arjun (1986), 'Introduction: Commodities and the Politics of Value', in Arjun Appadurai (ed.), *The Social Life of Things: Commodities in Cultural Perspective*, 3–63, Cambridge: Cambridge University Press.
Arnold, David (1979), 'European Orphans and Vagrants in India in the Nineteenth Century', *Journal of Imperial and Commonwealth History*, 7 (2): 104–27.
Ashcroft, Bill, Gareth Griffiths and Helen Tiffin, eds. (2013), *Postcolonial Studies: the Key Concepts*, 3rd edition, New York: Routledge.
Ashmore, Sonia (2008), 'Liberty and Lifestyle: Shopping for Art and Luxury in Nineteenth-Century London', in David Hussey and Margaret Ponsonby (eds.), *Buying for the Home: Shopping for the Domestic from the Seventeenth Century to the Present*, 73–90, Aldershot: Ashgate.
Aslin, Elizabeth (1969), *The Aesthetic Movement: Prelude to Art Nouveau*, London: Ferndale Editions.
Asquer, Enrica (2012), 'Domesticity and Beyond: Gender, Family and Consumption in Modern Europe', in Frank Trentmann (ed.), *The Oxford Handbook of the History of Consumption*, 568–84, Oxford: Oxford University Press.
Atkins, Annette (2007), *Creating Minnesota: A History from the Inside Out*, St. Paul, MN: Minnesota Historical Society Press.
Atkins, Gareth (2014), '"Idle Reading"? Policing the Boundaries of the Nineteenth-Century Household', in John Doran, Charlotte Methuen and Alexandra Walsham (eds.), *Religion and the Household* (*Studies in Church History* 50), 331–42, London: Boydell Press.
Atkins, Keletso (1988), '"Kafir Time": Pre-Industrial Temporal Concepts and Labor Discipline in Nineteenth Century Colonial Natal', *Journal of African History*, 29 (2): 229–44.
Attfield, Judy and Pat Kirkham, eds. (1995), *A View from the Interior*, London: Women's Press.
Auslander, Leora (2015), 'Reading German Jewry through Documentary Photography: From the Kaiserreich to the Third Reich', *Central European History*, 48 (3): 300–34.
Avery, Tracey (2007), 'Furniture Design and Colonialism: Negotiating Relationships between Britain and Australia, 1880–1901', *Home Cultures*, 4 (1): 69–92.
Aynsley, Jeremy and Charlotte Grant, eds. (2006), *Imagined Interiors: Representing the Domestic Interior since the Renaissance*, London: V&A Publications.
Banerjee, Swapna M. (2004), *Men, Women, and Domestics: Articulating Middle-class Identity in Colonial Bengal*, New Delhi: Oxford University Press.
Banivanua Mar, Tracey and Penelope Edmonds, eds. (2010), *Making Settler Colonial Space: Perspectives on Race, Place and Identity*, Basingstoke: Palgrave Macmillan.
Barson, Susie (1999), 'Infinite Variety in Brick and Stucco: 1840–1914', in Andrew Saint (ed.), *London Suburbs*, 61–102, London: Merrell.
Baudrillard, Jean (1994), 'The System of Collecting', in John Elsner and Roger Cardinal (eds.), *The Cultures of Collecting*, 7–24, London: Reaktion Books.

Beach, Harlan P. and Charles H. Fahs, eds. (1925), *World Missionary Atlas*, New York: Institute of Social and Religious Research.
Beddow, Tim and Natasha Burns (2002), *Safari Style*, London: Thames & Hudson.
Beese, A.K. (1971), *Coningsby Hospital*, Hereford: The Coningsby Trust.
Beetham, Margaret (1996), *A Magazine of Her Own?*, London: Routledge.
Benson, John (1994), *The Rise of Consumer Society in Britain 1880–1980*, London: Longman.
Berg, Maxine (1994), 'Factories, Workshops and Industrial Organization', in Roderick Floud and Donald McCloskey (eds.), *The Economic History of Britain Since 1700, vol. 1: 1700–1860*, 2nd edition, 123–50, Cambridge: Cambridge University Press.
Berg, Maxine (2004), 'In Pursuit of Luxury: Global History and British Consumer Goods in the Eighteenth Century', *Past and Present*, 182: 85–142.
Berger, Molly W. (1998), 'A House Divided: The Culture of the American Luxury Hotel, 1825–1860', in Roger Horowitz and Arwen Mohun (eds.), *His and Hers: Gender, Consumption and Technology*, 39–66, Charlottesville, VA: University of Virginia Press.
Black, Clementina (1915), *Married Women's Work*, London: G. Bell.
Blackburn, Sheila (2007), *A Fair Day's Wage for a Fair Day's Work? Sweated Labor and the Origins of Minimum Wage Legislation in Britain*, Aldershot: Ashgate.
Blassingame, John W. (1976), 'Status and Social Structure in the Slave Community: Evidence from New Sources', in Harry P. Owens (ed.), *Perspectives and Irony in American Slavery*, 137–51, Jackson, MS: University of Mississippi Press.
Bloch, Ruth H. ([1987] 2003), 'Republican Virtue: The Gendered Meanings of Virtue in Revolutionary America', in Ruth H. Bloch (ed.), *Gender and Morality in Anglo-American Culture, 1650–1800*, 136–53, Berkeley, CA: University of California Press, 2003.
Blunt, Alison (1999), 'Imperial Geographies of Home: British Domesticity in India, 1886–1925', *Transactions of the Institute of British Geographers*, 24 (4): 421–40.
Blunt, Alison and Ann Varley (2004), 'Geographies of Home', *Cultural Geographies*, 11 (3): 3–6.
Boos, Florence (2013), 'Under Physical Siege: Early Victorian Working-Class Women's Autobiographies', *Philological Quarterly*, 92 (2): 251–69.
Bourke, Joanna (1994), *Working-class Cultures in Britain 1890–1960: Gender, Class and Ethnicity*, London: Routledge.
Boyer, George R. (2004), 'Living Standards, 1860–1939', in Roderick Floud and Paul Johnson (eds.), *The Cambridge Economic History of Modern Britain, vol. 2: Economic Maturity, 1860–1939*, 280–313, Cambridge: Cambridge University Press.
Breward, Christopher (2001), 'Fashionable Living', in Michael Snodin and John Styles (eds.), *Design and the Decorative Arts, Britain 1500–1900*, 401–14, London: V&A Publications.
Briggs, Asa ([1963] 1993), *Victorian Cities*, Berkeley, CA: University of California Press.
Briggs, Asa (1990), *Victorian Things*, Harmondsworth: Penguin.
Brown, Callum G. (2009), *The Death of Christian Britain: Understanding Secularisation 1800–2000*, London: Routledge.
Buettner, Elizabeth (2004), *Empire Families: Britons and Late Imperial India*, Oxford: Oxford University Press.
Burnett, John (1978), *A Social History of Housing 1815–1970*, Newton Abbot: David & Charles.

Burnett, John (1980), *A Social History of Housing 1815–1970*, London: Methuen.
Burnett, John (1986), *A Social History of Housing 1815–1970*, 2nd edition, London: Methuen.
Burnett, John (1989), *Plenty and Want: A Social History of Food in England from 1815 to the Present Day*, 3rd edition, London: Methuen.
Burnett, John, ed. (1994), *Useful Toil: Autobiographies of Working People from the 1820s to the 1920s*, London: Routledge.
Burnett, John (2004), *England Eats Out: A Social History of Eating Out in England from 1830 to the Present*, Harlow: Pearson Education.
Burnett, John, David Vincent and David Mayall, eds. (1984), *The Autobiography of the Working Class: An Annotated Critical Bibliography, vol. 1: 1790–1900*, Brighton: Harvester.
Burr, Virgnia, I. (1990), *The Secret Eye: The Journal of Ella Gertrude Clanton Thomas, 1848–1889*, Chapel Hill, NC: University of North Carolina Press.
Burton, Antoinette (2003), *Dwelling in the Archive: Women Writing House, Home and History in Late Colonial India*, Oxford: Oxford University Press.
Bushman, Richard L. (1992), *The Refinement of America: Persons, Houses, Cities*, New York: Alfred A. Knopf.
Casella, Eleanor Conlin, Ellen Cornwall and Lucy Frost (2001), 'Your Unfortunate and Dutiful Wife', in Lucy Frost and Hamish Maxwell-Street (eds.), *Chain Letters: Narrating Convict Lives*, 105–18, Melbourne: Melbourne University Press.
Censer, Jane Turner (2003), *The Reconstruction of White Southern Womanhood*, Baton Rouge, LA: Louisiana State University Press.
Chandra, Satish (1987), *The Indian Ocean: Explorations in History, Commerce and Politics*, London: Sage.
Chattopadhyay, Swati (2000), 'Blurring Boundaries: The Limits of "White Town" in Colonial Calcutta', *Journal of the Society of Architectural Historians*, 59 (2): 154–79.
Chattopadhyay, Swati (2002), 'Goods, Chattels and Sundry Items: Constructing 19th-Century Anglo-Indian Domestic Life', *Journal of Material Culture*, 7 (3): 243–71.
Chattopadhyay, Swati (2005), *Representing Calcutta: Modernity, Nationalism and the Colonial Uncanny*, London: Routledge.
Chaudhuri, K.N. (1990), *Asia before Europe: Economy and Civilization of the Indian Ocean from the Rise of Islam to 1750*, Cambridge: Cambridge University Press.
Chaudhuri, N. (1994) 'Memsahibs and their servants in nineteenth-century India', *Women's History Review*, 3 (4): 549–62.
Christie, Nancy (2002), 'Introduction', in Nancy Christie (ed.), *Households of Faith: Family, Gender, and Community in Canada*, 3–36, Montreal / Kingston, McGill-Queen's University Press.
Christie, Nancy (2003), '"On the Threshold of Manhood": Working-Class Religion and Domesticity in Victorian Britain and Canada', *Histoire Sociale / Social History*, 36 (71): 145–74.
Clancy-Smith, Julia and Frances Gouda, eds. (1998), *Domesticating the Empire: Race, Gender and Family Life in French and Dutch Colonialism*, Charlottesville, VA: University Press of Virginia.
Cohen, Deborah (2006), *Household Gods: The British and Their Possessions*, New Haven, CT: Yale University Press.
Collingham, E.M. (2001), *Imperial Bodies: The Physical Experience of the Raj c. 1800–1947*, Cambridge: Polity Press.

Comaroff, John and Jean Comaroff (1997), *Of Revelation and Revolution, vol. 2: The Dialectics of Modernity on a South African Frontier*, Chicago, IL: University of Chicago Press.

Conrad, Sebastian (2010), *Globalisation and the Nation in Imperial Germany*, Cambridge: Cambridge University Press.

Cooper, Frederick and Ann Laura Stoler (1997), *Tensions of Empire: Colonial Cultures in a Bourgeois World*, Berkeley, CA: University of California Press.

Cott, Nancy ([1977] 1997), *The Bonds of Womanhood: 'Woman's Sphere' in New England, 1780–1835*, New Haven, CT: Yale University Press.

Cox, Jeffrey (1982), *The English Churches in a Secular Society: Lambeth, 1870–1930*, Oxford: Oxford University Press.

Crewe, Vicky and D.M. Handley (2013), '"Uncle Tom was there, in Crockery": Material Culture and a Victorian Working-Class Childhood', *Childhood in the Past: An International Journal*, 6 (2): 89–105.

Crisp, Zoe (2012), 'Housing and Private Outside Space in Nineteenth-Century England', *Cambridge Working Papers in Economic and Social History*, no. 3. Available online: http://www.econsoc.hist.cam.ac.uk/working_papers.html (accessed 20 May 2016).

Crocker, Ruth (2006), *Mrs. Russell Sage: Women's Activism and Philanthropy in Gilded Age and Progressive Era America*, Bloomington, IN: Indiana University Press.

Crossick, Geoffrey and Heinz-Gerhard Haupt (1995), *The Petite Bourgeoisie in Europe 1780–1914: Enterprise, Family and Independence*, London: Routledge.

Cruickshank, Dan and Neil Burton (1990), *Life in the Georgian City*, London: Viking.

Cruz, Jesus (2011), *The Rise of Middle-Class Culture in Nineteenth-Century Spain*, Baton Rouge, LA: Louisiana State University Press.

Daly, Suzanne (2011), *The Empire Inside: Indian Commodities in Victorian Domestic Novels*, Ann Arbor, MI: University of Michigan Press.

Daniels, Stephen (1981), 'Landscaping for a Manufacturer: Humphry Repton's Commission for Benjamin Gott at Armley in 1809–10', *Journal of Historical Geography*, 7 (4): 379–96.

Daunton, Martin J. (1983), *House and Home in the Victorian City: Working-Class Housing 1850–1914*, London: Edward Arnold.

Daunton, Martin J. (1990), 'Housing', in F.M.L. Thompson (ed.), *The Cambridge Social History of Britain, 1750–1950, vol. 2: People and their Environment*, 195–250, Cambridge: Cambridge University Press.

Daunton, Martin J., ed. (2001a), *The Cambridge Urban History of Britain, vol. 3: 1840–1950*, Cambridge: Cambridge University Press.

Daunton, Martin J. (2001b), 'Introduction', in Martin J. Daunton (ed.), *The Cambridge Urban History of Britain, vol. 3: 1840–1950*, 1–56, Cambridge: Cambridge University Press.

Davidoff, Leonore (1973), *The Best Circles: Society, Etiquette and the Season*, London: Croom Helm.

Davidoff, Leonore (1995), *Worlds Between: Historical Perspectives on Gender and Class*, Cambridge: Polity Press.

Davidoff, Leonore (2003), 'Gender and the "Great Divide": Public and Private in British Gender History', *Journal of Women's History*, 15 (1): 11–27.

Davidoff, Leonore (2012), *Thicker than Water: Siblings and Their Relations, 1780–1920*, Oxford: Oxford University Press.

Davidoff, Leonore and Catherine Hall (1987), *Family Fortunes: Men and Women of the English Middle Class 1780–1850*, London: Routledge.

Davidoff, Leonore and Catherine Hall ([1987] 2002), *Family Fortunes: Men and Women of the English Middle Class 1780–1850*, revised edition, London: Routledge.

Davin, Anna (1996), *Growing Up Poor: Home, School and Street in London, 1870–1914*, London: Rivers Oram Press.

Dejung, Christof and Niels Petersson (2013), *The Foundations of Worldwide Economic Integration*, Cambridge: Cambridge University Press.

Delap, Lucy (2011), *Knowing Their Place: Domestic Service in Twentieth-Century Britain*, Oxford: Oxford University Press.

Dennis, Richard (2008), *Cities in Modernity: Representations and Productions of Metropolitan Space, 1840–1930*, Cambridge: Cambridge University Press.

Desai, Madhavi, Miki Desai and Jon Lang (2012), *The Bungalow in Twentieth-Century India*, Farnham: Ashgate.

de Vries, J. (2008), *The Industrious Revolution: Consumer Behavior and the Household Economy, 1650 to the Present*, Cambridge: Cambridge University Press.

Digby, Anne (1985), *Madness, Morality and Medicine: A Study of the York Retreat, 1796–1914*, Cambridge: Cambridge University Press.

Donald, Moira (1999), 'Tranquil Havens? Critiquing the Idea of Home as a Middle-Class Sanctuary', in Inga Bryden and Janet Floyd (eds.), *Domestic Space: Reading the Nineteenth-Century Interior*, 103–20, Manchester: Manchester University Press.

Doolittle, Megan (2011), 'Time, Space, and Memories: The Father's Chair and Grandfather Clocks in Victorian Working-Class Domestic Lives', *Home Cultures*, 8 (3): 245–64.

Drews, Marie (2009), 'Catharine Beecher, Harriet E. Wilson, and Domestic Discomfort at the Northern Table', in Monika Elbert and Marie Drews (eds.), *Culinary Aesthetics and Practices in Nineteenth-Century American Literature*, 89–106, New York: Palgrave Macmillan.

Driver, Felix (1988), 'Moral Geographies: Social Science and the Urban Environment in Mid-Nineteenth Century England', *Transactions of the Institute of British Geographers*, N.S., 13: 275–87.

Dussart, F.C. (2005) 'The Master–Servant Relationship in 19th Century England and India', PhD thesis, University College London, University of London.

Dwyer, Ellen (1987), *Homes for the Mad: Life Inside Two Nineteenth-Century Asylums*, New Brunswick, NJ: Rutgers University Press.

Edmonds, Penelope (2010), 'The Intimate, Urbanizing Frontier: Native Camps and Settler Colonialism's Violent Array of Spaces', in Tracey Banivanua Mar and Penelope Edmonds (eds.), *Making Settler Colonial Space*, 129–54, Basingstoke: Palgrave Macmillan.

Edwards, Clive (2006), '"Home is where the art is": Women, Handicrafts and Home Improvements 1750–1900', *Journal of Design History*, 19 (1): 11–21.

Elbert, Monika M. (2000), 'Introduction', in Monika M. Elbert (ed.), *Separate Spheres No More: Gender Convergence in American Literature, 1830–1930*, 1–25, Tuscaloosa, AL: University of Alabama Press.

English Heritage (2011), *Designation Listing Selection Guide, Domestic 3: Suburban and Country Houses*, Swindon: English Heritage.

Facos, Michelle (1996), 'The Ideal Swedish Home: Carl Larrson's Lilla Hytannäs', in Christopher Reed (ed.), *Not at Home: The Suppression of Domesticity in Modern Art and Architecture*, 7–15, London: Thames & Hudson.

Faire, Lucy (1998), 'Making Home: Working-Class Perceptions of Space, Time and Material Culture in Family Life, 1900–1955', PhD thesis, University of Leicester.
Faust, Drew Gilpin (1996), *Mothers of Invention: Women of the Slaveholding South in the American Civil War*, New York: Vintage Press.
Fedorowich, Kent (2008), 'The British Empire on the Move, 1760–1914', in Sarah Stockwell (ed.), *The British Empire: Themes and Perspectives*, 63–100, Oxford: Blackwell.
Ferry, Emma (2003), '"Decorators May be Compared to Doctors": An Analysis of Rhoda and Agnes Garrett's *Suggestions for House Decorating in Painting, Woodwork and Furniture* (1876)', *Journal of Design History*, 16 (1): 15–33.
Fine, Agnes (1984), 'A Consideration of the Trousseau: A Feminine Culture?', in Michelle Perrot (ed.), *Writing Women's History*, 118–45, Oxford: Blackwell.
Finn, Margot (1996), 'Being in Debt in Dickens' London: Fact, Fictional Representation and the Nineteenth-Century Prison', *Journal of Victorian Culture*, 1 (2): 203–26.
Fliegelman, Jay (1982), *Prodigals and Pilgrims: The American Revolution Against Patriarchal Authority, 1750–1800*, Cambridge: Cambridge University Press.
Flint, Elizabeth (1963), *Hot Bread and Chips*, London: Museum Press.
Floud, Roderick, Jane Humphries and Paul Johnson, eds. (2014a), *The Cambridge Economic History of Modern Britain, vol. 1: 1700–1870*, Cambridge: Cambridge University Press.
Floud, Roderick, Jane Humphries and Paul Johnson, eds. (2014b), *The Cambridge Economic History of Modern Britain, vol. 2: 1870 to the Present*, Cambridge: Cambridge University Press.
Foley, Tricia (1993), *The Romance of British Colonial Style*, New York: Clarkson Potter.
Forty, Adrian (1987), *Objects of Desire: Design and Society 1750–1980*, London: Thames & Hudson.
Fowler, Simon (2007), *Workhouse: The People, The Places, Life Behind Doors*, Richmond: The National Archives.
Francis, Martin (2002), 'The Domestication of the Male? Recent Research on Nineteenth- and Twentieth-Century British Masculinity', *Historical Journal*, 45 (3): 637–52.
Franklin, Jill (1981), *The Gentleman's Country House and its Plan, 1835–1914*, London: Routledge & Kegan Paul.
Fraser, Craig and Mandy Allen (2007), *The New Safari: Design, Decor, Detail*, Cape Town: Quivertree.
Froide, Amy (2007), *Never Married: Singlewomen in Early Modern England*, Oxford: Oxford University Press.
Gamber, Wendy (2007), *The Boarding House in Nineteenth-Century America*, Baltimore, MD: Johns Hopkins University Press.
Gee, E. (2009), '"Where Shall She Live?": The History and Designation of Housing for Working-Women in London, 1880–1925', *Journal for Architectural Conservation*, 15 (2): 27–46.
Genovese, Eugene (1991), '"Our Family, White and Black": Family and Household in the Southern Slaveholders' View', in Carol Bleser (ed.), *In Joy and in Sorrow: Women, Family, and Marriage in the Victorian South*, 69–87, Oxford: Oxford University Press.
George, Susan (2000), *Liverpool Park Estates*, Liverpool: Liverpool University Press.
Gerber, David A. (2011), *American Immigration: A Very Short Introduction*, Oxford: Oxford University Press.

Gere, Charlotte and Lesley Hoskins (2000), *The House Beautiful: Oscar Wilde and the Aesthetic Interior*, London: Lund Humphries / The Geffrye Museum.

Gerritsen, Anne and Giorgio Riello (2016), *The Global Lives of Things: The Material Culture of Connections in the Early Modern World*, Oxford: Routledge.

Gestrich, Andreas and Margrit Schulte Beerbühl, eds. (2011), *Cosmopolitan Networks in Commerce and Society*, London: German Historical Institute.

Ghose, Indira, ed. (1998), *Memsahibs Abroad: Writings by Women Travellers in Nineteenth Century India*, New Delhi: Oxford University Press.

Ghosh, Devleena and Stephen Muecke, eds. (2007), *Cultures of Trade: Indian Ocean Exchanges*, Newcastle-upon-Tyne: Cambridge Scholars.

Gilbert, Christopher (1991), *English Vernacular Furniture 1750–1900*, New Haven, CT: Yale University Press.

Gilbert, Erik (2004), *Dhows and the Colonial Economy of Zanzibar, 1880–1970*, Oxford: James Currey.

Giles, Judy (2004), *The Parlour and the Suburb*, London: Berg.

Gillis, John R. (1997), *A World of Their Own Making: A History of Myth and Ritual in Family Life*, Oxford: Oxford University Press.

Girouard, Mark (1978), *Life in the English Country House: A Social and Architectural History*, New Haven, CT: Yale University Press.

Girouard, Mark (1980), *Life in the English Country House: A Social and Architectural History*, Harmondsworth: Penguin.

Girouard, Mark (2000), *Life in the French Country House*, London: Cassell.

Glazier, M. (1996), 'Common Lodging Houses in Chester, 1841–71', in R. Swift (ed.), *Victorian Chester: Essays in Social History, 1830–1900*, 53–83, Liverpool: Liverpool University Press.

Gleadle, Kathryn (2009), *Borderline Citizens: Women, Gender, and Political Culture in Britain, 1815–1867*, Oxford: Oxford University Press.

Glover, William J. (2004), '"A Feeling of Absence from Old England": The Colonial Bungalow', *Home Cultures*, 1 (1): 61–82.

Glymph, Thavolia (2008), *Out of the House of Bondage: The Transformation of the Plantation Household*, New York: Cambridge University Press.

Godley, Andrew (1995), 'The Development of the UK Clothing Industry, 1850–1950: Output and Productivity Growth', *Business History*, 37 (4): 46–63.

Goggin, Maureen Daly (2002), 'An Essamplaire Essai on the Rhetoricity of Needlework Sampler-Making: A Contribution on Theorizing and Historizing Rhetorical Praxis', *Rhetoric Review*, 21 (4): 309–38.

Goose, Nigel and Leanne Moden (2010), *A History of Doughty's Hospital Norwich, 1687–2009*, Hatfield: University of Hertfordshire.

Gordon, Beverly (1996), 'Woman's Domestic Body: The Conceptual Conflation of Women and Interiors in the Industrial Age', *Winterthur Portfolio*, 31 (4): 281–301.

Gordon, Eleanor and Gwyneth Nair (2003), *Public Lives: Women, Family and Society in Victorian Britain*, New Haven, CT: Yale University Press.

Gregory, Robert (1993), *South Asians in East Africa: An Economic and Social History, 1890–1980*, Boulder, CO: Westview Press.

Grier, Katharine C. (1988), *Culture and Comfort: People, Parlors, and Upholstery, 1850–1930*, Rochester, NY: The Strong Museum / University of Massachusetts Press.

Grier, Katharine C. (1997), *Culture and Comfort: Parlor Making and Middle-Class Identity, 1850–1930*, Rochester, NY: The Strong Museum / University of Massachusetts Press.

Griffin, Emma (2013), *Liberty Dawn: A People's History of the Industrial Revolution*, New Haven, CT: Yale University Press.

Griswold, Robert L. (1990), 'Divorce and the Legal Redefinition of Victorian Manhood', in Marc C. Carnes and Clyde Griffen (eds.), *Meanings for Manhood: Constructions of Masculinity in Victorian America*, 96–110, Chicago, IL: University of Chicago Press.

Gunderson, Joan R. (2006), *To be Useful to the World: Women in Revolutionary America, 1740–1790*, Chapel Hill, NC: University of North Carolina Press.

Gurney, Peter (2015), *Wanting and Having: Popular Politics and Liberal Consumerism in England, 1830–70*, Manchester: Manchester University Press.

Hall, Catherine (2002), *Civilizing Subjects: Metropole and Colony in the English Imagination, 1830–1867*, Cambridge: Polity Press.

Hall, Catherine and Sonya Rose, eds. (2006), *At Home with the Empire: Metropolitan Culture and the Imperial World*, Cambridge: Cambridge University Press.

Hall, David D. (1997), *Lived Religion in America: Toward a History of Practice*, Princeton, NJ: Princeton University Press.

Hallamore Caesar, Ann (2004), 'Women and the Public/Private Divide: The Salotto, Home and Theatre in Late Nineteenth-Century Italy', in Perry Willson (ed.), *Gender, Family and Sexuality: The Private Sphere in Italy, 1860–1945*, 105–121, Basingstoke: Palgrave Macmillan.

Hamerow, Theodore S. (1983), *The Birth of a New Europe: State and Society in the Nineteenth Century*, Chapel Hill, NC: University of North Carolina Press.

Hamlett, Jane (2009), 'The Dining Room should be the Man's Paradise and the Drawing Room is the Woman's': Gender and Middle-Class Domestic Space in England, 1850–1910', *Gender and History*, 21 (3): 576–91.

Hamlett, Jane (2010), *Material Relations: Domestic Interiors and Middle-Class Families in England, 1850–1910*, Manchester: Manchester University Press.

Hamlett, Jane (2015), *At Home in the Institution: Material Life in Asylums, Lodging Houses and Schools in Victorian and Edwardian England*, London: Palgrave Macmillan.

Hamlett, Jane and Rebecca Preston (2013), '"A Veritable Palace for the Hard-Working Labourer?" Space, Material Culture and Inmate Experience in London's Rowton Houses', in Jane Hamlett, Lesley Hoskins and Rebecca Preston (eds.), *Residential Institutions in Britain 1725–1970: Inmates and Environments*, 93–108, London: Routledge.

Harper, Roger H. (1985), *Victorian Building Regulations: 1840–1914*, London: Mansell Publishing.

Harvey, David (1990), 'Between Space and Time: Reflections on the Geographical Imagination', *Annals of the Association of American Geographers*, 80 (3): 418–34.

Harvey, Karen (2009), 'Men Making Home: Masculinity and Domesticity in Eighteenth-Century Britain', *Gender and History*, 21 (2): 520–40.

Heal, Felicity (1990), *Hospitality in Early Modern England*, Oxford: Clarendon Press.

Hemphill, C. Dallett (2011), *Siblings: Brothers and Sisters in American History*, Oxford: Oxford University Press.

Hewitt, Martin (1999), 'Domestic Visiting and the Constitution of Domestic Space in the Mid-Nineteenth Century', in Inga Bryden and Janet Floyd (eds.), *Domestic Space: Reading the Nineteenth-Century Interior*, 121–41, Manchester: Manchester University Press.

Hewitt, Martin (2004), 'Class and the Classes', in Chris Williams (ed.), *A Companion to Nineteenth-Century Britain*, 305–20, London: Blackwell.

Hickman, Claire (2009), 'Cheerful Prospects and Tranquil Restoration: The Visual Experience of Landscape as Part of the Therapeutic Regime of the British Asylum, 1800–1860', *History of Psychiatry*, 20 (4): 425–441.

Higgs, Edward (2005), *Making Sense of the Census Revisited*, London: Institute of Historical Research.

Hill, Bridget (1996), *Women Alone: Spinsters in England, 1660–1850*, New Haven, CT: Yale University Press.

Hilton, Boyd (1988), *The Age of Atonement: The Influence of Evangelicalism on Social and Economic Thought, 1785–1865*, Oxford: Clarendon Press.

Hobhouse, Mary (1906) *Letters from India 1872–1877*, Edinburgh: printed for private circulation.

Hoganson, Kristin L. (2002), 'Cosmopolitan Domesticity: Importing the American Dream, 1865–1920', *American Historical Review*, 107 (1): 55–83.

Hoganson, Kristen L. (2007), *Consumers' Imperium: The Global Production of American Domesticity, 1865–1920*, Chapel Hill, NC: University of North Carolina Press.

Holcombe, Lyanne (2013), 'Strand Palace Hotel, London', in Tom Avermaete and Anne Massey (eds.), *Hotel Lobbies and Lounges: The Architecture of Professional Hospitality*, 126–29, London: Routledge.

Holloway, Gerry (2005), *Women and Work in Britain since 1840*, London: Routledge.

Horn, Pamela (2004), *The Rise and Fall of the Victorian Servant*, Stroud: Sutton Publishing.

Hoskins, Lesley (2013), 'Social, Economic and Geographical Differences in Mid-Nineteenth-Century Homes: The Evidence from Inventories', *Regional Furniture*, xxvii: 93–119.

Hoskins, Lesley (2014), 'Household Inventories Reassessed', *Home Cultures*, 11 (3): 333–52.

Huber, Valeska (2013), *Channeling Mobilities: Migration and Globalisation in the Suez Canal Region and Beyond, 1869–1914*, Cambridge: Cambridge University Press.

Humphries, Jane (2004), 'Household Economy', in Roderick Floud and Paul Johnson (eds.), *The Cambridge Economic History of Modern Britain, vol. 1: Industrialisation, 1700–1860*, 238–67, Cambridge: Cambridge University Press.

Hunt, Leigh Ina (2006), 'Victorian Passion to Modern Phenomenon: A Literary and Rhetorical Analysis of Two Hundred Years of Scrapbooks and Scrapbook Making', PhD dissertation, University of Texas.

Hurt, R. Douglas (1998), *The Ohio Frontier: Crucible of the Old Northwest, 1720–1830*, Bloomington, IN: Indiana University Press.

Hussey, David and Margaret Ponsonby (2012), *The Single Homemaker and Material Culture in the Long Eighteenth Century*, Farnham: Ashgate.

Inglis, K.S. (1964), *Churches and the Working Classes in Victorian England*, London: Routledge & Kegan Paul.

Jafferji, Javed and Gemma Pitcher (2003), *Safari Living*, Zanzibar: Gallery Publications.

Johansen, Michelle (2006), 'The Public Librarian in Modern London (1890–1914): The Case of Charles Goss at the Bishopsgate Institute', PhD thesis, University of East London.

Johnson, Paul (1988), 'Conspicuous Consumption and Working-Class Culture in Late Victorian and Edwardian Britain', *Transactions of the Royal Historical Society*, 38: 27–42.

Jones, Frances M. (1968), 'The Aesthetics of the Nineteenth-Century Industrial Town', in H.J. Dyos (ed.), *The Study of Urban History*, 171–82, London: Edward Arnold.

Jones, Robin (2007), *Interiors of Empire: Objects, Space and Identity within the Indian Subcontinent, c. 1800–1947*, Manchester: Manchester University Press.

Jones, Timothy W. and Lucinda Matthews-Jones (2015), 'Introduction: Materiality and Religious History', in Timothy W. Jones and Lucinda Matthews-Jones, *Material Religion in Modern Britain: The Spirit of Things*, 1–16, London: Palgrave Macmillan.

Jordan, Bibi (2000), *Safari Chic: Wild Exteriors and Polished Interiors of Africa*, Layton, UT: Gibbs Smith.

Jordan, Bibi (2007), *Swahili Chic: The Feng Shui of Africa*, San Rafael, CA: Insight Editions.

Kann, Mark E. (1998), *A Republic of Men: The American Founders, Gendered Language, and Patriarchal Politics*, New York: New York University Press.

Kay, Alison C. (2003), 'A Little Enterprise of Her Own: Lodging House Keeping and the Accommodation Business in Nineteenth-century London', *The London Journal*, 28 (2): 41–53.

Kay, Alison C. (2008), 'Villas, Values and the Crystal Palace Company, c. 1852–1911', *The London Journal*, 33 (1): 21–39.

Keeble, Trevor (2013), 'Halls and Corridors: Spaces Between and Beyond', in Georgina Downey (ed.), *Domestic Interiors: Representing Homes from the Victorians to the Moderns*, 27–38, London: Bloomsbury.

Keen, Rosemary (n.d.), 'General Introduction and Guide to the Archive'. Available online: http://www.ampltd.co.uk/digital_guides/church_missionary_society_archive_general/editorial%20introduction%20by%20rosemary%20keen.aspx (accessed 3 January 2016).

Kelley, Victoria (2009a), '"The Virtues of a Drop of Cleansing Water": Domestic Work and Cleanliness in the British Working Classes, 1880–1914', *Women's History Review*, 18 (5): 719–35.

Kelley, Victoria (2009b), 'The Interpretation of Surface: Boundaries, Systems and Their Transgression in Clothing and Domestic Textiles, c. 1880–1939', *Textiles*, 7 (2): 216–35.

Kelley, Victoria (2010), *Soap and Water: Cleanliness, Dirt and the Working Classes in Victorian and Edwardian Britain*, London: I.B. Tauris.

Kemble, Frances Anne ([1863] 1984), *Journal of a Residence on a Georgian Plantation in 1838–1839*, ed. John A. Scott, Athens, GA: University of Georgia Press.

Kennedy, Dane (1987), *Islands of White: Settler Society and Culture in Kenya and Southern Rhodesia, 1890–1939*, Durham, NC: Duke University Press.

Kennedy, Lynn (2010), 'Out of Whole Cloth: Sewing and Family in the Old South', in Craig Thompson and Anya Jabour (eds.), *Family Values in the Old South*, 111–33, Gainesville, FL: University Press of Florida.

Kerber, Linda K. (1997), *Women of the Republic: Intellect and Ideology in Revolutionary America*, Chapel Hill, NC: University of North Carolina Press.

Kerber, Linda K. (2004), 'The Republican Mother and the Woman Citizen: Contradictions and Choices in Revolutionary America', in Linda K. Kerber and Sharron De Hart (eds.), *Women's America: Refocusing the Past*, 119–27, New York: Oxford University Press.

Kertzer, David I. (2002), 'Living with Kin', in David I. Kertzer and Marzio Barbagli (eds.), *The History of the European Family, vol. 2: Family Life in the Long Nineteenth Century, 1789–1913*, 40–72, New Haven, CT: Yale University Press.

Kertzer, David I. and Marzio Barbagli (2002), 'Introduction', in David I. Kertzer and Mario Barbagli (eds.), *The History of the European Family, vol. 2: Family Life in the Long Nineteenth Century, 1789–1913*, ix–xxxviii, New Haven, CT: Yale University Press.

Kinchin, J. (1996), 'Interiors: Nineteenth-Century Essays on the "Masculine" and "Feminine" Room', in Pat Kirkham (ed.), *The Gendered Object*, 12–29, Manchester: Manchester University Press.

King, Anthony (1995), *The Bungalow: The Production of a Global Culture*, 2nd edition, New Oxford: Oxford University Press.

Kirk-Greene, Anthony (2006), *Symbols of Authority: The British District Officer in Africa*, London: I.B. Tauris.

Koven, Seth (2002), 'How the Victorians Read *Sesame and Lilies*', in Deborah Epstein Nord (ed.), *Sesame and Lilies*, 165–204, New Haven, CT: Yale University Press.

Kowaleski, Maryanne and P.J.P. Goldberg, eds. (2008), *Medieval Domesticity: Home, Housing and Household in Medieval England*, Cambridge: Cambridge University Press.

Lalumia, Christine (2001), 'Scrooge and Albert: Christmas in the 1840s', *History Today*, 51 (12): 23–29.

Lambert, David (2002), 'The Prospect of Trade: The Merchant Gardeners of Bristol in the Second Half of the Eighteenth Century', in Michel Conan (ed.), *Bourgeois and Aristocratic Cultural Encounters in Garden Art, 1550–1850*, 123–45, Washington, DC: Dumbarton Oaks Research Library and Collection.

Lancaster, Bill (1995), *The Department Store: A Social History*, Leicester: Leicester University Press.

Laslett, Peter (1983), 'Family and Household as Work Group and Kin Group: Areas of Traditional Europe Compared', in Richard Wall, Jean Robin and Peter Laslett (eds.), *Family Forms in Historic Europe*, 513–64, Cambridge: Cambridge University Press.

LaViolette, Adria (2008), 'Swahili Cosmopolitanism in Africa and the Indian Ocean World, A.D. 600–1500', *Archaeologies: Journal of the World Archaeological Congress*, 4 (1): 24–49.

Lawrence, Dianne (2012), *Genteel Women: Empire and Domestic Material Culture, 1840–1910*, Manchester: Manchester University Press.

Lees-Maffei, Grace (2003), 'Studying Advice: Historiography, Methodology, Commentary, Bibliography', *Journal of Design History*, 16 (1): 1–14.

Leong-Salobir, C. (2011), *Food Culture in Colonial Asia: A Taste of Empire*, London: Routledge.

Levine, Caroline (2006), 'Strategic Formalism: Toward a New Method in Cultural Studies', *Victorian Studies*, 48 (4): 625–57.

Levitan, K. (2008), 'Redundancy, the "Surplus Woman" Problem, and the British Census, 1851–1861', *Women's History Review*, 17 (3): 359–76.

Lewis, Jan (1983), *The Pursuit of Happiness: Family and Values in Jefferson's Virginia*, Cambridge: Cambridge University Press.

Lewis, Jane (1986), 'Introduction: Reconstructing Women's Experience of Home and Family', in Jane Lewis (ed.), *Women's Experience of Home and Family, 1850–1940*, 1–24, Oxford: Blackwell.

Löfgren, Orvar (2003), 'The Sweetness of Home: Class, Culture and Family Life in Sweden', in Setha M. Low and Denise Lawrence-Zúñiga (eds.), *The Anthropology of Space and Place: Locating Culture*, 142–59, Oxford: Blackwell.

Logan, Thad (1995), 'Decorating Domestic Space, Middle-Class Women and Victorian Interiors', in V. Dickerson (ed.), *Keeping the Victorian House*, 207–34, New York: Garland.

Logan, Thad (2001), *The Victorian Parlour*, Cambridge: Cambridge University Press.

Long, Helen (1993), *The Edwardian House*, Manchester: Manchester University Press.

Longair, Sarah (2015), *Cracks in the Dome: Fractured Histories of Empire in the Zanzibar Museum, 1897–1964*, Farnham: Ashgate.
Longmate, Norman (2003), *The Workhouse: A Social History*, London: Pimlico.
Lystra, Karen (1989), *Searching the Heart: Women, Men, and Romantic Love in Nineteenth-Century America*, New York: Oxford University Press.
Machado, Pedro (2014), *Ocean of Trade: South Asian Merchants, Africa and the Indian Ocean, c. 1750–1850*, Cambridge: Cambridge University Press.
Mackenzie, John (1986), *Imperialism and Popular Culture*, Manchester: Manchester University Press.
MacLeod, Hugh (1996), *Religion and Society in England, 1850–1914*, London: Croom Helm.
MacLeod, Hugh (2007), *The Religious Crisis of the 1960s*, Oxford: Oxford University Press.
Macmillan, Margaret (1988), *Women of the Raj*, London: Thames & Hudson.
Magee, Gary B. and Andrew S. Thompson (2003), 'A Soft Touch? British Industry, Empire Markets, and the Self-Governing Dominions, c. 1870–1914', *Economic History Review*, 56 (4): 689–717.
Magee, Gary B. and Andrew S. Thompson (2010), *Empire and Globalisation: Networks of People, Goods and Capital in the British World, c. 1850–1914*, Cambridge: Cambridge University Press.
Majeed, Javeed (1992), *Ungoverned Imaginings: James Mill's 'The History of British India and Orientalism'*, Oxford: Oxford University Press.
Marcus, Sharon (1999), *Apartment Stories: City and Home in Nineteenth-Century Paris and London*, Berkeley, CA: University of California Press.
Mason, Shena (2005), *The Hardware Man's Daughter: Matthew Boulton and his 'Dear Girl'*, Chichester: Phillimore.
Mays, Kelly J. (2008), 'Domestic Spaces, Readerly Acts: Reading, Gender, and Class in Working-Class Autobiography', *Nineteenth-Century Contexts*, 30 (4): 343–68.
McBride, Theresa M. (1976), *The Domestic Revolution: The Modernization of Household Service in England and France 1820–1920*, London: Croom Helm.
McBride, Theresa M. (1978), '"As The Twig is Bent": The Victorian Nanny', in Anthony S. Wohl (ed.), *The Victorian Family: Structure and Stresses*, 44–58, London: Croom Helm.
McCrossan, Alexis (2000), *Holy Day, Holiday: The American Sunday*, Ithaca, NY: Cornell University Press.
McDannell, Colleen (1986), *The Christian Home in Victorian America, 1840–1900*, Bloomington, IN: Indiana University Press.
McGuire, Meredith B. (2008), *Lived Religion: Faith and Practice in Everyday Life*, Oxford: Oxford University Press.
McKellar, Elizabeth (2013), *Landscapes of London: The City, the Country and the Suburbs, 1660–1840*, New Haven, CT: Yale University Press.
McKeon, Michael (2005), *The Secret History of Domesticity: Public, Private, and the Division of Knowledge*, Baltimore, MD: Johns Hopkins University Press.
McPherson, Kathryn (2012), 'Home Tales: Gender, Domesticity and Colonialism in the Prairie West, 1870–1900', in Robin Jarvis Brownlie and Valerie J. Korinek (eds.), *Finding a Way to the Heart: Feminist Writings on Aboriginal and Women's History in Canada*, 222–40, Manitoba: University of Manitoba Press.
Menuge, Adam (2008), *Ordinary Landscapes, Special Places: Anfield, Breckfield and the Growth of Liverpool's Suburbs*, Swindon: English Heritage.

Metcalf, Thomas R. (1964), *The Aftermath of Revolt: India, 1857–1970*, Princeton, NJ: Princeton University Press.
Metcalf, Thomas R. (1995), *Ideologies of the Raj*, vol. 3 of The New Cambridge History of India, Cambridge: Cambridge University Press.
Milne-Smith, A. (2006), 'A Flight to Domesticity? Making a Home in the Gentleman's Clubs of London, 1880–1914', *Journal of British Studies*, 25 (4): 796–818.
Mitchell, Brian Redman and Phyllis Deane (1971), *Abstract of British Historical Statistics*, Cambridge: Cambridge University Press.
Mokyr, Joel (2000), 'More Work for Mother? Knowledge and Household Behavior, 1870–1945', *Journal of Economic History*, 60 (1): 1–41.
Moorthy, Shanti and Ashraf Jamal, eds. (2010), *Indian Ocean Studies: Cultural, Social and Political Perspectives*, New York: Routledge.
Morris, Jeremy (1992), *Religion and Urban Change: Croydon 1840–1914*, Woodbridge: Royal Historical Society.
Murrell Taylor, Amy (2005), *The Divided Family in Civil War America*, Chapel Hill, NC: University of North Carolina Press.
Muthesius, Hermann ([1904] 2007), *The English House, vol. II: Layout and Construction*, London: Frances Lincoln.
Muthesius, Hermann ([1904–5] 2007), *The English House*, trans. Janet Seligman, Oxford: BSP Professional Books.
Muthesius, Stefan (1982), *The English Terraced House*, New Haven, CT: Yale University Press.
Nash, Alice and Christoph Strobel (2006), *Daily Life of Native Americans from Post-Columbian through Nineteenth-Century America*, London: Greenwood Press.
Nash, Mary (1999), 'Un/Contested Identities: Motherhood, Sex Reform and the Modernization of Gender Identity in Early Twentieth-Century Spain', in Victoria Lorée Enders and Pamela Beth Radcliff (eds.), *Constructing Spanish Womanhood: Female Identity in Modern Spain*, 25–50, New York: State University of New York Press.
Neiswander, Judith (2008), *The Cosmopolitan Interior: Liberalism and the British Home 1870–1914*, London: Yale University Press.
Newton, Robert (1977), 'Exeter 1770–1870', in M.A. Simpson and T.H. Lloyd (eds.), *Middle Class Housing in Britain*, 12–42, Newton Abbot: David & Charles.
Nochlin, Linda (1989), 'The Imaginary Orient', in *The Politics of Vision: Essays on Nineteenth-Century Art and Society*, 33–59, Boulder, CO: Westview Press.
Norton, M.B. (1980), *Liberty's Daughters: The Revolutionary Experience of American Women, 1750–1800*, Boston, MA: Little, Brown.
Oldenziel, Ruth and Mikael Hård (2013), *Consumers, Tinkerers and Rebels: The People who Shaped Europe*, Basingstoke: Palgrave.
Oonk, Gijsbert (2013), *Settled Strangers: Asian Business Elites in East Africa 1800–2000*, London: Sage.
Parker, Rozsika (1984), *The Subversive Stitch: Embroidery and the Making of the Feminine*, London: The Women's Press.
Parker, Rozsika ([1984] 2010), *The Subversive Stitch: Embroidery and the Making of the Feminine*, London: I.B. Tauris.
Pelletier, Yvonne Elizabeth (2009), 'Strawberries and Salt: Culinary Hazards and Moral Education in *Little Women*', in Monika Elbert and Marie Drews (eds.), *Culinary Aesthetics in Nineteenth-Century American Literature*, 189–204, New York: Palgrave Macmillan.

Perrot, Michelle (1990), *A History of Private Life, vol. IV: From the Fires of Revolution to the Great War*, Cambridge, MA: Harvard University Press.

Perry, Adele (2010), '"Is Your Garden in England, Sir": James Douglas's Archive and the Politics of Home', *History Workshop Journal*, 70 (1): 67–85.

Ponsonby, Margaret (2007), *Stories from Home: English Domestic Interiors, 1750–1850*, Aldershot: Ashgate.

Pooley, Colin G. (2001), 'Patterns on the Ground: Urban Forms, Residential Structure and the Social Construction of Space', in Martin Daunton (ed.), *The Cambridge Urban History of Britain, vol. 3: 1840–1950*, 427–66, Cambridge: Cambridge University Press.

Porter, Roy (1997), *The Greatest Benefit to Mankind: A Medical History of Humanity from Antiquity to the Present*, London: Fontana.

Potvin, John, ed. (2015), *Oriental Interiors: Design, Identity, Space*, London/New York: Bloomsbury.

Presthold, Jeremy (2008), *Domesticating the World: African Consumerism and the Genealogies of Globalization*, Berkeley, CA: University of California Press.

Preston, Rebecca (1999), '"The Scenery of the Torrid Zone": Imagined Travels and the Culture of Exotics in Nineteenth-Century British Gardens', in Felix Driver and David Gilbert (eds.), *Imperial Cities: Landscape, Display and Identity*, 194–211, Manchester: Manchester University Press.

Preston, Rebecca (2014), 'The Pastimes of the People: Photographing House and Garden in London's Small Suburban Homes, 1880–1914', *The London Journal*, 39 (3): 205–26.

Prochaska, Frank (1990), 'Philanthropy', in F.M.L. Thompson (ed.), *The Cambridge Social History of Britain, 1750–1950, vol. 3: Social Agencies and Institutions*, 357–94, Cambridge: Cambridge University Press.

Procida, M. (2002), *Married to the Empire*, Manchester: Manchester University Press.

Raine, Katherine (2000), 'Domesticating the Land: Colonial Women's Gardening', in Bronwyn Dalley and Bronwyn Labrum (eds.), *Fragments: New Zealand Social and Cultural History*, 76–96, Auckland: Auckland University Press.

Ralph Lauren Home Cape Lodge Collection. Available online: http://qa.ralphlaurenhome.com/rlhome/collection/sp08_capelodge_explore.asp (accessed 28 March 2016).

Reed, Christopher (1996), 'Introduction', in Christopher Reed (ed.), *Not at Home: The Suppression of Domesticity in Modern Art and Architecture*, 7–17, London: Thames & Hudson.

Reiter, Christiane and Deidi von Schaewen (2004), *Safari Style: Exteriors, Interiors, Details*, Cologne: Taschen.

Rich, Rachel (2011), *Bourgeois Consumption: Food, Space and Identity in London and Paris, 1850–1914*, Manchester: Manchester University Press.

Richmond, Vivienne (2016), 'Stitching Women: Unpicking Histories of Victorian Clothes', in Hannah Greig, Jane Hamlett and Leonie Hannan (eds.), *Gender and Material Culture in Britain since 1600*, 90–103, London: Palgrave Macmillan.

Richter, Amy G. (2015), *At Home in Nineteenth-Century America: A Documentary History*, New York: New York University Press.

Riley, Noel (1991), *Gifts for Good Children: The History of Children's China, 1790–1890*, London: Richard Dennis.

Robertson, Priscilla (1982), *An Experience of Women: Pattern and Change in Nineteenth-Century Europe*, Philadelphia, PA: Temple University Press.

Romines, Ann (1992), *The Home Plot: Women, Writing, and Domestic Ritual*, Amherst, MA: University of Massachusetts Press.
Rose, Jonathan (2010), *The Intellectual Life of the British Working Classes*, New Haven, CT: Yale University Press.
Ross, Ellen (1993), *Love and Toil: Motherhood in Outcast London, 1870–1918*, Oxford: Oxford University Press.
Rothman, Ellen K. (1984), *Hands and Hearts: A History of Courtship in America*, New York: Basic Books.
Rubinstein, William D. (1988), 'The Size and Distribution of the English Middle Classes in 1860', *Historical Research*, 61 (144): 65–89.
Said, Edward (1978), *Orientalism*, New York: Pantheon Books.
Said, Edward (1993), *Culture and Imperialism*, New York: Knopf.
Salmi, Hannu (2008), *Nineteenth-Century Europe: A Cultural History*, Cambridge: Polity Press.
Sambrook, Pamela A. (1999), *The Country House Servant*, Stroud: Sutton Publishing / The National Trust.
Sandoval-Strausz, A.K. (2007), *Hotel: An American History* New Haven, CT: Yale University Press.
Scannell, Dolly (1975), *Mother Knew Best: An East-End Childhood*, London: Pan.
Schilling, Britta (2014), 'Design Advice for the African Home: Translating "Colonial Style", 1945–1962', *Interiors*, 5 (2): 179–98.
Schmiechen, James (1984), *Sweated Industries and Sweated Labor: The London Clothing Trades, 1860–1914*, Beckenham: Croom Helm.
Schwartz Cowan, Ruth ([1983] 1989), *More Work for Mother: The Ironies of Household Technology from the Open Hearth to the Microwave*, London: Free Association Books.
Scott, Joan W. (1983), 'On Language, Gender, and Working-Class History', *International Labor and Working-Class History*, 31 (1): 1–13.
Segalen, Martine (1996), 'The Industrial Revolution: From Proletariat to Bourgeoisie', in André Burguière, Christiane Klapisch-Zuber, Martine Segalen and Françoise Zonabend (eds.), *A History of the Family, vol. 2: The Impact of Modernity*, 377–415, Cambridge: Polity Press.
Segalen, Martine (2002), 'Material Conditions of Family Life', *The History of the European Family, vol. 2: Family Life in the Long Nineteenth Century, 1789–1913*, 3–39, New Haven, CT: Yale University Press.
Sen, Indrani (2002), *Women and Empire: Representations in the Writings of British India (1858–1900)*, New Delhi: Longman Orient.
Shammas, Carole (2002), *A History of Household Government in America*, Charlottesville, VA: University of Virginia Press.
Shapiro, Laura ([1986] 2001), *Perfection Salad: Women and Cooking at the Turn of the Century*, New York: Modern Library.
Sharpe, Pamela (1999), 'Dealing with Love: The Ambiguous Independence of the Single Woman in Early Modern England', *Gender and History*, 11 (2): 202–232.
Sheehan-Dean, Aaron (2007), *Why Confederates Fought: Family and Nation in Civil War Virginia*, Chapel Hill, NC: University of North Carolina Press.
Sheriff, Abdul (2010), *Dhow Cultures in the Indian Ocean*, London: Hurst.
Shoemaker, Robert B. (1998), *Gender in English Society, 1650–1850: The Emergence of Separate Spheres?*, London: Longman.
Simonton, Deborah (2002), *A History of European Women's Work*, London: Routledge.

Sinha, Mrinalini (1995), *Colonial Masculinity: The 'Manly' Englishman and the 'Effeminate' Bengali*, Manchester: Manchester University Press.

Sklar, Kathryn Kish (1976), *Catharine Beecher: A Study in American Domesticity*, New York: W.W. Norton.

Slater, T.R. (1978), 'Family, Society and the Ornamental Villa on the Fringes of English Country Towns', *Journal of Historical Geography*, 4 (2): 129–44.

Sluga, Glenda and Julia Horne (2010), 'Cosmopolitanism: Its Pasts and Practices', *Journal of World History*, 21 (3): 369–74.

Smith, Virginia (2007), *Clean: A History of Personal Hygiene and Purity*, Oxford: Oxford University Press.

Smitley, Megan (2009), *The Feminine Public Sphere: Middle-Class Women and Civic Life in Scotland, c. 1870–1914*, Manchester: Manchester University Press.

Snell, K.D.M (2012), 'Belonging and Community: Understandings of "Home" and "Friends" among the English Poor, 1750–1850', *Economic History Review*, 65 (1): 1–25.

Soja, Edward (1996), *Thirdspace: Journeys to Los Angeles and Other Real-and-Imagined Places*, Oxford: Basil Blackwell.

Southgate, Walter (1982), *That'd the Way it Was: A Working Class Autobiography, 1890–1950*, ed. Terry Philpot, London: New Clarion Press.

Stearns, Peter N. (2010), *Globalization in World History*, London: Routledge.

Steedman, Carolyn (2013), *An Everyday Life of the English Working Class: Work, Self, and Sociability in the Early Nineteenth Century*, Cambridge: Cambridge University Press.

Stevenson, Christine (2000), *Medicine and Magnificence: British Hospital and Asylum Architecture, 1660–1815*, New Haven, CT: Yale University Press.

Stoler, Ann Laura (1995), *Race and the Education of Desire: Foucault's History of Sexuality and the Colonial Order of Things*, Durham, NC: Duke University Press.

Stoler, Ann Laura (2002), *Carnal Knowledge and Imperial Power: Race and the Intimate in Colonial Rule*, Berkeley, CA: University of California Press.

Stone, Lawrence (1977), *The Family, Sex and Marriage in England 1500–1800*, London: Weidenfeld & Nicolson.

Strange, Julie-Marie (2005), *Death, Grief and Poverty in Britain 1870–1914* (Cambridge Social and Cultural Histories Series, No. 6), Cambridge: Cambridge University Press.

Strange, Julie-Marie (2015), *Fatherhood and the British Working Class, 1865–1914*, Cambridge: Cambridge University Press.

Styles, John and Amanda Vickery, eds. (2006), *Gender, Taste and Material Culture in Britain and North America, 1700–1830*, New Haven, CT: Yale University Press.

Sugg-Ryan, Deborah (1997), *The Ideal Home through the Twentieth Century*, London: Hazar.

Tapaninen, Anna-Maria (2004), 'Motherhood through the Wheel: The Care of Foundlings in Late Nineteenth-Century Naples', in Perry Willson (ed.), *Gender, Family and Sexuality: The Private Sphere in Italy, 1860–1945*, 51–70, Basingstoke: Palgrave Macmillan.

Tarn, J.N. (1977), 'Sheffield', in M.A. Simpson and T.H. Lloyd (eds.), *Middle Class Housing in Britain*, 170–91, Newton Abbot: David & Charles.

Thomas, Julia (2000), *Victorian Narrative Painting*, London: Tate Publishing.

Thomas, Nicholas (1991), *Entangled Objects: Exchange, Material Culture and Colonialism in the Pacific*, Cambridge, MA: Harvard University Press.

Thompson, F.M.L. (1988), *The Rise of Respectable Society: A Social History of Victorian Britain, 1830–1900*, London: Fontana.

Thornton, Peter (1984), *Authentic Décor: The Domestic Interior 1620–1920*, London: Weidenfeld & Nicolson.

Tiersten, Lisa (2001), *Marianne in the Market: Envisioning Consumer Society in Fin-de-Siecle France*, Berkeley, CA: University of California Press.

Titus, Mary (1997), 'The Dining Room Door Swings Both Ways: Food, Race, and Domestic Space in the Nineteenth-Century South', in Anne Goodwyn Jones and Susan Van D'Elden Donaldson (eds.), *Haunted Bodies: Gender and Southern Texts*, 243–56, Charlottesville, VA: University Press of Virginia.

Tonkovich, Nicole (1997), *Domesticity with a Difference: The Nonfiction of Catharine Beecher, Sarah J. Hale, Fanny Fern, and Margaret Fuller*, Jackson, MS: University Press of Mississippi.

Tosh, John (1999), *A Man's Place: Masculinity and the Middle-Class Home in Victorian England*, New Haven, CT: Yale University Press.

Tosh, John (2015), 'Home and Away: The Flight from Domesticity in Late-Nineteenth-Century England Revisited', *Gender and History*, 27 (3): 561–75.

Tristram, P. (1989), *Living Space in Fact and Fiction*, London: Routledge.

Tugendhat, Julia (2011), *My Colonial Childhood in Tanganyika*, London: Choir Press.

Umbach, Maiken and Bern Hüppauf, eds. (2005), *Vernacular Modernism: Heimat, Globalization and the Built Environment*, Stanford, CA: Stanford University Press.

Unwin, Sheila (2006), *The Arab Chest*, London: Arabian Publishing.

Utica Daily Press (1915), 'Chapter Day is Celebrated – Oneida Chapter Daughters of the American Revolution', 15 October, article reprinted, sourced from the Family Archives courtesy of Kathy Wright Fowler.

Valenze, Deborah (1985), *Prophetic Sons and Daughters: Female Preaching and Popular Religion in Industrial England*, Princeton, NJ: Princeton University Press.

Van Osselaer, Tine and Patrick Pasture, eds. (2014), *Christian Homes: Religion, Family and Domesticity in the 19th and 20th Centuries*, Leuven: Leuven University Press.

Vickery, Amanda (1993), 'From Golden Age to Separate Spheres: A Review of the Categories and Chronology of English Women's History', *Historical Journal*, 36 (2): 383–414

Vickery, Amanda (2008), 'An Englishman's Home is His Castle? Thresholds, Boundaries and Privacies in the Eighteenth-Century London House', *Past and Present*, 199: 147–73.

Vickery, Amanda, (2009), *Behind Closed Doors: At Home in Georgian England*, New Haven, CT: Yale University Press.

Vincent, David (1980), 'Love and Death and the Nineteenth-Century Working Class', *Social History*, 5 (2): 223–47.

Vincent, David (1981), *Bread, Knowledge and Freedom: A Study of Nineteenth-Century Working-Class Autobiography*, London: Methuen.

Vollenbröker, Nina (2014), '"Home on the Range": Rootedness and Identity in the Borderlands of the Nineteenth-Century American West', Paul Readman, Cynthia Radding and Chad Bryant (eds.), *Borderlands in World History, 1700–1914*, 293–311, London: Palgrave Macmillan.

Wanhalla, Angela (2012), 'Beyond the Borders: The "Founding Families" of Southern New Zealand', in Robin Jarvis Brownlie and Valerie J. Korinek (eds.), *Finding a Way to the Heart: Feminist Writings on Aboriginal and Women's History in Canada*, 98–101, Manitoba: University of Manitoba Press.

Weatherill, Lorna (1988), *Consumer Behavior and Material Culture in Britain, 1660–1760*, London: Routledge.

Welter, Barbara (1966), 'The Cult of True Womanhood: 1820–1860', *American Quarterly*, 18: (2): 151–74.

White, Jerry (2007), *London in the Nineteenth Century*, London: Vintage.

Wickham, E.R. (1964), *Church and the People in an Industrial City*, London: Lutterworth Press.

Wildman, Charlotte (2011), 'Religious Selfhoods and the City in Inter-War Manchester', *Urban History*, 38 (1): 103–23.

Wilk, Christopher (1980), *Thonet: 150 Years of Furniture*, Woodbury, NY: Barron's.

Williams, Sarah C. (1999), *Religious Belief and Popular Culture: A Study of the South London Borough of Southwark*, Oxford: Oxford University Press.

Williams, Sarah C. (2010), 'Is there a Bible in the House? Gender, Religion and Family', in Sue Morgan and Jacqueline deVries (eds.), *Women, Gender and Religious Culture, 1880–1940*, 11–31, London: Routledge.

Williams, Susan (1996), *Savory Suppers and Fashionable Feasts: Dining in Victorian America*, Knoxville, TN: University of Tennessee Press.

Willis, Frederick (1960), *A Book of London Yesterdays*, London: Phoenix House.

Willson, Perry (2004), 'Introduction: Gender and the Private Sphere in Liberal and Fascist Italy', in Perry Willson (ed.), *Gender, Family and Sexuality: The Private Sphere in Italy, 1860–1945*, 1–19, London: Palgrave Macmillan.

Wood, Natasha (2013), "Inspired by the British Empire: Colonial-Inspired House and Interior Design', *My Luscious Life Blog*, 9 February. Available online: http://www.mylusciouslife.com/british-empire-style-colonial-inspired-design-decor/ (accessed 28 March 2016).

Wright, Gwendolen (1981), *Building the Dream: A Social History of Housing in America*, New York. Pantheon Books.

Wrigley, E.A. and R.S. Schofield (1981), *The Population History of England, 1541–1871: A Reconstruction*, London: Edward Arnold.

Yanni, Carla (2007), *The Architecture of Madness: Insane Asylums in the United States*, Minneapolis, MN: University of Minnesota Press.

Yeo, Eileen (2002), 'Gender in Working-Class and Labor History', in M. Van Der Linden and L.H. Van Voss (eds.), *Class and Other Identities: Gender, Religion and Ethnicity in the Writing of European Labor History*, 73–87, Oxford: Berghahn.

Yoshihara, Mari (2003), *Embracing the East: White Women and American Orientalism*, Oxford: Oxford University Press.

Young, Alfred F. (2005), *Masquerade: The Life and Times of Deborah Sampson, Continental Soldier*, New York: Vintage.

Young, Linda (2003), *Middle-Class Culture in the Nineteenth Century: America, Australia and Britain*, Basingstoke: Palgrave Macmillan.

Zafar, Rafia (2009), 'Recipes for Respect: Black Hospitality Entrepreneurs Before World War I', in Anne L. Bower (ed.), *African American Foodways: Explorations of History and Culture*, 139–52, Urbana, IL: University of Illinois Press.

Zhao, Bing (2012), 'Global Trade and Swahili Cosmopolitan Material Culture: Chinese-Style Ceramic Shards from Sanje ya Kati and Songo Mnara (Kilwa, Tanzania)', *Journal of World History*, 23 (1): 41–85.

CONTRIBUTORS

Marie Drews is an Assistant Professor of English at Luther College in Iowa, USA. Her research focuses on domestic and kitchen narratives in nineteenth- and twentieth-century American women's writing. Along with Monika Elbert, she co-edited the collection *Culinary Aesthetics and Practices in Nineteenth-Century American Literature* (Palgrave Macmillan, 2009). Her current project examines American writers' representations of women's subordination and subversion within commodity-driven kitchen spaces during the mid-twentieth century.

Fae Dussart is Lecturer in Human Geography at the University of Sussex, UK. British, imperial and colonial identity, and the intersection of these with the formation of spaces and places, are major themes of Dussart's teaching and research. These have focused on domestic service in nineteenth-century India and Britain, and on humanitarianism and colonialism in the British Empire. She is the co-author, with Alan Lester, of *Colonization and the Origins of Humanitarian Governance: Protecting Aborigines Across the Nineteenth-Century British Empire* (Cambridge University Press, 2014) and is currently working on a monograph to be published by Bloomsbury on domestic service and empire in Britain and India in the nineteenth century.

Rebecca J. Fraser is an Associate Professor of American History and Culture at the University of East Anglia, UK. She has published several books including *Courtship and Love among the Enslaved in North Carolina* (University Press of Mississippi, 2007) and *Gender, Race and Family in Nineteenth Century America: From Northern Woman to Plantation Mistress* (Palgrave Macmillan, 2012). Her most recent research concerning Black female intellectuals in nineteenth-century America has been published in *Slavery and Abolition* and the *Journal of American Studies*.

Jane Hamlett is Professor of Modern British History at Royal Holloway University of London, UK. Her research interests include histories of society and culture in modern Britain, women and gender, the family, intimacy and emotion, and material and visual culture. Her first book, *Material Relations: Domestic Interiors and Middle-Class Families in England, 1850–1910* (Manchester University Press, 2010), explored the relationship between middle-class families and their material worlds, and her second monograph, *At Home in the Institution: Material Life in Asylums, Lodging Houses and Schools in Victorian and Edwardian England* (Palgrave Macmillan, 2015) explored material culture and domesticity in institutional space. With Julie-Marie Strange, she is currently writing a book on the history of pets in modern Britain, based on their collective work for the AHRC Pets and Family Life Project.

Lesley Hoskins is Research Associate (Bucks New University) on 'Woodlanders' Lives and Landscapes', a community social history project (supported by the Heritage Lottery Fund and Chilterns Landscape Partnership Scheme) that is investigating the everyday working and domestic lives of people who were occupied in rural and home-based industries in the central Chilterns. Her research and publications focus on the material culture of 'ordinary' domestic and quasi-domestic life from the mid-nineteenth to the mid-twentieth century.

Victoria Kelley is Director of Research and Education and Professor of the History of Design and Material Culture at the University for the Creative Arts, UK. She is co-editor (with Glenn Adamson) of *Surface Tensions: Surface, Finish and the Meaning of Objects* (Manchester University Press, 2013), and author of *Soap and Water: Cleanliness, Dirt and the Working Classes in Victorian and Edwardian Britain* (I.B. Tauris, 2010), *Cheap Street: London's Street Markets and the Cultures of Informality, c. 1850–1939* (Manchester University Press, 2019), as well as chapters and papers on aspects of the material culture of Britain from the mid-nineteenth to mid-twentieth century.

Lucinda Matthews-Jones is a Senior Lecturer at Liverpool John Moores University, UK, where she teaches nineteenth-century gender and urban history. She has published articles in *Cultural and Social History*, *The Historical Journal*, *Victorian Studies* and *Journal of Victorian Culture*. She is co-editor (with Timothy W. Jones) of *Material Religion in Britain: The Spirit of Things* (Palgrave Macmillan, 2015). She is currently writing a book provisionally entitled 'Settling: The Making of the British Settlement Movement, 1880–1920'.

Rebecca Preston is Historian with the English Heritage London Blue Plaques scheme. Recent publications include, with Clare Hickman, 'Cultivation in Captivity: Gender, Class and Reform in the Promotion and Practice of Women's Prison Gardening in England, 1900–1939', *Women's History*, 2(13), 2019, 27–32 and, with Fiona Fisher, 'Light, Airy and Open: the Design and Use of the

Suburban Public House Garden in England Between the Wars', *Studies in the History of Gardens and Designed Landscapes*, 39(1), 2019, 5–21.

Margaret Ponsonby is an Honorary Research Fellow at the University of Wolverhampton, UK. Her background is in design history and material culture. Her research has focused on the history of domestic interiors and her publications include *Stories from Home: English Domestic Interiors, 1750–1850* (Ashgate, 2007); *Faded and Threadbare Historic Textiles and their Role in Houses Open to the Public* (Ashgate, 2015); and, with David Hussey, *The Single Homemaker and Material Culture in the Long Eighteenth Century* (Ashgate, 2012).

Britta Schilling is Assistant Professor of Cultural History at Utrecht University, the Netherlands, specializing in European colonialism, memory and material culture. She is the author of *Postcolonial Germany: Memories of Empire in a Decolonized Nation* (Oxford University Press, 2014) and is currently working on a comparative history of colonial homes in British, French and German territories in sub-Saharan Africa. Her contribution draws on work supported by the Leverhulme Trust.

INDEX

accommodation
  almshouses 36–7
  boarding houses 172, 175
  charitable institutions providing 35–6
  council housing 42
  diseases and 31–2, 119
  for domestic servants 124
  furnished rooms 8
  lodging houses/night shelters 8, 31–2, 33–4, 68, 159, 172, 173
  rented 31, 68
  shared accommodation 8
  for unmarried shop girls and boys 32–3
  workhouses 26, 37, 38, 173–4, 178
activism, of northeast middle-class women 155
Acts of Uniformity (1559, 1662) 179
Adams, Abigail 135
Adams, John 135
Addison Act 41
Adkins, Ida 145
advice manuals
  advice for homemakers 26–31
  African home-making 90
  the colonies and 28
  dining rituals and 158
  domestic regimes 121
  the efficacy of 167
  furnishings 27, 41–2
  home and fashion 119
  hospitality and 160–6
  for men 139
  ranges and 115
  the role of a hostess and 163
  the role of women and 120
  store cupboard staples 116
  variety of available 205n.2
  for women in India 40, 46–7, 52, 60
  written by people of colour 171
Aesthetic Movement 30
aesthetics
  Picturesque 71
  villas and 87
African Americans, homes of 171
afternoon tea 164, 166
agency
  of colonized people 65
  of indigenous peoples 108–9
  of readers of advice manuals 160
  sewing and 16–17
agri-towns, Southern Europe 7–8
Aitken, E.H. 56
Alas! And Did My Saviour Bleed? At the Cross 194
alcohol, the working-classes and 26
Alcott, Louisa May 137, 167–8, 177
Alcott, William A. 138, 139
almshouses 36–7
Amateur Gardening 81
The American Frugal Housewife 168

'American Negro' exhibit 171
The American Woman's Home 153
Ammerman, Nancy T. 181
ancien régime 14
'The Angel in the House' 5, 20, 21, 113
Anglo-Indian homes 15, 65
apartments, France, Spain and 6
Appadurai, Arjun 108
apprentices, live-in 11
apprenticeships, East Africa 104
architectural features, terraced housing 78
aristocracy, displaced by the middle classes 20 (*see also* elites)
Aristotle's Complete Works 192
Army and Navy stores 94
Arnold, David 51
art
    Islamic art and architecture 98
    narrative paintings 21
    the portraying of the working classes 26
Art Nouveau 30, 161
The Art of Beauty 119
The Art of Housekeeping 121
arts and crafts 14, 105
Arts and Crafts Movement 30–1
Astor House, New York 171
'At Homes' 164
Atkins, Gareth 187
Atkins, Keletso 104
Auslander, Leora 14
Australia
    furniture 104
    migration to 2
    obtaining furnishings 39
    settlement of 38
authority
    Anglo-Indian 65
    of employers of servants 52, 59
    of fathers 1
    female in the home 5, 125
    of husbands over dependents 134
    religious, of men 183
    western moral 7
Avery, Tracey 39, 104
ayahs 53–5, 58, 63

back-to-back housing 77–8 (*see also* terraced housing)
back yards 80, 82
Baganda ruling elite 107

Baker, Delphine P. 154
baking 115–16
balloon frame technologies 13
banda 92
bathrooms 25
Baudrillard, Jean 96, 97
bearers 53, 59, 62
Bedfordshire Times 65
bedrooms 74–5, 83, 87
Beecher, Catherine 133, 138, 153, 155, 170
Beeton, Mrs 164, *166*
Berlin wool work 30
Bethlem hospital, London 175
Bibles, in working-class homes 189
Birmingham, Edgbaston 71
births, taking place in the home 16
Black, Clementina 119, 126
Bleak House 19, 32
Blunden, Anna *129*
Blunt, Alison 40, 198
boarding houses 172, 175
Bohemian style 14
books (*see also* titles of individual books)
    advice on homemaking 27 (*see also* advice manuals)
    awarded as prizes from Sunday schools 196–7
Books for the Bairns 187
Booth, Charles 78–9, 128
Borup, K.E. 104
Bosanquet, Helen 131
Bosse, Sara 169
Boston Manufacturing Company 175
Boston, Tremont House 171
Boulton, Anne 33
bourgeoisie 4, 6, 13, 14, 15 (*see also* elites)
Bournville Almshouse 37
Braddon, Edward 50–1, 52
Bradley, Emily 90
bread production 115–16
bricolage 108
Briggs, Asa 115
Britain
    childcare practices 16
    class 6, 48
    detached houses 6
    dining practices 15
    hotels 172
    housing in England 67–8
    Lancashire cotton towns 10

INDEX 241

lodging houses 8, 31, 33–4, 68, 172, 173
lower classes; shared accommodation 8
lower middle-classes 6
middle-classes 4–5
religion 179 (*see also* religion)
secularism 179–80
social transformation 5
terraced housing 12, 68, 69, 77–86
urbanization 7, 8, 20, 67, 112
villas 68, 69–77, 86–7, 124
British East Africa. *See* East Africa
British Empire
colonial homemaking 38–40
East Africa. *See* East Africa
expansion of 43
ideal of the home and 7
British World economy 109
Brontë, Charlotte 32
Brookwood Hospital, Surrey 175–6
Broom Hall estate, Sheffield 71
Brown, Callum 181, 182, 183
Brown, James 139
Browne, Phillis 114, 120, 121, 128
Buettner, Elizabeth 64
bungalows 90, 92
Bunyan, John 187, *188*, 189
Burnett Archives of Working-Class Autobiographies 182, 200–1
Burnett, John 115
Burton, Harry McGuire 81, 85, 87
Bushman, Richard 140
Butler, Piece 149–50
Butler, Samuel 199
Buxton, Mary Aline 90, 97, 105
Buxton, T.F. Victor 105
byelaw housing 78, 80, 82, 87, 117

calling cards 164
calling practices 15, 164
camp furniture 94
Can You Forgive Her? 35
Canada 2, 38
capitalism 68, 136
Carpenter, Edward 199
Cassell's Household Guide 27
Castle, John 184, 194
Catholicism 6, 58
celibacy 32
Censer, Jane Turner 154–5

Central Europe 2
Chadwick, Edwin 119
chairs, Thonet model 95, 106
Chambers Journal 36
change, socio-economic 4
charitable institutions, providing accommodation 35–6
charitable organizations, the deserving poor and 26
Charitable Trusts Act (1853) 36
Chase, Alice Maud 182–3, 184
Chattopadhyay, Swati 110
chests, Arab or Zanzibar 99–102
Child, Lydia Maria 168
childbirth, class and 16
children
advice to girls on being a hostess 163, 164
childhood 1
cultural differences in childcare practices 16
education of American 135–6
of elites in India 12, 50, 53–5
infant/child mortality 11, 119, 134
labour of 134
nurseries 16, 74
parents maintaining a distance from 74
placed in institutional care in France 11
relationships with servants in India 57–9
religion and 182, 184, 186, 197
of slave women 149
terraced housing and 81–2
of working-class working mothers 127, 131
The Children's Bible 184
The Children's Friend 192
Christian Globe 192
The Christian World 192
Christianity 58, 181–2, 199–200
Christmas 24, 25, 49
Church Missionary Society (CMS) 91–2, 96, 104
Church, Richard 81
civic duty, in the home 136
civic virtue 135
civil servants, East Africa 91, 93–4, 95, 98, 106
civilising mission
to the American West 153
imperial 44, 47, 65, 143

civilization, the home and 49
Claridge's, London 172
class
   Britain 6, 48
   childbirth, death and 16
   class difference and hospitality in the United States 159
   domesticity and 6, 118, 119–20
   furniture and 93
   growth of the middle-classes 2, 4, 41, 136
   hospitality and 167–8, 177
   housework and 116–17, 118
   lower middle classes 6
   performance of 168
cleanliness 25, 37, 41
climate, housing and 12
clothing, respectability/status and 196
Cohen, Deborah 20, 98, 195
Collet, Clara 128, 130
colonial style 89–90, 91, 92, 93–7, 106, 109–10
colonialism (*see also* imperialism)
   advice manuals on homemaking in the colonies 28
   Anglo-Indian returnees 64–5
   British in India 43–4 (*see also* India)
   colonial homemaking 38–40
   colonial homes 90–1
   colonial identity 64, 65, 110
   colonial style. *See* colonial style
   domesticity and 47
   East Africa. *See* East Africa
   global relationships and 109
   justification of 63
   justification of violence and 60–2
   migrants to colonies 2
   power and 110
   role of servants in the colonial household 51–6
Colored American Magazine 171
Comaroff, John and Jean 108
commercial living spaces, hospitality in 158, 171–3
Common Lodging House Act 32
communications
   imperialism and 44
   migration and 9
The Complete Indian Housekeeper and Cook 47, 52, 59

Coningsby 30
Coningsby Hospital in Hereford 37
consumption
   conspicuous religious 197
   of elites in East Africa 106–9
   middle-classes and 20, 27, 28
cooking equipment 115
cooks
   in India 55
   slaves in the American South 146
cosmopolitanism, diverted 110
council housing 42
craft production, women 30
craftsmen 103, 105
Cranworth, Lady 103
Crosse, Andrew 35
Crystal Palace 77
culture(s)
   American bourgeois ideals in Northern homes 136–41
   aristocratic 157
   cult of domesticity 4
   cultural anchors 24
   cultural capital 168
   cultural difference 14, 17
   cultural differences in childcare practices 16
   cultural hybridity 9
   cultural imperialism 7
   cultural media 21
   cultural redefinition of manhood 139
   feminine 16
   French 4
   homes as a cultural phenomenon 2
   households as places of cultural pedagogy 49
   indigenous 7
   material culture 13, 24, 27, 39, 91, 110, 169
   middle-class 139, 158
   print culture 4, 30, 158, 160
   public 172
   superiority of Western 2
   working-class 197
Cummin, Maria Susanna 137
cutlery and tableware 158

Daily Mail Ideal Homes exhibition (1908) 28
Daly Goggin, Maureen 196

INDEX 243

Daly, Suzanne 164
Darley, Sarah Ann 185
Daudi Chwa II of the Baganda (r. 1896–1939) 106–7, *108*
Daudi Kasagama, King of Toro in Uganda (r. 1891–1928) 106
Davidoff, Leonore 11, 20, 75, 113, 158, 180
day rooms 75–6 (*see also* dining rooms; drawing rooms)
deaths, taking place in the home 16
decoration(s) (*see also* furnishings)
    choice of 17
    decorative objects in elite homes 76
    of living rooms 13
Delap, Lucy 122–3, 125
demographics
    changing demographic patterns 10–11
    East Africa 92
    population expansion 8, 10–11, 67, 112
design advice 28
Design and Industries Association 42
destitution 21
Devonshire Declaration (1922) 104
dhobies 56
Dickens, Charles 19, 32, 197
difference
    cultural 14, 17
    racial 45, 90
dining à la Russe 163
dining practices, Britain 15
dining rituals 158
dining rooms
    furnishings of 75
    hospitality and 160–1
    in hotels 172
    as a male domain 28
    as spaces of resistance 170
dining spaces and practices
    North America 157–8
    in North American novels 166–71
dinner parties 161, 163
diseases
    accommodation and 31–2, 119
    cleanliness and 25
Disraeli, Benjamin 28
diverted cosmopolitanism 110
divorce 6
Domestic Duties 27
A Domestic Guide to Mothers in India 57
domestic inclusion and exclusion 198

domestic interiors, colonial 13
domestic life, Anglo-Indian 64
domestic practices 9–10, 14–17
domestic science 159
domestic servants
    accommodation for 124
    colonial violence towards 61–2
    decrease in 41
    the duties of housemaids 121
    in English villas 74, 88
    enslaved 145
    exploitation of 123
    housework as paid work 122–5
    India *34*, 40, 43, 45, 48, 49–51, 52–3, 55–6, 56–7, 59–60, 62–4
    industrialization and 122
    lack of in colonies 40
    middle-classes and 2, 11–12, 44
    mistress of the house and her servants 169–70
    the moral threat of servants 57–8
    paternalism, Indian servants and 59–60
    power of 57
    privacy and 124
    relationships between servants and children 57–9
    role of in the colonial household 51–6
    rules for 125
    terraced housing 87
    Western Europe 2, 11–12
    women 32, 45
domestic service, the development of 122
domestic sociability, women and 163–4
domestic womanhood, United States 5
domestication, of manhood 139
domesticity
    in the American South 142, 144
    class and 6, 118, 119–20
    colonization and 47
    cult of 4
    evangelical 180
    expected standards of 119–20
    feminine 166
    gender and 114
    gendered notions of in hotels 172
    housework and 119
    ideal of 41
    imperial 43
    the work of 114
    working women and 131

Doolittle, Megan 189, 195
dormitories, for unmarried shop girls and boys 32–3
Douglass, Frederick 170
Dover stoves 95
drawing rooms 21, 23, 24, 28, 29, 75, 160–1, 172
dress and appearance, of women 140
Drews, Marie 235 (*see also* chapter 7)
DuBois, W.E.B 171
dukas 102
Dundas, Anne 102, 105
Dussart, Fae 235 (*see also* chapter 2)

East Africa
    apprenticeships 104
    civil servants 91, 93–4, 95, 98, 106
    consuming elites 106–9
    demographics 92
    East African Women's League 101
    education 104–5
    furniture imports to 103–6, 109
    hybridity 110
    local global markets 97–102
    material culture of the home in 13, 91–2
    middle-classes and 91–2
    missionaries 91–2, 95, 106
    Public Works Departments 98, 103, 104, 105
    South Asians in 103–4
East India Company 43, 45, 48, 76, 91, 92
Eastlake, Charles Locke 166
economic growth 112
economic impact, of housework 114
education
    East Africa 104–5
    Education Act 1870 189
    in the moral codes of middle-class behaviour 153
    National Schools 184
    Sunday schools 184, 196–7
    women and 5, 135–6
    working-classes and 189
Egg, Augustus 21
Elbert, Monika 159
elites
    advice on hospitality and dining for 160–6
    Baganda ruling elite 107
    children of elites in India 12, 50, 53–5
    consuming, in East Africa 106–9
    elite Anglo-Indian living practices 12
    elite families 12
    European aristocracy, moral excesses of the 14
    hospitality and 75
    hotel hospitality and 171–2
    housing of 68, 69–70, 71–2, 73–6
    Revolutionary era America 135
    status of elites in India 12
    white southern American 141
embroidery 30
emotional responsibility, of household management 28
empire
    British Empire. *See* British Empire
    empire-building, homemaking and 40
    homes and the production of 92
    political establishment of 2
employment (*see also* work)
    domestic servants. *See* domestic servants
    housekeepers 35
    middle-class female 41
    stipulating that women remain unmarried 33
    for women 32, 33
energy sources
    technological change and 112, 115
    terraced housing 83
Engels, Friedrich 117
The English House 86
The Englishman 62
Enlightenment 134
entertaining, at home 157–8, 161 (*see also* 'At Homes'; dinner parties; hospitality)
Ernest George & Yates 92
An Essay on the Education of Female Teachers 153
ethnic groups, marginalization of 168–9, 177 (*see also* race)
etiquette, dinner-table 163
European and African Trade Organization 104
European aristocracy, moral excesses of the 14
The Europeans 14

exclusion, domestic 198
Exeter, villas and 76
exoticism 102
exploitation
   of female home workers 128, 131
   of servants 123
exports to colonies 13

Family Fortunes 113, 180
family(ies)
   in the American South 144
   domestic faith in working-class families 182–5
   elite 12
   family composition, Italy 10
   hybrid 12
   industries, family composition and 10
   the institution of 5
   the limiting of family size 11
   the long family 11
   Mediterranean countries 10
   nineteenth-century America 134
   nineteenth-century family life 24
   nuclear 20, 32
   patriarchal 1
   power of the home and family 3, 17
   the trans-local family 12
farming, modernization of 1
fashion 112, 119
fashion trades 128
fathers, Victorian 114
Faust, Drew Gilpin 154
Fay, Eliza 46, 48
feminine public sphere 126
femininity 16, 119
feminism 41, 113, 155
fertility rates 10
Fitzhugh, George 141–2
5 o'clock tea 164, 166
Flint, Dr. and Mrs 145–6
Flint, Elizabeth 119–20
food
   foreign 168
   industrial production of 115–16
For Only One Short Hour (The Song of the Shirt) 129
Fowler, Hilda Rose 182, 186, 189, 197
Fox, Tryphena 143–4
Foxe's Book of Martyrs 189, 190, 191, 192

France
   ancien régime 14
   apartments and 6
   childcare practices 16
   children placed in institutional care 11
   culture of 4
   female participation in the public world 5
   the 'Femme de Foyer' 5
   French bourgeois homes, the *petit salon* 14
   home and work places 8–9
   the limiting of family size 11
   middle-classes 4–5
   Paris World's Fair (1900) 171
   taste and 14
   the term 'home' and 3–4
   the trousseau 16
   urban expansion 7
Fraser, Rebecca J. 235 (*see also* chapter 6)
Frisby, Minnie 186–7, 195
From the Young Wife 138
fundis 103, 105
Furley, E.M. 96
furnished rooms 8
furnishings
   advice publications 27, 41–2
   American homes 140–1
   brought from Europe 95–6
   colonial style 89–90, 91, 92, 93–7, 106, 109–10
   in colonies 39
   of dining rooms and drawing rooms 161
   gender and 41, 75
   gendered usage of rooms and 28
   home and 90
   indigenous artefacts 106
   individuality and 98
   local global markets and 97–102
   mass production of 20
   middle-class 41, 91
   minority groups and 14
   Orientalism and 169
   production and labour and 103–6
   styles of 14
   symbolic role of 19, 25, 30
   table decorations 163, 169
   taste and 27
   travelling objects 93–7
   Victorian era 24

furniture
    Arab or Zanzibar chests 99–102
    Australia 104
    camp furniture 94
    class and 93
    colonial style 89–90, 92, 93–7, 109–10
    in colonies 39
    imports to East Africa 103–6, 109
    mobility and 95, 98
    pianos 24, 95
    small wooden octagonal tables 98
    Thonet model chair 95, 106
    travelling objects 93–7
    Victorian 24

gabinettes (family rooms), Spain 14
Gamber, Wendy 172
Gardenesque style 77
gardens
    in colonies 39
    terraced housing 80–1, 82, 84, 87
    villas and 69, 70–1, 73, 77, 87
Gardiner, G. 47, 48, 52, 55, 56, 59
garment industry 128
Garrett, Agnes and Rhoda 161
Garrett, Elizabeth 53, 55, 58, 59
gas cookers 115
gender
    domestic role of women 1
    domesticity and 114
    furnishings and 41, 75
    gender roles 5, 27, 113
    gender roles in the home 5, 20, 30, 121–2, 133, 140, 154, 155
    gender roles in the United States 133, 134, 135, 140, 141
    gendered activities 44
    gendered judgements of the working-classes 113
    gendered and racial power dynamics 145–6
    gendered power relations in the home 5
    gendered usage of rooms 25, 28, 33, 75, 86, 161
    home as a gendered space 136
    hospitality rituals and 159
    the male breadwinner 1, 27
    morality and 5
    public and private spheres and 44, 159
    religion and 20, 183–4
    servant characteristics of in India 59–60
    Southern homes. Maintaining racial/gendered hierarchies 141–50
    zoning of bedrooms and 83
Genovese, Eugene 144
gentility
    in the colonies 40
    domestic servants and 44
    homemaking and 38–9
    leisure time and 30
    middle-class culture of 158
    new standards of 15
The Gentleman's House 117, 161
germ theory 119
Germany
    home and work places 8–9
    industrialization 7
    the term 'home' and 4
Ghose, Indira 45
gift exchange, hand-worked objects 16
Gilbert, Erik 102
Gilchrist Gibb, Alexander 95
Gillman, Caroline Howard 142
The Girl's Own Paper 163, 164, 172–3
Glasgow 125, 158
globalization 13, 89–90, 95, 97–102, 169
Glymph, Thavolia 143, 144
Godey's Lady's Book 136, 137, 138, 140
Goffin, Arthur Frederick 192, 195, 199
Good Housekeeping Institute 42
Gordon, Beverly 119
Gordon, Eleanor 125–6, 158–9
governance
    colonial 48
    indirect rule 91
    of slaves 142–3
Gregory, George 187, 200
Gregory, Robert 103
Griswold, Robert 139
A Guide to Indian Household Management 53

Hale, Sarah J. 138, 140
Hall, Catherine 20, 113, 158, 180
Hall, David D. 181
Hamlett, Jane 35, 91, 236 (*see also* Introduction; chapter 7)
Hampton, Nora 184, 198
Handbook of British East Africa 103
Hardy, Frederick Daniel 21

harmoniums 95
Harvey, David 185
Hattersley, Charles 106
Haweis, Eliza 119, 121
Haydon, Benjamin Robert 35
Heal, Felicity 157
health (*see also* mortality rates)
   germ theory 119
   industrialization and 70–1
   infectious diseases 25
   institutions for the mentally ill 175–7
   poverty and 119
   public health movement 77, 78, 117, 119
   villas and 87
Heath House, London 70, 73–6, 77
Hebert, Daniel 189
heimat 4
Hemphill, C. Dallett 134
Henderson, Katherine 195
Herschel, Caroline 35
Hewitt, Cecil 82, 84–5
Hicks, Samuel 139, 140–1
Hicks, Sarah Parmelee 140–1
hierarchies
   racial/social in India 49, 51
   servants in India 52–3, 55–6, 62
   Southern homes. Maintaining racial/gendered hierarchies 141–50
Hobhouse, Mary 51, 61, 63
Hoganson, Kristin 168
Hogg, Edith 130
Holloway Sanatorium, London 176–7
'Home Sweet Home' (song) 21
homelessness, the fear of 22
homemaking
   advice for homemakers 26–31
   colonial 38–40
   ideals of 26
   making a home in an institution 35–8
   migration and 10
   morality and 38–9
   one style of 24
   the practice of 21
   the reality of 1800–1920 31–2
   single people and 32–5
   women and 20
home(s) (*see also* homemaking; houses; housing)
   African American in the South 171
   Anglo-Indian 15, 65
   births and deaths taking place in 16
   as a building block of 'Britishness' 90
   Christian 199–200
   civic duty in the 136
   civilization and 49
   colonial 90–1
   the concept of 21
   conceptions of home in the American West 152–3
   as a cultural phenomenon 2
   East Africa 92
   external appearance of the 140
   gender roles in the home 5, 20, 30, 121–2, 133, 140, 154, 155
   home workers 128–30
   home and workshops 8
   the idea of 3–7
   the ideal home 21–6, 27, 31
   identity and 90
   leisure and 111
   life-cycles and 17
   the material culture of 13, 24, 91–2
   as a material space 12–14
   the meaning of 17, 19–20, 38, 39, 41
   middle-class 41
   of missionaries 106
   nineteenth-century America 133
   North American homes 6
   paid work in the home 111–12, 126–31
   place and 7–10
   post civil war America 154
   power of the home and family 3
   public and private sphere and 112
   religion and 5–6, 180
   respectability and 140–1
   semi-public role of 20
   Southern American homes 141–50
   Southern homes of disrepair 150–2
   as spaces of 'global encounter' 168
   the term 'home' 3–4
   transnational bourgeois homes 13
   urban expansion and 8
   Victorian era 15, 19–21
   who lived in them? 10–12
   women and 27, 30, 119, 138
   work and 24, 111, 113, 122, 130
   working-class 42, 114
   zoning of the interior 25, 124–5
Hoskins, Lesley 21, 236 (*see also* chapter 3)

hospitality
  advice manuals and 160–6
  class and 167–8, 177
  in commercial living spaces 158, 171–3
  dining rooms and 160–1
  elites and 75
  gender and hospitality rituals 159
  hotels and 171–2
  in lodging houses 159, 172, 173
  middle-classes and 75, 157–8, 160–6, 177
  nineteenth century 157
  in North American novels 166–71
  performance of 158
  private/public nature of 158–9
  in residential institutions 158, 173–7
  rituals 159, 167
  United States and 159
  working-classes and 159
Hostess and Guest 163, 164
hostesses 160, 163, 177
hotels 171–2
The House Beautiful 161
House magazine 163
The House Servant's Directory; or, A Monitor for Private Families 171
household management, emotional responsibility of 28
households
  imperial 48–51
  as a place of cultural pedagogy 49
  role of servants in the colonial household 51–6 (*see also* domestic servants)
housekeepers 35
houses (*see also* home(s); housing)
  Anglo-Indian residences 46–7
  bathrooms 25
  dining rooms/ drawing rooms/parlours/ sitting rooms. *See* individual rooms
  privacy and 15, 69, 74, 76
  sod houses 13
  verandas 40
housework 112, 113–25
housing (*see also* home(s); houses)
  back-to-back housing 77–8 (*see also* byelaw housing; terraced housing)
  bungalows 90, 92
  byelaw housing 78, 80, 82, 87, 117 (*see also* back-to-back housing; terraced housing)
  council housing 42
  crumbling and decrepit housing stock 8
  of elites 68, 69–70, 71–2, 73–6
  England 67–8
  industrialization and 8, 67
  inequalities between rich and poor 12
  lodging houses 8, 31, 33–4, 68, 159, 172, 173
  of middle-classes 8, 68, 69–77
  model housing 26
  multi-occupancy 8, 83, 84, 85
  new housing forms 13
  philanthropy and 68
  of poor people 67
  public health movement 77, 78, 117, 119
  reform of 174
  rented accommodation 31, 68
  of servants in India 55, 60
  shared accommodation. *See* multi-occupancy
  slum housing 41
  suburban 71
  temporary or community-based housing models 158
  terraced housing 12, 68, 69, 77–87 (*see also* back-to-back housing; byelaw housing)
  United States 13
  villas 68, 69–77, 86–7, 124
  working-class 31, 41, 68, 77–86, 116, 117
Hughes, Anita 192, 197
Hughes, Francis 193
Huxley, Elspeth 100
hybridity 9, 110
hygiene reform 13, 25, 119
hygiene, working class housing and 31
Hymns and Pictures 193
Hymns and Poems 189, 192

identity(ies)
  Anglo-Indian 47
  the British Raj and 9
  colonial 64, 65, 110
  dining rooms, drawing rooms and 161
  Englishness/Britishness 48–9, 64, 65, 90
  global 106, 107–8
  homes and 90
  ideal of the home and 6

middle-class 20, 180
moral identity 8
national 14
religious 180, 183, 201
Ilford, Cranford Park *81*
Illustrated London News 24
imagery, of the home 21
immigration, re-immigration 9 (*see also* migration)
imperialism (*see also* colonialism)
  British imperial dominance 7
  the civilizing mission 44, 47, 65, 143
  cultural 7
  power of 7, 40, 48–51
  technological change, communications and 43
Incidents in the Life of a Slave Girl 170
indentured labour 2
India
  Anglo-Indian society 46
  the British Raj and 9, 45
  calling practices 15
  caste designations 52
  children of elites in 12, 50, 53–5
  colonial homes in 110
  Crown control of 45
  domestic servants *34*, 40, 43, 45, 48, 49–51, 52–3, 55–6, 56–7, 59–60, 62–4
  elite Anglo-Indian living practices 12
  imperial households as a symbol of power 48–51
  Indian craftsmen 103
  Indian home life 5
  indigenous living practices 7
  justification of colonial violence 60–2
  nationalist movements 45
  pejorative attitudes to Indian people 46
  the problem of proximity of servants 56–7
  racial/social hierarchies in 49, 51
  reform of Indian society 48
  relationships between servants and children 57–9
  religion 57–8
  role of servants in the colonial household 51–6
  'Sepoy Mutiny' of 1857 45, 57
  settlement of 38
  small wooden octagonal tables 98
  social ranking 48
  women in 46, 48, 57, 63
Indian Ocean trade system 97, 102, 106
Indian Outfits and Establishment 47, 54, 63
indigenous peoples
  colonialism and 3
  indigenous Africans, apprenticeships 104
  indigenous artefacts 106
  indigenous crafts 105
  indigenous living practices, India 7
  intermarriage between settlers and indigenous groups 12
  Pacific Islanders 108–9
individuality
  architectural features and 78
  furnishings and 98
industrial missions/training 104, 105
industrialization
  domestic lives and 1
  domestic servants and 122
  health and 70–1
  home working and 112
  housing and 8, 67
  social turbulence and 20
  United States 136
  urbanization and 7
  women's factory working 127
industries, family composition and 10
inequalities, housing stock and 12
infant mortality 11, 119 (*see also* mortality rates)
infectious diseases 25
infrastructure, urban 115
Inglis, K.S. 180
institutions
  hospitality in residential institutions 158, 173–7
  making a home in an 35–8
  for the mentally ill 175–7
  prisons and penitentiaries 38
  privacy and 37
interior-decorating 30
interior designers 161
Ireson, Alfred 183
Ireson, Hannah 183, 195
ironing 116, *117*
Irving, Beryl 64
Islamic art and architecture 98
Italy 5–6, 10

Jacobs, Harriet 145–6, 170
James, Henry 14
Jane Eyre 32
Jennings, H.J. 28, 29, 161
Johnston, Harry 95, *96*
Jones, Frances M. 80
Jones, John 187
Jones, Robin 90
Jones, Timothy W. 196, 201
Jordan, Thomas 193–4
Journal of a Residence on a Georgian Plantation in 1838–39 149

Kann, Mark E. 135
Kelley, Victoria 236 (*see also* chapter 5)
Kemble, Fanny 148–50
Kenya 91, 93, 97, 98, 103, 105
Kerber, Linda 135
Kerr, Robert 6, 69, 74, 76, 117, 124, 161
King, Anthony 92
knowledge, held by Indian servants 52
Koven, Seth 126

labour
    of children 134
    domestic servants. *See* domestic servants
    the duties of housemaids 121
    furniture production and 103–6
    home workers 128–30
    housework 112, 113–22
    indentured labour 2
    skilled South Asian 103
    sweated labour 127–8
    women's waged outside the home 116, 125–6
Ladies Sanitary Association 125
Lady Assistant Commissioners 127, 128
Lalumia, Christine 24
Lambert, David 71
The Lamplighter 137
Langley, Amy 197
Lanigan, Jack 195
Larsson, Carl 14
laundry 116
Lawrence, Dianne 39
law(s)
    Acts of Uniformity (1559, 1662) 179
    Addison Act 41
    building byelaws 68, 78
    Charitable Trusts Act (1853) 36
    Common Lodging House Act 32
    Education Act 1870 189
    leasehold laws 80–1
    New Poor Law 1834 173
    Public Health Act (1875) 117
    slum housing and 41
    women's work and 127
leadership etiquette, for women 170
leasehold laws 80–1
Lecture to Young Men 192
Leech, John *162*, 163
Leigh, Linda 102
leisure
    gentility and 30
    home as a place of 111
    Sunday observance and 187
letter writing 9, 12, 39
Lewis, Jane 31
liberalism 126
Liberty's 28, 98
libraries 76
Life and Labour of the People in London 128
life-cycles
    homes and 17
    rituals related to 15
literacy 9, 135, 184
literature, advice literature. *See* advice manuals
Little Women 137, 167–8, 177
Liverpool
    housing 86
    Rock Park estate 70, 71–2, 76, 77
    terraced housing 83
    Wirral peninsula 71
living rooms 13 (*see also* dining rooms; drawing rooms; parlours)
living standards, rising 112
Locke, John 192
lodgers 83, 87
lodging houses 8, 31, 33–4, 68, 159, 172, 173
Loftie, Mrs 163
Logan, Thad 24, 28
London
    Battersea 81
    Bermondsey 86
    Bethlem hospital 175
    East End 128
    Fulham 85

Heath House 70, 73–6, 77
Holloway Sanatorium 176–7
hotels 172
Islington 84
Lambeth 82, 117–18
Rowton Houses 174–5
Southwark 195
Longair, Sarah 102
Loudon, John Claudius 27, 71, 72, 77
Lovekin, Emmanuel 184
Lowell, Frances Cabot 175
lunatic asylums 175
Lyons and Co., London 172
Lytton, Lord 61, 62

Mackay, Alexander 104
Maddocks, Sydney 76
Magee, Gary 109
The Magic Mountain 16
Maitland, Julia 51, 61
Manchester 115–16, 117
manhood, domestication of 139
Mann, Horace 180
Mann, Thomas 16
manufacturing, paid work in the home and 111–12
marriage
 Catholicism and 6
 divorce 6
 intermarriage between settlers and indigenous groups 12
 the meekly submissive wife 5
 national variations in 16
 romantic love as the only justification for 136–7
 the unmarried state 32
 wifely duty to obey 142
Married Women's Work 126
Marryat, Florence 58, 62, 63
masculinity
 domesticity and 114
 religious 183
mass production 1, 13, 20
material culture 13, 24, 27, 39, 91, 110, 169
material spaces, homes as 12–14
maternalism, slavery and 144, 145
Matthews-Jones, Lucinda 236 (*see also* chapter 8)
Maynard, Bertie 53, 63
Mays, Kelly 183

McGregor Ross, William 98, 99
McGuire, Meredith B. 181
McLauchlan, Thomas 197
McPherson, Kathryn 40
media, cultural 21
Mediterranean countries, family composition 10
Membrey, Jemima 197
memory objects 100
men
 located in the public world of work 138–9
 single homemaking and 34–5
 mental illness, institutions for 175–7
Menuge, Adam 86
Metcalf, Thomas 90
Methodism 184, 185, 187
Methodist Times 192
middle-classes
 advice on hospitality and dining for 160–6
 Britain 4–5
 consumption and 20, 27, 28
 cult of domesticity 4
 the cultural codes of gendered conduct and 140
 cultural ideals of American 139
 culture of gentility 158
 domestic divisions and 15
 domestic servants and 2, 11–12, 44
 East Africa 91–2
 France 4–5
 furnishings and 41, 98
 growth of 2, 4, 41, 136
 homes of 41
 hospitality and 75, 157–8, 160–6, 177
 housing of 8, 68, 69–77
 identity 20, 180
 importance and decoration of living rooms 13
 middle-class female employment 32, 41
 the moral codes of middle-class behaviour 153
 philanthropy 36
 poor people and the 6
 respectability 20, 44
 rise of 20, 26–7, 41
 Spain 4–5
 Sweden 4

United States 5
unmarried women 32, 33
women in the public sphere 126
women's paid work 41, 130–1
the work of domesticity 131
migration
    to the colonies 2
    domestic practices and 9–10
    homemaking activities and 10
    hotels and 171
    intermarriage between settlers and indigenous groups 12
    voluntary mass 9
Millington, Mrs 105
minority groups, furnishings and 14
missionaries, East Africa 91–2, 95, 106
mobility
    furniture and 95, 98
    hotels and 171, 172
    increasing 89
    social 75
model housing 26
The Modern Housewife or Ménagére 27
modernization, of farming 1
Monsieur, Madame et Bebe 4
Moody, Reuben 182–3
Moorish style 98
morality
    consumption of goods and 20
    gender and 5
    homemaking and 38–9
    the ideal home and 25
    the moral codes of middle-class behaviour 153
    moral guardianship of America by it's women 136, 137, 138
    moral identity 8
    moral motherhood 5
    moral obligation of parents 24–5
    the moral threat of servants 57–8
    moral treatment of the mentally ill 175
    moral well-being 20
    religious 180
    taste and 27, 31
    the unmarried state and 32
    women, home and 119
    western moral authority 7
More Work for Mother 114
Morning Hours in India 59

mortality rates
    amongst the poor 10–11
    infant/child mortality 11, 119, 134
    nineteenth-century America 134
motherhood 5, 119
Mrs Beeton's Cookery Book and Household Guide 164, 166
Mtesa of Buganda 107
Mukasa of Buganda 107
multi-occupancy housing 8, 83, 84, 85
Murray Mitchell, J. 46, 58
Muthesius, Hermann 86
Muthesius, Stefan 80
Mwanga II of Buganda 107

Nair, Gwyneth 125–6, 158–9
Nairobi 93, 98, 99
National Romantic interiors, Sweden 14
National Schools 184
nationalist movements, India 45
needlework 16–17, 30 (*see also* sewing)
neighbourhoods, zoned 88
networks, global trade 13
New York, hotels 171
New York State Asylum, Utica 175
New Zealand
    migration to 2
    obtaining furnishings 39
    settlement of 38
night shelters 31
North American style 14
Notes for officers appointed to East Africa and Uganda 93–4
novels, dining spaces/practices in North American 166–71 (*see also* names of individual novels)
nuclear families 20, 32
nurseries 16, 74

objects
    hand-worked 16
    memory objects 100
    object systems 97
    oriental 13
    religious 194–8
    social life of 108
    travelling objects 93–7
Ohio 152
Olmsted, Frederick Law 150
oriental style 98

Orientalism 48, 98–9, 169
Orme, Eliza 127
Others/otherness
    colonial style and 90, 106
    domestic servants in India and 58
    in the home 110
    objects as 108
    racialized 59, 61
    Zanzibar chests and 102
Our Homes and How to Beautify Them 29
Our Nig 170
outside spaces, terraced housing 80–2 (*see also* gardens)

Pacific Islanders 108–9
Panton, Jane Ellen 164
Paris World's Fair (1900) 171
Park, Benjamin 138
parlours
    furnishings 24
    in hotels 172
    imagery of 21, *23*
    terraced housing 83, 85, 86, 87
Past and Present series 21
paterfamilias 114
paternalism
    Indian servants and 59–60
    slavery and 144
Patmore, Coventry 5, 21, 113
patriarchy
    America 139
    empire and 2
    in families 1
    hotels and 172
    religion and 180, 182, 183, 189, 199
    slavery and 141
Peace Treaty of Paris (1783) 134
Pelletier, Yvonne Elizabeth 168
performances
    of class 168
    of hospitality 158
Perrin, Alice 46
Perry, Adele 12
personal services, performed by servants 50
petit salon, French bourgeois homes 14
philanthropy 26, 36, 68
pianos 24, 95
Pictures of Life and Character. . . from the Collection of Mr Punch 162
piety 144

Pilgrim's Progress 137, 187, *188*, 189, 192
The Pioneer 61, 62
place, home and 7–10
plantation households, sewing and 17
plantation mistresses 143–4
politics, women's work and 127
Ponsonby, Margaret 75, 237 (*see also* chapter 1)
poor people (*see also* poverty)
    deserving poor 26
    the housing of 67
    the middle-classes and 6
    mortality rates and 10–11
    poor relief 4, 173, 174
    Victorian era 19
population expansion 8, 10–11, 67, 112 (*see also* demographics)
porcelain 96–7
postal services 9
poverty (*see also* poor people)
    family composition and 11
    health and 119
power
    colonialism and 110
    of the concept of home 21
    gendered and racial power dynamics 145–6
    gendered power relations in the home 5
    of the home and family 3, 17
    imperial 7, 40, 48–51
    mistress of the house and her servants 169–70
    of servants in India 57
    white 170–1
Powys-Cobbs of Kerenget 103
Presthold, Jeremy 97
Preston *196*, 197
Preston, Rebecca 236–7 (*see also* chapter 3)
print culture 4, 30, 158, 160
printed materials, religious 189–92
prisons and penitentiaries 38
privacy
    back-garden space and 82
    domestic servants and 124
    English houses and 15, 69, 74, 76
    furnished rooms/lodging houses and 8
    India 57
    institutions and 37
    terraced housing 78, 80, 88
    villas and 88

Prochaska, Frank 159
Procida, Mary 46
professional middle-class women 126
Protestantism 6, 179
public and private spheres
  gender and 44, 159
  home and 112
  home and work and 44, 113, 122
  public role of Southern women 154–5
  religious public sphere 196
  'separate spheres' of 28
  United States 136
  women in the public sphere 5, 126, 154–5
  the world as divided into 5
public health movement 77, 78, 119
  Public Health Act (1875) 117
public nature of hospitality 158–9
Public Works Departments, East Africa 98, 103, 104, 105
publishing industry 187–9
Punch 163, 172
punishment, religion and 199
"The Puzzling Pair" 197

quilt making 17

race
  ethnic groups, marginalization of 168–9, 177
  gendered and racial power dynamics 145–6
  racial difference 45, 90
  racial privilege 144
  racial status, India 51
  racial stereotypes held by slaveholders 149
  racialized Others 59, 61
  racism in the domestic sphere 170–1
  rule of difference 90
  Southern homes. Maintaining racial/gendered hierarchies 141–50
railway hotels 172
railways, Uganda 102
Raine, Katherine 39
reading
  books awarded as prizes from Sunday schools 197
  religious 187–9, 189–92
Reeves, Maud Pember 82, 114, 117

reform,
  of housing 174
  of Indian society 48
  social reform 174
regulation
  almshouses and 37
  of childhood 1
  of the working-classes 26
relationships
  global and colonialism 109
  between servants and children 57–9
  between servants and employers 55, 56–7, 59–60, 61–3, 65
religion
  almshouses and 36, 37
  Britain 179
  Catholicism 6, 58
  children and 182, 184, 186, 197
  church attendance 200
  domestic 6, 181
  domestic faith in working-class families 182–5
  everyday/religion-as-lived 181
  gender and 20, 183–4
  the home and 5–6, 180
  the ideal home and 25
  India 57–8
  institutionalization of Evangelicalism 187
  Methodists 184, 185, 187
  non-conformist groups 6, 179, 186–7
  patriarchy and 180, 182, 183, 189, 199
  praying 193–4
  Protestantism 6, 179
  punishment and 199
  Religious Census (1851) 186
  religious identities 180, 183, 201
  religious morality 180
  religious objects 194–8
  religious printed materials 189–92
  religious public sphere 196
  religious subjectivity 181–2
  religious toleration 5, 179–80
  rhythms of working-class domestic religion 185–94
  sewing and 195–6
  society and 181
  spiritual well-being 20
  states and 5–6

Sunday observance 186–7, 192
Sunday schools 184, 196–7
unhomely religious households 198–200
women and 183, 196
working-classes and 6, 180–1, 194–8, 200–1
rented accommodation 31, 68
The Report of the Enquiry . . . into Working-Class Rents, Housing and Retail Prices 78, 83, 85
Report on the Sanitary Conditions of the Labouring Population 119
representations, of the parlour 24
republican motherhood 136
Republican Womanhood 135
residential institutions, hospitality in 158, 173–7
resistance, kitchen and dining rooms as spaces of 170, 177
respectability
    the American home and 140–1
    Christian 199
    clothing and 196
    the cultural codes of gendered conduct and 140
    domestic 6
    home circumstances and 112
    middle-class 20, 44
    single men and 35
    unmarried women and 32
    working-class 80
Rich, Rachel 160, 163
Riddell, R. 51–2, 62–3
rights, for married women 1
Rignall, Elizabeth 186, 187, 195, 197
rituals
    construction of 160
    death in the home 16
    dining 158
    domestic 2, 16
    hospitality 159, 167
    new social 163–4
    related to the life-cycle 15
    religious 186
The Ritz, London 172
Roberts, Emma 58
Roberts, Robert 171
Rock Park estate, Liverpool 70, 71–2, 76, 77

rooms (*see also* specific rooms)
    the function of 15
    gendered usage of 25, 28, 33, 75, 86, 161
Rose, George 173
Ross, Ellen 119
Rowton Houses, London 174–5
Royal Commission on Labour (1891–94) 127
royal family, Christmas and 24
Ruete, Rudolf Heinrich and Emily 100–1
Rush, Benjamin 135–6
Ruskin, John 27, 31, 113, 126

Sabin, Edwin L. 169
sanitation 80, 84, 85, 86, 112, 115
The Savoy, London 172
Sayyid Sultan bin Said al-Said 103
Sayyida Salme, Princess of Zanzibar and Oman 100–1
Schilling, Britta 237 (*see also* chapter 4)
Schleinitz, Kurt Freiherr von 106, *107*
Schmiechen, James 127, 128, 130
Schwartz Cowan, Ruth 114, 119
scrapbooks 195
sculleries 31, 78, 80, 83, 85
secularism, Britain 179–80
Seebohm-Rowntree, B. 44
self, presentation of 120
sentimental portrayals of the home 21
sentimentalization, early-nineteenth-century America 137
separate spheres 113, 124
Sesame and Lilies 113, 126
sewing (*see also* needlework)
    agency and 16–17
    home sewing work 128
    religion and 195–6
shame, women's paid work in the home and 130–1
sharecroppers, Italy 10
Sheehan-Dean, Aaron 154
Sheffield, Broom Hall estate 71
Shore, Frederick 57
Simonton, Deborah 122
single people, homemaking and 32–5
sitting rooms 21, 23, 24, *107*
slavery
    abolitionism 150
    in the American South 141

children of slave women 149
governance of slaves 142–3
gradual removal of 2
justification of 150
maternalism and 144, 145
paternalism and 144
patriarchy and 141
plantation mistresses 143–4
power and 170–1
violence towards slaves 145–6
women sewing and 17
sleeping arrangements 25
slum housing 41
Smitley, Megan 126
sociability, domestic 158–9, 163–4
social activism 155
social democracy 123
social etiquette 15
social exclusion 178
social expression, sewing and 17
social injustice 174
social life, of objects 108
social mobility 75
social ranking, India 48
social reform 174
social relations, domestic space and 74
social relationships 1
social status 11, 15, 20, 25, 51, 163
social stratification, dining rituals and 158
social transformation 5, 157
social turbulence; industrialization, urbanization and 20
social value, of hospitality 160
society, religion and 181
socio-economic change 4
Sociology for the South 141–2
sod houses 13
Soja, Edward 185
Soldier Settlement Scheme, East Africa 91
Solon; or, The Rebellion of '61: A Domestic and Political Tragedy 154
South Africa, calling practices 15
South Asia, colonial homes 91
South Asians
   in East Africa 103–4
   the furniture trade and 102
Southern Europe, agri-towns 7–8
Southgate, Walter 120
Soyer, Alexis 27
spaces, new ordering of household space 15

Spain 4–5, 6, 14
St. Mary's Almshouses in Shrewsbury 36
state(s)
   regulation of childhood by 1
   religion and 5–6
status
   clothing and 196
   domesticity and 120
   of elites in India 12
   home circumstances and 112
   hospitality and 158
   ideal of the home and 6
   personal appearance and 120
   social 11, 15, 20, 25, 51, 163
Steel, F.A. 47, 48, 52, 55, 56, 59
stereotypes
   the indulged European aristocrat 48
   racial stereotypes held by slaveholders 149
Stocqueler, J.H. 46
Stoler, Ann Laura 59
Stone, Kate 146–7
Stowe, Harriet Beecher 147–8, 153
Strand Palace Hotel, London 172
Strange, Julie-Marie 195
style(s)
   colonial 89–90, 91, 92, 93–7, 106, 109–10
   French historic styles 14
   North American 14
   oriental or Moorish 98–9
   variations in 17
suburban growth, urban expansion and 8
suburban housing 71 (*see also* villas)
Suez Canal 89
suffrage 155
Sunday observance 186–7, 197
Sunday schools 184, 196–7
surveillance, almshouses and 37
Swainbank, Lavinia 123
Sweden 4, 14
System of Theology 192

table decorations 163, 169
table d'hôte 172, 176
tables 24
A Tale of Two Cities 197
Tanganyika 91
Tanzania 102

taste
- France as the leader of 14
- furnishings and 27
- homemaking and 28
- individual 30
- morality and 27, 31

Taylor, Benjamin 189, 199–200
tea 164
'Tea from Japan' 169
technological change
- amenities 112, 115
- balloon frame technologies 13
- imperialism and 43
- laundry and 116

tenants, gardens and 81
terraced housing 12, 68, 69, 77–87
terroir 4
Terry, Isaac 184–5
textiles 24, 30
Thomas, Gertrude Clanton 147
Thomas, Nicholas 108–9
Thompson, Andrew 109
Thonet, Michael 95
Thonet model chair 95, 106
'Thoughts on Married Life' 136–7
Thoughts Upon Female Education 135
Tilley lamps 95
Tilyard, Elizabeth 51
time
- religious rituals and 186
- spent on housework 119

Tonkovich, Nicole 159
Tosh, John 166, 180, 182, 199
trade
- global networks of 13
- Indian Ocean trade system 97, 102, 106
- South Asian furniture trade 102

trade union movements 6
transport, migration and 9
travel abroad 168–9, 177
A Treatise on Domestic Economy 153, 170
Tremont House, Boston 171
Trollope, Anthony 35, 36
Trollope, Frances 152
trousseaus 16
'The True Rights of a Women' 138
true womanhood 5, 137–8, 140

Uganda
- the British Empire and 91
- elites 106–7, 108
- furnishings in 95, 96
- industrial missions/training 105
- Public Works Department 104
- railway 102
- South Asians in 103

Uncle Tom's Cabin 148
United States
- American bourgeois ideals in Northern homes 136–41
- changing ideologies in revolutionary America 134–7
- Civil War of 1861–65 137, 153–5
- conceptions of home in the American West 152–3
- the cult of true womanhood 5, 137–8, 140
- domestic revolution 134–5
- domestic womanhood and 5
- gender roles in 133, 134, 135, 140, 141
- home management by women 159
- hospitality and 159
- hotels 171–2
- housing 13
- industrialization 136
- the limiting of family size 11
- middle-classes 5
- migration to 2, 9
- moral guardianship of America by it's women 136, 137, 138
- moral motherhood 5
- North American homes 6
- North American style 14
- novels and dining spaces/practices 166–71
- Orientalism 169
- patriarchy 139
- public and private sphere 136
- quilt making 17
- Revolutionary War for Independence 1776 134–5
- Southern homes. Maintaining racial/gendered hierarchies 141–50
- Southern homes of disrepair 150–2
- Thirteenth Amendment 1865 146
- urban expansion 8

Unwin, Sheila 100
upper classes, advice on hospitality and dining for 160–6 (*see also* elites)
urban infrastructure 115
urbanization 7, 8, 20, 67, 112

Valenze, Deborah 187
values, of British civilization 47
Van Osselaer, Tine 185–6
Varley, Ann 198
verandas 40
Vickery, Amanda 91, 199
Victoria and Albert Museum 98
Victorian era
    furniture/furnishings 24
    homes and 15, 19–21
views, from villas 71–2
villas 68, 69–77, 86–7, 88, 124
Villette 32
violence
    justification of colonial violence 60–2
    to slaves 145–6
virtue
    civic 135
    feminine 30
    virtuous womanhood 177
vulgarity 140

Waldemar Leverton, Mrs 121
Walter, Emma 51
Ward, Thomas 73, 75, 76
The Warden 36
warfare, the gendered home justifying 154
washing machines 116
Washington, Booker T. 171
water closets 80
Watts, Isaac 194
welfare provision 174
Welter, Barbara 137
West, Alfred 189, 192
West, Harry 194
Westall, Lillian 123
Western Europe 1, 2, 5, 10, 11
Western Female Institute in Cincinnati 153
white domination 170–1
Wickham, E.R. 180
Williams Parkes, Mrs 27
Williams, Sarah C. 180, 183, 186, 189, 195
Williams, Sarah Hicks 137, 143, 146, 148
Willis, Frederick 86
Willis, Nathaniel 172
Wilson, Anne 46, 55, 63, 64
Wilson, Harriet 170
Wilson, Lady 53

Windsor castle 24
Winnington-Ingram, Arthur 192
Wirral peninsula 71
womanhood
    in the American South 142, 144
    ideal 137–8
    Republican Womanhood 135
    revised notions of 155
    virtuous 177
women
    activism and 155
    advice manuals for 40, 46–7, 52, 60, 120
    as the 'Angel in the House' 5, 20, 21, 113
    boarding houses for 175
    in colonies 40
    craft production of 30
    domestic conventions and 15
    domestic practices and 159
    domestic role of 1
    domestic servants 32, 45
    domestic sociability and 163–4
    domesticity and working women 131
    dress and appearance of 140
    duties of 30
    education and 5, 135–6
    employment for 32, 33
    exploitation of female home workers 128, 131
    factory working 127
    feminine virtues 30
femininity 16, 119
feminism 41, 113, 155
    home and 119
    home, family and 27, 30, 138
    hostesses 160, 163, 177
    in India 46, 48, 57, 63
    institutional lodgings and 175
    leadership etiquette for 170
    legal rights for married women 1
    in lodgings 172–3
    male domestic servants and 58–9
    managing slaves 143–4
    married women working 126–7
    the meekly submissive wife 5
    middle-class female employment 32, 41
    mistress of the house and her servants 169–70
    model republican 135

moral guardianship of America by it's women 136, 137, 138
as mothers and homemakers 113
new women 155
paid work in the home 111–12, 126–31
paid work outside the home 116, 125–6, 127
plantation mistresses 143–4
professional middle-class 126
in the public sphere 5, 126, 154–5
religion and 183, 196
Revolutionary era America 135
true womanhood 5, 137–8, 140
unmarried/surplus women 32–3
wifely duty to obey 142
work and 5, 111–12
Wood, Minnie 52, 57, 59, 60
work (*see also* employment)
domestic servants. *See* domestic servants
home and 24, 111, 113, 122, 130
home and workshops 8
housework 112, 113–22
industrialization, home working and 112
live-in workers 11
married women working 126–7
middle class women and 32, 41
nineteenth-century America 134
paid work in the home 111–12, 126–31
paid work outside the home 116, 125–6, 127
Southern women and 155
urban workers 8
women and 5, 111–12
women's factory working 127
working-class women and 126–31
workhouses 26, 37, 38, 173–4, 178
working-classes
art portraying the 26
alcohol and 26

culture 197
death in the home 16
domestic faith in working-class families 182–5
dress and appearance 120
education and 189
gardens of 80–1, 82, 84, 87
gendered judgements of 113
homes of 42, 114
hospitality and 159
housing 31, 41, 68, 77–86, 116, 117
living standards of 112
regulation of the 26
religion and 6, 200–1
religious domesticity of 180–1
respectability 80
rhythms of working-class domestic religion 185–94
the term 'home' and 4
unhomely religious households 198–200
unmarried women 32
women's work 111–12
working-class material religion 194–8
working-class women and work 126–31
The Workwoman's Guide 30
World Wars, First and Second, domestic service and 123
Wright, Thomas 86

Yeo, Eileen 126, 131
Young Man's Guide 139

Zafar, Rafia 171
Zakaria Kisingiri 108
Zanzibar 97, 100–1, 102, 103, 107
Zanzibar chests 99–102
zoned neighbourhoods 88
zoning of rooms 25, 83, 124–5